THE SOCIOLOGY OF CONTEMPORARY WORK

What It Is, and Why We Need It

Marek Korczynski

BRISTOL
UNIVERSITY
PRESS

First published in Great Britain in 2024 by

Bristol University Press
University of Bristol
1–9 Old Park Hill
Bristol
BS2 8BB
UK
t: +44 (0)117 374 6645
e: bup-info@bristol.ac.uk

Details of international sales and distribution partners are available at bristoluniversitypress.co.uk

British Library Cataloguing in Publication Data
A catalogue record for this book is available from the British Library

ISBN 978-1-5292-2912-7 hardcover
ISBN 978-1-5292-2913-4 paperback
ISBN 978-1-5292-2914-1 ePub
ISBN 978-1-5292-2915-8 ePdf

Cover design: Lyn Davies Design
Front cover image: Getty/LeoPatrizi
Bristol University Press uses environmentally responsible print partners.
Printed and bound in Great Britain by CPI Group (UK) Ltd, Croydon, CR0 4YY

In memory of Dariusz Korczynski

Contents

List of Figures and Tables

Figures

Tables

For: The Sociology of Contemporary Work

For ...

This book makes the argument *for* the sociology of contemporary work. If we want to understand society and the economy that is embedded in it, we have to understand the world of work, and if we want to understand work, we need sociology. The book highlights the great strengths of the sociology of work – for example its engagement with theory as a holistic world-view, its ability to unearth patterns of power and resistance, its ability to analyse the contextual meanings of work for people, its ability to illuminate how key patterns of inequality in society are often based on patterns of inequality in the arena of work. In sum, the sociology of work considers work as a substantively meaningful arena for analysis. In the current times, this, in itself, is a vital, political step. It is a step going up on a down escalator. The down escalator is a perspective that regards the organization, nature and meaning of work as secondary, as peripheral, in comparison with the central issue of the outcomes of that work for consumers and for employers. As long ago as 1971, the UK sociologist Alan Fox argued that there was a systematic marginalizing of what happens in the arena of work – or 'producer values' as he put it (1971: 19): 'The very nature of industrial society ... gives its major centres of power a variety of motives for promoting consumer values at the expense of producer values.' If that was an important observation at the beginning of the 1970s, arguments in subsequent decades about the increasing importance of consumption and consumerism (Bauman, 2004) suggest that it is likely to be even more important now.

Sociologists of work, however, question the marginalizing of the arena of work. Sociologists of work take seriously that work is something that many of us do for large parts of our adult lives. Many people create important meanings in their lives in relation to work. Some people do not. Both of these positions should be dignified with careful and engaged analysis. At its best, the sociology of work provides such analysis. This book makes the case for the sociology of work in its own right. The final chapter also considers the strengths of the sociology of work against gaps and weaknesses in neighbouring disciplines that also consider the arena of work – human resource management, organizational behaviour, work psychology and labour economics.

Before we start looking at the threads running through the book, I outline what I mean when I write about 'the sociology of contemporary work'.

Sociology ...

There are several ways in which people define sociology. A useful starting point is to think of sociology as the study of people as social beings. Plummer (2016: 237) invites the reader into sociology by defining it as 'the systematic, sceptical and critical study of the social, investigating the characteristics, construction and consequences of the human social world'. It is also useful to see sociology as a way of thinking about the world. A key starting point for thinking sociologically is the assumption that no human action takes place in a social vacuum, or, as John Donne puts it with more grace and poetry (and more challenging punctuation) in 'Meditation XVII' in 1624:

> No man is an island entire of itself; every man is a piece of the continent, a part of the main; if a clod be washed away by the sea, Europe is the less, as well as if a promontory were, as well as if a manor of thy friend's or of thine own were; any man's death diminishes me, because I am involved in mankind, and therefore never send to know for whom the bell tolls; it tolls for thee.

Sociology allows us to see beyond current myths of ourselves as purely self-made individuals. Although contemporary songs may intimate that it's just 'Me, Myself and I', we are all essentially social beings. Who we are is fundamentally influenced by the social contexts in which we live.

Another central element of thinking sociologically is to 'denaturalize' the social world: sociology asks us not to accept as natural that which appears to be natural. Thinking sociologically requires us to consider the taken for granted in our social worlds as socially created. As Giddens and Sutton (2021: 4) put it, sociology 'teaches us that much of what appears to us as natural, inevitable ... may not be so, and that things we take for granted are shaped by historical events and social processes'. Thinking sociologically changes the way you see the world, and, in so doing, changes you. Plummer (2016: 237) states: 'Sociology brings a way of thinking – an imagination, a form of consciousness – that can/will change your life. It defamiliarises the familiar, questions the taken for granted, and destroys the myths we choose to live by.' For instance, it seemed natural, obvious, even, to John Donne that he should use the word 'man' in the quote above to refer to a person. Feminist sociology has shown such assumptions in our language to be loaded with social and political history and implications.

Giddens and Sutton (2021), in their introduction to the wider topic of sociology, give a nice example of how sociology can denaturalize in their discussion of an everyday, 'natural' thing – drinking coffee. This book is about the sociology of work, so, let's explore how thinking sociologically can help denaturalize the coffee or tea break in the workplace.

First, we can consider the coffee break itself as a social and political creation. As Upchurch (2020) shows, there is a rich history in UK industrial relations regarding disputes between workers and employers over the length of, timing of and payment for tea and coffee breaks in workplaces. The break for a drink in the workplace can be seen as an important part of contests at the 'frontier of control' in the workplace, for, when workers are taking time out to drink tea or coffee, they are not working, especially if theirs is manual or service work. This starkly comes out in the celebratory song from the 1930s, 'Everything Stops for Tea', that Upchurch quotes at the start of his article:

> Oh, the factories may be roaring
> With a boom-a-lacka, zoom-a-lacka, wee
> But there isn't any roar when the clock strikes four
> Everything stops for tea.

This is a celebration not of tea, but of what tea is *not* in the factory workplace.

Second, we can think of the social process of the coffee break and how that informs wider workplace relations. Stroebaek (2013) made a sensitive sociological analysis of coffee breaks in a Danish family law/social work office and found that coffee breaks were a key forum where workers came together to form 'communities of coping' in this emotionally taxing work setting. Here, workers shared stories of angry and abusive clients, helped each other, leant on each other and supported each other. These autonomous, deep-lying but informal and invisible communities of coping formed a key texture of workplace relations. To link back to coffee breaks as part of the frontier of control between workers and employers, Stroebaek's study also notes that the employer had sought to stop coffee breaks occurring – and workers were findings ways around this.

... of contemporary work

It may appear natural to think of work as equivalent to paid employment. But we know that thinking sociologically asks us to denaturalize – to examine how the taken for granted is socially created. Edgell and Granter (2020) argue that thinking of work as equivalent to paid employment represents the 'dominant conception of work' wrought by industrial capitalism, linked to a form of patriarchy. Prior to the growth of industrial capitalism, there was nothing of the contemporary association of work with paid employment. The rural, household-based family working was torn apart by the growth of factories – and the separation of the (mainly male) workers finding paid employment outside the house, in these new factories. What then came of the tasks still being undertaken in the household – child-rearing, cooking, washing, cleaning? As Blyton and Jenkins (2007) note, the fact that these work activities do not receive payment acts to reduce their visibility as work such that, somehow, they may even become invisible when we think about work. The fact that the overwhelming majority of people doing this domestic work were, and still are, women meant that the visibility and recognized significance of such work was further marginalized. This was sharply exposed in Oakley's (1974) pioneering study of unpaid domestic work. Oakley noted that the term 'housewife' only began to be commonly used from the mid-19th century.

Although the main focus of this book is upon paid employment – and its relationship to domestic work – there are other forms of activity that we can also usefully think of as constituting work. First, there is the recent growth of 'free labour' undertaken by people in peer production networks, facilitated by social sharing aspects of internet technology for 'the digital commons'. The digital commons is an internet repository of code, information, knowledge and culture that is collectively produced and freely available to everybody who wants to use or modify these resources. It has spread from the peer production of software and code to the peer production of text, sound, images and moving images, with iconic sites such as Wikipedia, WikiLeaks, Pirate Bay and Creative Commons (Korczynski and Wittel, 2020).

Second, although industrial capitalism drew a sharp and strong dividing line between work and consumption/leisure (Gabriel and Lang, 2015), in recent decades, commentators have begun to argue that this divide is becoming increasingly blurred and porous. Academics have put forward labels such as the *working consumer* (Cova and Dalli, 2009) and the *working customer* (Rieder and Voß, 2010). Sociologists Ritzer, Dean and Jurgensen (2012) construct the word 'prosumer' from the two words, producer and consumer, to point to certain activities as new forms of self-service and new forms of do-it-yourself tasks. They are essentially arguing that firms are increasingly putting consumers to work. For instance, mass customization and internet technology have positioned consumers to become involved in the design of products that they later purchase. Gabriel et al (2015: 637) note that 'new technologies like 3D printing or electronics assembly enable consumers to develop and produce all kinds of objects that are usually assembled in factories or workshops'.

Third, it is appropriate to include volunteering as a form of work. Important forms of formal voluntary work include working for a charity, running a youth group, and sitting as a school governor. Although much voluntary work can be considered a 'gift' related to a 'sense of community', it is also the case that some voluntary work is undertaken by people as a bridge to help them find paid employment (Hirst, 2001). Current debates over the ethics of firms expecting young people, often students, to work as unpaid interns are clearly relevant here (Shade and Jacobson, 2015).

Key threads in the book and why they are there
Focus on three important contemporary forms of paid employment

A danger for an overview sociology of work book is that it can provide too many bits and pieces about too many things, such that a reader can easily become lost in a sea of detail, without a map to guide them through. There is, after all, a lot of sociology of work out there. To guard against that danger, there is a focus throughout the book on three important types of work: client/customer-facing service work, knowledge work and platform-mediated work. These three growing types of work in contemporary advanced economies form a thread that runs through the book. When examples are used to illustrate ideas, developments or debates, the first option is to call on studies of these three types of work.

Client/customer-facing service work

Here, the focus is on work *below* the level of senior professional (such as doctor, lawyer or academic) in which a central element involves the presence of a service recipient within the labour process. The service recipient can be given a range of labels according to the context of the work – customer, client, patient, passenger, guest, diner, fan, punter and so on. Important examples of such service jobs are bartenders, hairdressers, barristas, nurses, healthcare aides, flight attendants, waiters, shop workers, sales assistants and call-centre operators. Although there can be significant differences between these jobs, there are also important shared aspects that may allow us to talk about broad tendencies and commonalities across this type of work (Korczynski, 2002; Korczynski and MacDonald, 2009). Customer-facing service jobs are a central element of contemporary economies. MacDonald and Merrill (2009) calculated that around 29 per cent of workers in the US work in such jobs. In Korczynski (2009a), I estimated that 28 per cent of the UK labour force were in jobs below the level of senior professional and in which the central job requirement involved interacting with a service recipient. Many readers who are students will have had direct experience of working part time in such service jobs.

Knowledge work

One of the most basic ways of thinking about work is to consider the key item that is worked upon. Essentially, jobs can involve working on three elements – information/ symbols (broadly defined), people and materials. Although there are debates about how knowledge work should be defined (Hislop et al, 2013), for our purposes, it is useful to think of *knowledge work* as where information is a central element that is worked upon and where task complexity tends to be high. Work in traditional professions such as law, accounting, science, architecture and medicine is included within this definition of knowledge work. Knowledge work also encompasses many managerial, consultant and analyst roles and many roles in technology-centred parts of the economy, such as software designers and engineers.

'Knowledge work' somehow sounds like great work, and, two or three decades ago, when the term was first used, some commentators used it to imply that the world of work was making a fundamental shift for the better (see Noon and Blyton, 2013). Studies by sociologists of work who were (rightly) sceptical about such claims, however, brought clarity to bear. An inflated sense of the extent of knowledge work can be generated by identifying knowledge work through proxy indicators such as job titles and education levels of job-holders, so Brinkley et al's (2009) study of the importance of knowledge work in the UK economy dug deeper by focusing on the tasks undertaken within jobs. The authors analysed the level of complexity of tasks in jobs and the degree to which people drew on tacit knowledge they had. On this basis, the authors pointed to seven groups of jobs, which they ranked in a hierarchy from least to most knowledge-intensive. The most knowledge-intensive group of roles – labelled 'expert thinkers, innovators, and leaders' – comprised 11 per cent of the total UK labour force. Overall, the study estimated that 30 per cent of the workforce was made up of knowledge workers in the sense that their jobs had high knowledge content.

Platform work

Here, the focus is upon work that is mediated by a digital platform. Important examples of labour platforms are Uber, Deliveroo, UpWork, Freelancer and Amazon Mechanical Turk. A central, shared aspect of platform work is that the platform seeks to mediate a relationship between a worker (service-provider) and a client (service-user), and the platform seeks to do this in such a way that the work is undertaken outside an employment relationship with the platform company. So, for instance, Uber provides a platform to connect a worker (taxi driver) and a client (who wants to be driven somewhere), but claims that 'Uber drivers' are not employed by, or in an employment relationship with, Uber. As I am writing, there are important battles being fought over whether this claim of the platform not being an employer is tenable.

Research is quickly catching up with the rise of labour platforms that launched around 2010 (Forde et al, 2017; Vallas and Schor, 2020), and this research shows that there are many important different types of platform work. Vallas and Schor (2020) provide a typology of platform work by mapping such work against two dimensions: 1) whether it is rooted in a given locality or globally dispersed; and 2) whether it involves low or high skill. This book concentrates on locally rooted work that involves low to medium skill – such as couriers and taxi drivers – as these are the forms of platform-mediated work that are more likely to constitute the basis for a person's main (rather than side) form of income.

Although some commentators predicted that platform-mediated work would sweep through the economy to become the dominant form of work, the percentage of the labour force engaging in platform work is low, although continuing to expand. In the UK, Lepanjuuri et al (2018) found that 4.4 per cent of adults had undertaken platform work in the previous year and 2.4 per cent of adults did so at least monthly. These figures cover people who undertake platform work as their main generator of income and those for whom platform work is not their main income. Despite these low numbers, platform work is becoming an important form of work, and, as we will explore in subsequent chapters, it can be seen as the leading edge of a wider logic driving the organization and nature of work.

While the first two types of work – service work and knowledge work – are defined according to level of task complexity and what is worked upon (people or information), *platform work* is defined in relation to different dimensions – in relation to whether the work is mediated by a digital platform. This means that there can be overlaps between service work and platform work, and between knowledge work and platform work. When these overlaps occur in the studies discussed in the book, they tend to be placed under consideration of platform work.

Having a clear thread in the book regarding three important contemporary types of work gives the book greater focus, and allows analysis to go into greater depth. However, it is also the case that something is lost. Important types of work may be marginalized in the book because of this focus. Most notably, *manual work* – where the labour process involves work upon materials – is not included in the thread, except for those manual jobs that are becoming platform-mediated. Three important points need to be considered here. The first is that there has been a global redistribution of manual jobs in factory production away from advanced economies to countries with lower labour costs. I am writing in the city of Nottingham. A few decades ago, this city hosted many factories producing clothing. It no longer does. Bangladesh has become a global centre of garment manufacture. This global redistribution of manual jobs in manufacturing is discussed in more detail in Chapter 3. Second, not only have manual jobs slumped in advanced economies in recent decades, but they continue to fall. Third, many of the foundational studies in the sociology of work focused on the manual labour of factory workers, and this book calls on these studies where appropriate.

The sociological imagination at work

C. Wright Mills wrote *The Sociological Imagination* in 1959. It has endured as a classic book within sociology. This canonical status within sociology is somewhat ironic given that Mills spends much of the book railing against major tendencies within sociology at the time. He criticizes the 'arid formalism' of sociological theorizing where 'the splitting of concepts and their endless rearrangement becomes the central endeavour' (p 23). He attacks empirically oriented sociology as so methodologically inhibited that sociology was in danger of failing to tell substantively meaningful stories about people's experiences of social life. The key aspect that most readers take from the book is not these critiques, but his positive and passionate arguments for the sociological imagination – the ability to make the connection between the experience of individuals and the social structures that they inhabit. Mills puts it this way (1959: 5): 'The sociological imagination enables its possessor to understand the larger historical scenes in terms of the meaning for the inner life and the external career of a variety of individuals.' Only by being able to make the connections between individuals' 'private troubles' and wider 'public issues of social structure' (p 8) can we expose and respond to social injustice.

In keeping with the impulse of imagination, we can use Mills' approach as a starting point to develop a wider sense of the sociological imagination. I use an expanded idea of the sociological imagination as a thread that runs throughout the book. The following sections explain the elements of this expanded idea.

Connecting individual experience to wider social structure

This is the essence of how Mills first used the concept. A great example of sociology of work informed by this idea is Hochschild's groundbreaking 1983 book on emotional labour, *The Managed Heart: Commercialisation of Human Feeling*. The social structure that

Hochschild focused on was the employment relationship for customer-facing service workers, particularly management's increasing control over the emotional displays from service workers to customers. Management was not just seeking to control the bodily actions of workers, but also to manage workers' hearts. It is through the analysis of increasing management demands for, and measurement of, smiling empathy to customers that Hochschild points to the tensions and unease that service workers experience in their working lives. She ends the book (p 198) by reflecting on the private 'troubles' of people's emotional experiences and how, in order to understand this, we need to understand the social structure in which their work is embedded: 'And so in the country that most celebrates the individual [the US], more people privately wonder, without tracing the question to its deepest social root: What do I really feel?' The sociological imagination is exactly about acknowledging people's experiences and tracing the ensuing questions to their 'deepest social root'.

Considering alternative ways of organizing work

Imagination opens up the possibility to consider how different things might be. The sociological imagination opens up the possibility to consider how differently work may be organized. This could be in terms of comparing how the same task has been done in different historical periods. Consider first Adam Smith's (1776) description of pin manufacture in the immediate aftermath of the industrial revolution in Britain:

> One man draws out the wire, another straightens it, a third cuts it, a fourth points it, a fifth grinds it at the top for receiving, the head; to make the head requires two or three distinct operations; to put it on is a peculiar business, to whiten the pins is another; it is even a trade by itself to put them into the paper; and the important business of making a pin is, in this manner, divided into about eighteen distinct operations, which, in some manufactories, are all performed by distinct hands, though in others the same man will sometimes perform two or three of them. … Ten persons, therefore could make among them upwards of 48,000 pins in a day.

Next, consider that, prior to the industrial revolution, under the craft system, one craft worker would have undertaken all of these 18 distinct operations as a skilled, highly respected occupation. The sociological imagination at work asks us to compare the nature and meaning of work for the people in these different systems of manufacture.

While this example points to a degradation in the nature of work, we can also use the sociological imagination to consider the potential for positive changes in the nature of work. Workers' cooperatives are organizations that are owned and run democratically by the member-workers. They use their social imagination to find alternative ways to organize work that are centred on principles of equality, participation in decision-making and the importance of meaningful work. This contrasts sharply to many private, capitalist organizations in contemporary economies such as the US and the UK, which have severe and increasing forms of inequality of income, where hierarchy is still important (albeit sometimes in a reconfigured way) and where measurement is more important than meaning with regard to work. Some of the texture of this contrast comes across in the following quotation from a Swedish worker-cooperative member (Wiksell and Henriksen, 2023: 1283):

> When you think about how much, globally, is based on dominance and that you do what you're told and what you must do, and all this very strict hierarchy and control by bosses and middle managers. ... And [we have] this that one can bring along one's kids and that we all like to take care of each other's kids and ... [the cooperative] has managed to realise ... organic ways of distributing responsibility and rotating responsibilities, and that you feel it's genuinely equal. ... Because we know each other so well, have gone through incredibly much, like, privately as well.

Even though we may be told otherwise, with our sociological imagination at work, we can see that it doesn't have to be the way that it is. The idea of the social imagination as offering alternative possibilities is an important thread in this book.

Towards postcolonial understandings

Another constructive way to expand the sociological imagination at work is to consider: the role of sociology itself within structures of power, how sociology may be shaped by structures of power and, in turn, how it may contribute to the reproduction of those structures of power. Postcolonial sociology points to the importance of colonialism as a structure of power. We need to consider how sociology itself has developed through implicit links to colonial structures of power and may continue to contribute to the playing out of some of the consequences of those structures of power. Most notably, sociology is centrally structured by the voices of academics from dominant countries. The sociology *of work* is no different here. The canon – the foundational and dominant texts – of the sociology of work is structured by colonialism.

Applying a sociological imagination asks us to move towards a *post*colonial sociology of work. There are likely to be two main elements in this endeavour. First, we should question the canon and look for alternatives to it. Second, we should open our ears to the marginalized voices of those from the dominated countries. For instance, when thinking sociologically about coffee breaks, we should consider the workers undertaking the labour that leads to the coffee being available to be drunk at a break in work. West's (2012) anthropological study of Papua New Guinea in the global value-chain in coffee production and marketing is notable for how it contrasts, on the one hand, the 'fantasy formation' marketing imagery of the Papua New Guinea workers as 'chiselled warriors in Bird of Paradise headdresses' (p 39) that suggests an 'enforced subsistence primitivism' with, on the other hand, the voices of these workers regarding their lived experience of their work.

The sociological imagination – your turn

At their worst, textbooks can be part of the problem. Through an emphasis on simplification, some textbooks can encourage thin, rote learning. This emphasis often finds its visual expression in the use of bullet points and boxes. Metaphorically, this, sadly, can box up students' understanding and limit their imaginative thinking. This book is informed by a rather different impulse, and it asks something different of the reader. It shares Charles Lemert's (2012: 3) understanding of people as 'everyday sociologists' in the way that they exhibit 'this quality of human resilience, this competence that sustains and enriches human life, even against the odds'. People are everyday sociologists in that they often intuit a deep understanding of social structures that they journey through. In a similar vein, Cohen and Taylor (2003: 31) have a lovely phrase about how people often bring 'spontaneous wisdom ... to bear upon the concrete problem of living'.

This book, therefore, aims to develop the capacity of the reader as an everyday sociologist, to help the reader to call on their felt-knowing and spontaneous wisdom in articulating arguments concerning the sociology of work. This finds a specific expression in the section at the end of each following chapter, titled 'Sociological imagination – your turn'. As everyday sociologists, readers can call on their sociological imagination not to rote-learn bullet points in boxes but to think beyond boxes, to bring to bear their own experiences (perhaps in service or platform work), knowledge and imagination. The questions asked of readers in the 'your turn' sections are designed to open up the reader's sociological imagination and capacity as an everyday sociologist.

The importance of debate

Much of social science, including the sociology of work, features debate. It is unusual for topics to have a clear, unambiguous consensus among social scientists. A key reason for this is that, as Chapter 2 shows, there is a range of sociological perspectives or theories that present alternative ways of understanding society and of seeing the key patterns in how societies function. Many of these sociological perspectives have significant areas of incompatibility, so, they present competing approaches to understanding society. Furthermore, sociologists often disagree about how to study people's behaviour and how to interpret research findings. All this necessarily gives rise to debate. Debate in the sociology of work is not something that should be shied away from. Rather, it should be embraced. A key element of this book, therefore, is about explaining the key areas of debate on topics, outlining why those debates are important and, sometimes, giving a reading of the balance of strengths and weaknesses on the sides of the debate. Such a reading of the balance in a debate cannot be, and is not put forward as, the definitive reading of the debate. It is an informed evaluation, but that evaluation will still be a contested one.

There might be two reactions from readers to this. One, perhaps immediate, reaction could be frustration. Readers might ask what the point is of a sociology of work overview book that does not give definitive evaluations of debates. A second, wiser, reaction is one of actively developing your own role as an informed evaluator of debates. The book is not about closing down debates; it is about opening up important debates for readers to engage in. Students who perform well in social science modules at university are those who actively engage in debates and develop their own, original reading of the debates. As such, I invite readers to construct informed disagreements with my reading of debates (informed agreements are welcome too).

The book includes many references to articles, books and reports. These serve a double purpose. First, they show what is informing the point being made. Second, they are inviting the reader to go to the referenced work and critically evaluate it. Perhaps the reader will then see other relevant articles or books that cite the article being read, or that are cited by the article. The book, therefore, offers a doorway into debates for the reader to step through.

The aim is to communicate

I write this book to communicate. I am a sociologist of work, and I want to tell other people about the great insights that the sociology of work can give us. This means that I seek to avoid sociological jargon – terms that sociologists have become accustomed to use but which are awkward for non-sociologists to get their heads around. Often, there are more straightforward, more easily understood terms that can be used. I aim to use those straightforward terms. If I do include sociological jargon, I explain the meaning in an easily understood way. I seek to avoid esoteric vocabulary – language that is intended for, or likely to be understood by, only a small number of people with specialized knowledge. This puts me at odds with the communication approach of French social philosopher and writer Michel Foucault, whose work is called upon by some sociologists of work. Burrell (1988: 222) gives a very clear description of Foucault's writing style:

> His style is ornate and like a thicket, often impenetrable – but deliberately and consciously so … Foucault's writings are … the product of a long European tradition in which philosophical idealism is strongly represented … where a complex, convoluted writing style is self-consciously adopted to escape from what is seen as the limitations and constraints of clear prose.

Yes, Foucault *deliberately* adopted an impenetrable style. Unfortunately, Foucault is not alone in having this approach to social science writing. Michael Billig (2013) has written a lovely exposé and examination of such writing in the cleverly (but depressingly) titled book *Learn to Write Badly: How to Succeed in the Social Sciences*. Remarkably, as Billig shows, using jargon made up of long words and esoteric vocabulary (or 'puffed-up language', as he puts it) can make writers *appear* more intelligent in their analysis and more profound in their thinking, and can lead to their reputation as academics growing. Well, I hope that I am not a sociologist who has learnt to write badly. I invite readers to email me if they spot me using esoteric language or unexplained jargon, or, more generally, writing in a puffed-up way.

Overview and structure of the book

The book offers an analytical, celebratory overview of the sociology of contemporary work. Chapter 2 provides a theoretical grounding by outlining key social theories and their relevance to the analysis of work. Flowing from this, Chapters 3 and 4 examine the key social structures of work: macro–structures relating to forms of capitalism, and workplace-level structures relating to forms of work organization. As a necessary companion to the analysis of the social structures of work, Chapters 5 and 6 analyse the agency and voice of workers. These chapters consider how workers use their agency and voice both within and upon the social structures of work. The book then turns (Chapters 7 and 8) to consider key outcomes relating to inequality: inequality of outcome in terms of income inequality, and important inequalities of opportunity in terms of class, gender, ethnicity and migration. The final chapter analyses artificial intelligence in progress, and the progress made by the sociology of work. It points to key strengths in the sociology of work, and highlights these by pointing to corresponding weaknesses and gaps in neighbouring disciplinary fields. Overall, the book shows what the sociology of work is and why we need it.

2

Social Theory at Work

One of the great strengths of the sociology of work is that it is informed by a wide range of social theories that put forward some deeply insightful ways of understanding the social world. In this chapter, we are concerned with theories that provide an understanding of the key nature of the structures and patterns of the social world. They articulate a world-view. They present a picture of the deep structures underpinning the social world. They offer a way of seeing beneath the surface events of everyday life. This is theory as abstractions that cover a whole range of arenas of the social world. Work is just one of the arenas to which these social theories are applied.

In this chapter, for each social theory covered, I outline the key relevant aspects of the general theory before focusing on the theorizing in relation to the analysis of work. In outlining the theories, I present extensive quotes from the theorists themselves. Too often, textbooks summarize methodically rather than quote flashpoints of brilliance. Burrell (2006: 176) has written about approaching social theorists in terms of 'the excitement of reading something so fresh and thrilling that it changes one's life'. This chapter is written with that spirit in mind.

While some of these social theories have been put forward as closed statements, with an emphasis on the internal logic of the system outlined, in practice, these theories have become living, breathing things in the sense that sociologists are constantly using them, applying them, modifying them, developing them and making connections between them. This is an approach to theory that sits well with the call of the sociological imagination. Galtung (1990: 102) celebrates this approach thus: 'A good theory should never leave us with the idea that the world is made once and for all. A good theory will always have some empty spaces for the reality not yet there … for potential as opposed to empirical reality.' Again, that spirit informs this chapter.

After I have outlined six key social theories at work, I offer a brief overview of important points of comparison and contrast between the theoretical approaches and important dimensions or aspects that underpin many of the approaches. Applying the sociological imagination to the contents of this chapter means a consideration of how far we need to decolonize social theory at work. Following that, there is a section that examines how these social theories have been applied to the three types of work focused on in this book: service work, knowledge work and platform work. Then it is over to you, with the first 'Sociological imagination – your turn' section.

Social theories at work

Marx

Karl Marx is the most influential social theorist the world has known. He is also one of the social theorists whose work is least well understood. Marx lived from 1818 to 1883, in Germany, France, Belgium and England, and was an active revolutionary, rather than just a theorist or social analyst. As he put it, 'the philosophers have hitherto only interpreted the world in different ways; the point is to change it' (1845/1978: 422). He often wrote with his collaborator, Friedrich Engels. His most famous works are *Economic and Philosophical Manuscripts* (1844), *The Communist Manifesto* (1848) and *Capital* (three volumes in 1867, 1885 and 1894). With Marx having written over many decades, it is little surprise that commentators can point to a range of points of ambiguity and inconsistency in his work. There can still be heated debates over whether the younger or the older Marx created the 'real' Marxism. Such debates even occurred during Marx's lifetime – but without Marx's participation. 'Moi, je ne suis pas marxiste' was a famous and irritated observation of his (Draper, 1978). As Hyman (2006) notes, debate over Marx's legacy has been so intense because, uniquely among social theorists, Marx's writings inspired a mass movement. His writings were a central pillar for European social-democratic parties in the late-19th century and were embraced by the Russian Bolsheviks in their 1917 revolution and subsequent creation of a communist state. As different political factions have battled for dominance, so Marx's legacy has been a heated object of contest. Although there is no unambiguous body of thought called Marxism, it is still appropriate to give an overview of key elements in Marx's writings.

Marx worked at a number of levels of analysis or abstraction. He had a general theory of history, within which he located his theory of capitalism, within which he located his analysis of labour and production. I outline each in turn. At the most abstract level is his theory of history. Marx's political philosophy here has become known as 'historical materialism' or 'dialectical materialism'. He borrowed from Hegel, a leading German philosopher, the concept of history moving forward *dialectically* through the clash of contradictions. The dialectical movement of history involves a thesis giving rise to its antithesis; the clash of which is resolved in a new synthesis, which itself becomes the new thesis, which gives rise to its own antithesis … and so on. Marx's approach was materialist in the sense that he argued for the primacy of *economic* forces, rather than ideas, as driving forward history. For Marx, people's consciousness is conditioned by their material, economic conditions (1970: 2):

> In the social production which men carry on they enter into definite relations that are indispensable and independent of their will; these relations of production correspond to a definite stage of development of their material

powers of production. The totality of these relations of production constitutes the economic structure of society – the real foundations, on which legal and political superstructures arise and to which definite forms of social consciousness correspond. The mode of production of material life determines the general character of the social, political, and spiritual processes of life. It is not the consciousness of men that determines their being, but, on the contrary, their social being determines their consciousness.

Taking this materialist logic forward, he identified the clash of economic classes within economic development as the key driving dialectic of human history (Marx and Engels, 1848: 1):

> The history of all hitherto existing society is the history of class struggle. Freeman and slave, patrician and plebeian, lord and serf, guild-master and journeyman, in a word, oppressor and oppressed, stood in constant opposition to one another, carried on an uninterrupted, now hidden, now open fight, a fight that each time ended, either in a revolutionary reconstitution of society at large, or in the common ruin of the contending classes.

Class was centrally defined in terms of a relationship between those who own the means of production and those who do not, who only own their own capacity to labour. A certain form, or mode, of production would give rise to class formations (one exploitative, owning the means of production, and one exploited, without ownership of the means of production). The political and legal superstructure erected by the dominant class at first supports the development of production. However, as production develops into a new mode, the old superstructure becomes a 'fetter' on economic development. Hence revolutionary pressures arise, based on class conflict.

Marx identified capitalism as the mode of production following feudalism. Capital – the factory, the mill, the office – is the key means of production in capitalism. The owners of the means of production, the exploiting class, the employers, are the *bourgeoisie*, or capitalist class. The exploited class, who own only their own labour, were labelled the *proletariat*, or working class. Capitalism was a new mode of production that involved the systematic creation of profit and its reinvestment in further capital to generate further profit. Marx identified the creation of profit as lying within the exploitation of labour. Capitalists only employed labour if they could extract *surplus value* from that labour – that is, if they could pay them less than the value they generated within the labour process. Further, Marx identified capitalism as a system in which the creation of surplus value was *hidden* within the terms of an apparently 'free' exchange in the employment relationship: workers are 'free' to leave a job and find another employer. Applying his dialectical materialism to capitalism, Marx saw the following dynamics leading to its downfall and replacement by communism, where exploitation would be ended. One important way in which capitalism would provide the conditions for its own downfall was by bringing together the exploited en masse within work. The exploited must eventually join together, see their common interests in ending their exploitation and overthrow the capitalist class. In this sense, capitalism creates the diggers of its own grave: 'What the bourgeoisie therefore produces, above all, are its own grave-diggers' (Marx and Engels, 1848: 6).

Central to Marx's analysis of work, or labour, within capitalism are exploitation, conflict and alienation. Because work in capitalism is exploitative, it is potentially fraught with *conflict* – class conflict in its essence. On the other hand, as just noted, Marx saw the *hidden* nature of exploitation within capitalism – so there was the possibility that workers would not see their interests here. It was the role of the practical theorists and political activity, and indeed, Marx's role, to educate workers regarding their exploited status in order to foster revolutionary consciousness (recall that the point was to change the world, not just interpret it). At an abstract political philosophical level, Marx argued that labour within capitalism was alienated labour. There are four elements to *alienation*. First, workers are divorced from the products of their labour. People put themselves into the goods they produce, but under capitalism the goods are then expropriated and sold for profit. Second, the process of production becomes fragmented; labour becomes an uninteresting chore, meaningless, unfulfilling and unrewarding, a means to an end, rather than an end in itself. Third, people become alienated from each other as relationships between people come to be dominated by competition and the market. Finally, Marx argued that humans become alienated from their 'species being' (for Marx, self-conscious creative activity was the defining characteristic of humanity), in the sense that more and more work is made mindless and uncreative – to allow a better control of the crucial labour process by capitalists and their servants, management.

The above is just an outline of key currents in Marx's writing. There are multiple-volume analyses of Marx's work, so, inevitably, I have passed over much in the hope of presenting a clear picture of Marx's challenging, revolutionary (in more senses than one) theorizing. For a longer, but clear and readable examination of Marx in relation to the analysis of work, readers are invited to turn to Hyman (2006). Such is the reach of Marx's analysis that it is difficult for sociologists generally, and especially for sociologists of work, not to engage with Marx at some level. Indeed, Marx's work became a pillar against which other key social theorists of work subsequently defined themselves.

Weber

Max Weber lived from 1864 to 1920 in Germany and Austria. He is still regarded as one of the, if not *the*, greatest social theorists of the modern era. He was a contemporary of the rise of industrial capitalism and of burgeoning communist movements that took inspiration from Marx. Much of Weber's work is implicitly arguing against the forms of Marxism that existed around him that emphasized the determinism of economic forces. Weber's major works are *The Protestant Ethic and the Spirit of Capitalism* (1904) and *Economy and Society* (1921). There are many strands to Weber's writing, not all of which knit coherently together. Here, the focus is only on the strands that have direct relevance to the sociology of contemporary work: his writing on rationality and bureaucracy.

Authority is a key concept in Weber's writing. *Authority* refers to legitimate power, or 'legitimate domination', as Weber put it. Legitimate power exists where people accept the basis for decisions. It is different from power that functions through coercion – through people being compelled to do things. Taking a long historical view (such as Marx also did), Weber pointed to three 'pure' forms of authority as underlying the history of human society and organizations:

1. Traditional authority – resting on an established belief in the sanctity of immemorial traditions and the legitimacy of those exercising authority;
2. Charismatic authority – resting on devotion to the exceptional sanctity, heroism or exemplary character of an individual person and of the behaviour and beliefs revealed or ordained by them;
3. Rational-legal authority – resting on a belief in the 'legality' of rules and the rights of those elevated to authority under such rules to issue commands. (Weber's use of the word 'legal' here is a little confusing. He does not use it to pertain to state or government laws that define what constitutes crimes. Rather, this form of authority is 'legal' in that it functions on the basis of procedures that could be judged as correct or incorrect through reference to a body of rules by those subject to its authority.)

Weber argued that traditional and charismatic authority had been the key forms of authority in the pre-modern era, but rational-legal authority was becoming dominant in the modern era. Arguably, the word *rational* is the most important in Weberian analysis, and it requires some careful consideration, not least because Weber's approach to the concept of rationality was inconsistent, 'scattered and fragmented' (Kalberg, 1980: 1146). Indeed, Kalberg meticulously documents that Weber used the term 'rationality' in four distinct ways. By far the most important is 'formal rationality'. This relates to a calculation of an efficient means to attain an end, undertaken through an application of universal rules and regulations. So, formal-rational legal authority, which is what Weber centrally meant by 'rational-legal authority', relates to an acceptance of a system of power, where that power is legitimate because it is part of an efficient way to attain an end, and where the structure follows accordingly systematic rules. If this sounds complicated, think of formal-rational legal authority existing in a firm, with a structure set up to create profits through efficient production. A supervisor or line manager in this firm does not have authority because of traditional or charismatic authority, but because the rules of the firm set out the decision-making power of the role of supervisor/manager – the supervisor has rational-legal authority.

Weber theorized that formal-rational legal authority finds its purest organizational manifestation in a 'bureaucracy'. Now, to understand Weber's important ideas here, we have to cast aside how we use the word bureaucracy pejoratively in our everyday language to refer to red tape and an unwanted over-emphasis on undertaking the exact letter of the law. In Weberian sociology, bureaucracy is an organizational form based on formal-rational legal authority. The focus in a bureaucracy, therefore, is upon calculating an efficient means to an end through a systematic application of universal rules. Weber (1978: 973) used a metaphor of bureaucracy as a machine to highlight its qualities:

A fully developed bureaucratic apparatus compares with other organizations as does the machine with the non-mechanical mode of production. Precision, speed, unambiguity, knowledge of the files, continuity, discretion, unity, strict subordination, reduction of friction and of material and personal costs – these are raised to the optimum point in the strictly bureaucratic administration.

The rise of capitalism was intimately tied to the rise of bureaucracy. According to (Weber, 1978: 224): 'The capitalistic system has undeniably played a major role in the development of bureaucracy. Indeed, without it capitalistic production could not continue … capitalism is the most rational economic basis for bureaucratic administration and enables it to develop in the most rational form.' Weber saw bureaucracy being played out in modern enterprises: 'the very large modern capitalist enterprises are themselves unequalled models of strict bureaucratic organization' (1978: 974). Weber assumed that bureaucracy was the most efficient form of organization and hence would come to dominate the world.

Although the economy and public administration would be efficient, Weber saw that there would be significant negative consequences of the dominance of bureaucracy. Indeed, his metaphor of the machine forewarned us of this part of his analysis. Narrower, less skilled or more 'specialized' jobs were an inevitable part of the logic of formal rationality and bureaucracy: 'Bureaucratization offers … the optimum possibility for carrying through the principle of specializing administrative functions according to purely objective considerations. Individual performances are allocated to functionaries who have specialized training and who by constant practice increase their [efficiency]' (Weber, 1978: 975). At its heart, bureaucracy is a dehumanized structure: 'Bureaucracy develops the more perfectly, the more it is "dehumanized", the more completely it succeeds in eliminating from official business love, hatred, and all purely personal, irrational and emotional elements which escape calculation' (1978: 975).

In his most famous phrase, Weber stated that society was dominated by 'iron cages' of formal-rationality, of bureaucracy in which 'machine production … determine[s] the lives of all the individuals who are born into this mechanism' (1976: 181). People who have no choice but to live in these iron cages are dehumanized. They become 'specialists without spirit, sensualists without heart' (1976: 182). In one of the most devastating pieces of sociology ever written, Bauman (1989) argued that Weber's pessimism had not gone far enough in the sense that the lowest point of dehumanization – the industrially organized murder of millions of Jewish people by the Nazis in the Holocaust – can be seen to be informed by the bureaucratic form. The prioritizing of the means over the ends, the ethical indifference to the ends, the impersonalization of processes – all these, Bauman argues, are essential parts both of bureaucracy and the organization of the Holocaust. Bureaucracy was a necessary basis for the Holocaust: 'the choice of physical extermination as the right means to the task of Enfernung [removal of Jews from the German lifeworld] was a product of routine bureaucratic procedures: means-end calculus, budget balancing, universal rule application' (Bauman, 1989: 17).

Durkheim

Marx, Weber and Durkheim stand as the three main founding theorists for sociology. Emile Durkheim lived in France from 1858 to 1917. He sought to establish a new scientific sociology capable of helping France overcome the moral crisis reflected in the turmoil, violence and discontent that pervaded French society during his lifetime. So, like Marx, and Weber, Durkheim lived on the cusp of momentous social changes – a position that allowed him the opportunity to examine the social meaning of the development of capitalism.

Starting at the most abstract level, Durkheim is commonly regarded as a functionalist sociologist. Functionalists assume that society is a complex system and that the parts of the system tend to work together to produce stability. Here, the primary task of the sociologist is to investigate *how* the parts work together towards stability. Notably, Durkheim compared society to the human body, in which the different organs work together towards the survival of the whole. We can see the logic of functionalism underpinning much of Durkheim's arguments in *The Division of Labour in Society* (1893), his only major book directly pertaining to work. The key issue that Durkheim addressed in this book was the ever-increasing division of labour, or specialization, in the economy and society, and the consequences of that for overall social cohesion. The rise of industrial capitalism, that Durkheim lived through, saw a dramatic increase in the division of labour. Think of the example in Chapter 1 of how the industrial manufacture of pins broke up pin production from the job of a single craft worker into 18 distinct tasks. Often, jobs consisted of repeatedly undertaking just one of these tasks. Durkheim (1893: 39) noted: 'Modern industry … advances steadily towards powerful machines, towards great concentrations of forces and capital, and consequently to the extreme division of labour. Occupations are infinitely separated and specialized, not only inside the factories, but each product is itself a specialty dependent upon others.'

Durkheim argued against a common view at the time that the increasing division of labour would lead to the collapse of social life – for instance, see Tonnies' (1887) argument that modern society was disintegrating under the transition to industrial life, conceptualized as a shift from *Gemeinschaft*, in which real community existed, to *Gesselschaft*, in which social solidarity was being ripped apart, where 'everyone is out for himself alone and living in a state of tension against everyone else … there is no such thing as "common good"' (p 52).

Durkheim argued that social cohesion was not being dismantled but simply being reconstructed in a different form. The rise of industrial capitalism represented a shift from *mechanical solidarity* to *organic solidarity*. In the pre-industrial era, where there was no advanced division of labour, the mechanical solidarity of society was based on similarities between people. There was a form of suffocating uniformity of experience and thought, in which powerful moral rules were made that brooked no challenge (Durkheim, 1893: 129):

> Solidarity which comes from likenesses is at its maximum when the collective conscience completely envelops our whole conscience and coincides in all points with it … when this solidarity exercises its force, our personality vanishes, as our definition permits us to say, for we are no longer ourselves, but the collective life.

In the era of the increasing division of labour linked to industrial capitalism, a new form of social cohesion emerges. This is organic solidarity in society, based on mutual dependence – the very mutual dependence created by the ever-increasing division of labour. Durkheim notes that individualism, based on different experiences and thoughts, can flourish without a breakdown in social cohesion. People with complementary differences interact and come to realize that they rely on each other:

> The members [of societies with a high division of labour] are united by ties that go well beyond the ever so brief moments during which exchange actually takes place. … Because we exercise this or that domestic or social function, we are caught in a network of obligations which we do not have the right to forsake. (1893: 207)

> If the division of labour produces solidarity, this is not only because it makes of each person an exchanger, to speak the language of the economists; it is because the division of labour creates among men a comprehensive system of rights and duties which tie them to one another in a durable fashion. (1893: 402–403)

Durkheim used the adjective 'organic' in relation to this form of social cohesion because he saw the analogy of the functioning organism as applying well to the process: 'The unity of the organism is as great as the individuation of the parts is more marked. Because of this analogy, we propose to call the solidarity which is due to the division of labour, organic' (1893: 131).

In this (central) part of his argument, Durkheim's approach is explicitly functionalist. In the meantime, however, he had to contend with the evidence of the turmoil of his own times – a turmoil which he analysed in terms of 'anomie' and the 'forced division of labour'. These existed in the period of transition between the death of mechanical solidarity and the rise of organic solidarity. This would be a period of turmoil, but the turmoil would be temporary. Anomie is the state in which there is no effective form of social cohesion that ties individuals to society, or workers to others (including employers) in the workplace. It is an anarchy of selfishness, in which individuality is not yet tied to others through a recognition of mutual dependence and complementary differences. For Durkheim, class conflict in the workplace through strikes was an example of anomie in action. In addition, in the temporary state of anomie, work often appeared meaningless to people.

Anomie would only be temporary, however, as organic solidarity would emerge. This could be helped by institutions and regulation, not least through the removal of the forced division of labour. The forced division of labour effectively perpetuates anomie. The forced division of labour exists when patterns of inequality fail to mirror the normal or inevitable distribution of personal inequalities. Social cohesion from the division of labour would only exist 'if society is constituted in such a way that social inequalities exactly express natural inequalities' (Durkheim, 1893: 377). Further, 'there cannot be rich and poor at birth without there being unjust contracts' (p 384). These (ultimately radical) arguments about the forced division of labour and its link to the continuation of anomie stand less easily with the functionalist logic in Durkheim's writing.

Polanyi

Karl Polanyi (1886–1964) was born in Hungary, and lived in Austria, the UK and the US. He was a newspaper editor, academic and writer. His great work is *The Great Transformation: The Political and Economic Origins of Our Time* (1944). Although for many decades Polanyi only had a marginal presence in sociology of work scholarship, increasing numbers of work sociologists see his theorizing as shedding light on key aspects of contemporary work (see Silver, 2003). Notably, Block (2001: xiii) writes: '*The Great Transformation* remains fresh … it is indispensable for understanding the dilemma facing global society at the beginning of the twenty-first century.'

Like Marx, Weber and Durkheim, Polanyi's theorizing is based on seeing the essential nature of the economy and society of his time by comparing it with forms of economy and society historically. Here, Polanyi's key starting point is his observation of the persistent embeddedness of the economy within society. Polanyi observed that, for the vast majority of human history, the economy has not been autonomous from society but has been embedded in it, subordinated to politics, religion, social norms and social relations. For instance, up until the 19th century in Britain, the law, local values and customs and religious authorities placed numerous restrictions on the activities of merchants and workshop owners and many other forms of economic activity. Polanyi puts it (1944: 73):

> Under the guild system, as under every other economic system in previous history, the motives and circumstances of productive activities were embedded in the general organisation of society. The relations of master, journeyman and apprentice; the terms of the craft; the number of apprentices, the wages of the workers were all regulated by the custom and rule of the guild and town.

The economic sphere was understood as being part of the wider social world. Writers have examined this phenomenon using slightly different terminology. The great social historian, E.P. Thompson (1991), wrote of 'the moral economy' that occurred in Britain prior to the advent of industrial capitalism. Particularly important here were norms of reciprocity and mutual obligation and recognition that should exist between an employer and workers. There was a commitment from both sides of the 'master–servant' relationship of a diffuseness quite at odds with current understandings of the social contract of employment (Fox, 1985). It was this deep social embedding of work and the economy that informed the considerable forms of state regulation that operated in many industries. In the 17th century, there were already movements by merchants and others to rid themselves of such restrictions. The tensions around this are brilliantly explored by Shakespeare in *The Merchant of Venice*. As Long (2012) puts it, 'in the play, Antonio, Shylock and Portia play out the apprehension of a society witnessing the falling away of ritual constraints and the empowerment of individuals at the periphery *to act without regard to community values*' (emphasis added).

For Polanyi, the 'great transformation' of human history was the advent of market capitalism, which rested on the idea of disembedding the economy from society (1944: 67):

The disembedded economy of the nineteenth century stood apart from the rest of society, more especially from the political and governmental system. In a market economy the production and distribution of material goods in principle is carried on through a self-regulating system of price-making markets. It is governed by laws of its own, the so-called laws of supply and demand, and motivated by fear of hunger and hope of gain. Not blood-tie, legal compulsion, religious obligation, fealty or magic creates the sociological situations which make individuals partake in economic life but specifically economic institutions such as private enterprise and the wage system.

At the same time as the laws and customs of the social embedding of the economy were being dismantled, the economics profession was creating an intellectual map of what the free market – free from social and political restrictions – should look like. A famous quote from political economist Adam Smith captures the distance of the idea of the free market from ideas of morality. Smith (1776: 14) argued that the only norm that should govern the running of the economy is the appeal to economic self-interest:

> It is not from the benevolence of the butcher, the brewer and the baker, that we expect our dinner, but from their regard to their own interest. We address ourselves not to their humanity, but to their self-love, and never talk to them of our necessities but of their advantages.

Polanyi argued that the disembedded market could only exist as an idea because, in practice, it would inevitably have self-destructive tendencies. At the heart of his argument is that central to the running of a disembedded economy is the commodification of three 'fictitious commodities': labour, land and money. For Polanyi, a true commodity is something that is created to be bought and sold. Because human labour, land (or natural resources) and money are not created so they can be bought and sold, they are fictitious commodities (1944: 72):

> Labour is only another name for human activity which goes with life itself, which is in its turn not produced for sale but for entirely different reasons, nor can that activity be detached from the rest of life, be stored or mobilised, land is only another name for nature, which not produced by man, actual money, finally, is merely a token of purchasing power. ... None of them is produced for sale. The commodity description of labour, land and money is fictitious.

For the study of the sociology of work, Polanyi's big argument here is his challenge to the orthodox economic view that human labour could be treated as a simple commodity, like anything that is bought and sold on the market. Human beings are not commodities, and the labour of human beings cannot be treated as a commodity. The character of Willy Loman in Arthur Miller's play *Death of a Salesman* (1949) puts it thus, as he realizes that his boss is firing him without any dignity near the end of his long career: 'You can't eat the orange and throw the peel away – a man is not a piece of fruit!' Treating any of these three fictitious commodities as pure commodities, Polanyi argued, will lead to their ruin. Yet, the economists' idea of the free market exactly treats them as commodities. The logic of Polanyi's argument is that any attempt to make perfect free markets is not sustainable.

Polanyi argued that attempts to create a disembedded free market, in which labour, land and money are treated as commodities, inevitably give rise to a counter-movement that seeks to re-embed economic activity within the social, to stop the treatment of labour, land and money as simple commodities. Polanyi calls the move to disembed and the reaction against this, the 'double movement'. Writing about the 19th century, Polanyi (1944: 79) observes that:

> Social history in the nineteenth century was thus the result of a double movement: the extension of the market organization in respect to genuine commodities was accompanied by its restriction in respect to fictitious ones. While on the one hand markets spread all over the face of the globe and the amount of goods involved grew to unbelievable proportions, on the other hand a network of measures and policies was integrated into powerful institutions designed to check the action of the market relative to labour, land, and money.

His analysis suggests that society would inevitably protect itself from destruction through the free market: 'society protected itself against the perils inherent in a self-regulating market system'. Unlike Marx, Polanyi does not assume that counter-movements (to disembedding) will be led by the labour movement.

We can understand why Polanyi's analysis has become more pressing and more pertinent for sociologists of work if we consider the argument that we are living in an era of disembedding of the economy from society. The intellectual map for disembedding is given by free-market economists – something that sociologists sometimes call neoliberalism. Globalization can be understood as disembedding production systems from their previously anchored nation-based locations. In addition, a key element in the rise of platform capitalism involves the (attempted) disembedding of labour from employment rights regulations. It is on these bases that Sallaz (2013: 159) insists – in line 'with the spirit of *The Great Transformation*' – that 'the contested processes by which labor is disembedded from and re-embedded within the social' should be at the heart of the sociology of work.

Feminist perspectives

The term 'feminism' was first used in the 1880s, to refer to the struggle for legal and political equality for women. Since then, it has become one of the key political, social and theoretical movements of the 20th and 21st centuries. Feminists such as Arlie Hochschild, Cynthia Cockburn and Sylvia Walby have produced some of the most important sociology of work studies in recent decades, highlighting the institutionalized subordination of women in the workplace and in domestic labour, but also women's resistance to such inequalities. Notably, the growth of feminist sociological theorizing from the 1970s onwards has been informed both by women resisting their restriction to the domestic sphere by entering paid employment in unprecedented numbers (Fevre, 2003) and by women resisting their subordination within paid employment through fighting for equal pay.

There is a range of feminist theoretical perspectives, and there is no one dominant strand of feminist theorizing. Nevertheless, there are some core shared elements across the range of feminist perspectives, and this overview concentrates on those shared elements. It proceeds from a discussion of key elements of general feminist theorizing to then focus on theorizing in relation to the sociology of work.

A common starting point in feminist theorizing is the critique of the main social theories as gender-blind. Feminist analyses point to the inadequacies of the classic social theorists (Marx, Weber, Durkheim and Polanyi) as ignoring a vital aspect of social reality at work – the subordination of women. There is a deafening silence in the work of these theorists regarding the position of women in society and work. Here is a piquant quotation from Jennifer Marx, wife of Karl (in Wheen, 1999: 292):

> In all these struggles we women have the harder part to bear because it is the lesser one. A man draws strength from his struggle with the world outside, and is invigorated by the sight of the enemy, be their number legion. We remain sitting at home, darning socks.

Weber and Durkheim both regarded women as 'naturally' fitted for domestic responsibilities. Indeed, Durkheim went so far as to argue that the gender-based domestic division of labour was a good example of social harmony (organic solidarity) generated when social inequalities simply mirrored 'natural' inequalities. Abbott et al (2005: 3) put the feminist challenge to social theorizing thus:

> The feminist challenge to malestream sociology is one that requires a radical rethink of the content and the methodology of the whole enterprise; one that recognises the need, not simply to see society from the standpoint of women as well as from the standpoint of men, but to see the world as fundamentally gendered.

Also common across feminist perspectives is the focus on the systematic patterns of restriction and subordination that women experience in the social world. Much feminist theorizing has used the concept of patriarchy to explain these patterns. A common thread in the understanding of patriarchy is presented by Bilton et al (2002: 147):

> In most societies, males ... have more power and more authority over women; more than that, they have power over women. Men and women are, then, not merely different but in relations of subordination and domination. The structure of subordination and domination is called patriarchy. Although there is a great deal of controversy about the precise connotations of the term, at least it implies a hierarchy of social relations and institutions in which and through which men are able to dominate women.

More recently, some feminist writers have noted important limitations in such a concept of patriarchy as too universal and trans-historical, preferring to make use of related terms of (types of) 'gender regimes' (Walby, 2011) and 'gender orders' (Connell, 2005). Feminist theorizing also shares an understanding of the importance of the distinction between sex and gender. Sex has been used to refer to a person's physical characteristics, such as male or female genitalia. Gender is a different concept – it refers to the social and cultural differences between sexes that are shaped within social processes, involving the playing out of power. Traditionally, masculine and feminine have been the main types of gender that have been discussed by feminist sociologists. Overall, a key point developed by feminist analysis is that 'gender is linked to socially constructed norms of masculinity and femininity and is not a direct product of biology' (Giddens and Sutton, 2021: 245).

Joan Acker used this concept of gender to develop the sociology of work, and argued that employment is a key sphere in which gender is socially constructed. She argued for the importance of seeing the 'gendered organisation' (1990: 146):

> To say that an organisation ... is gendered means that advantage and disadvantage, exploitation and control, action and emotion, meaning and identity, are patterned through and in terms of a distinction ... between male and female, masculine and feminine. Gender is not an addition to those processes, conceived as gender neutral. Rather, it is an integral part of those processes, which cannot be properly understood without an analysis of gender.

Acker argues that organizational design and established norms are far closer to men's lives and assumptions about men (for instance as rational, goal-oriented and with a primary commitment to the workplace) than to women's lives and the assumptions made about women (for instance as emotional and with a primary commitment to home and family). The power of the gendered organization lies in the fact that it is rarely recognized. Established organizational practices are usually simply assumed to be the best way of organizing and, as such, are assumed to be gender-neutral. Feminist analyses have argued that the concept of 'skill' is, in large part, socially constructed, and in this social construction there is considerable gendering – see Phillips and Taylor's (1986: 63) conclusion that 'it is the sex of those who do the work, rather than its content, which leads to its identification as skilled or unskilled'.

Another fundamental insight from feminist theorizing for the sociology of work was to show the domestic arena as a key sphere of work, and to point to the need to consider the overall unequal position of women in terms of the relationship between domestic work and paid employment. While some schools of feminist theory debate whether the domestic sphere or the sphere of paid employment is the more fundamental basis of women's overall unequal position in society, there is also widespread support for a focus on how inequality in one sphere informs inequality in the other. For instance, consider Bond and Sales' (2001: 245) conclusion from their analysis of a large UK survey, that women were 'disadvantaged in the labour market due to their domestic responsibilities and their disadvantaged position in employment leads to a continuation of these domestic responsibilities'.

Foucault and postmodernism

A number of French philosophers have been associated with postmodernism, including Derrida, Baudrillard and Lyotard. Although Michel Foucault (1926–84) was not a self-declared postmodernist, there are a number of clear affinities between his writing and postmodernism. These authors wrote their major works in the 1970s and 1980s. Legge (2005) suggests that the timing of the rise of postmodern theory was not accidental. She argues that postmodernism theory reflected the falling away of key structures of modern capitalism (Lash and Urry, 1987) and the advent of the postmodern period and organization (see Offe's *Disorganized Capitalism*, 1985). Clegg (1990: 181) summarizes the differences between these periods for the nature of organizations and work:

> Where the modernist organisation was rigid, postmodern organisation is flexible. Where modernist consumption was premised on mass forms, postmodernist consumption is premised on niches. Where modernist organisation was premised on technological determinism, postmodernist organisation is premised on technological choices made possible through 'de-dedicated' micro-electronic equipment. Where modernist organisation and jobs were highly differentiated, demarcated and de-skilled, postmodernist organisation and jobs are highly de-differentiated, de-demarcated and multiskilled. Employment relations ... give way to more complex and fragmentary relational forms, such as subcontracting and networking.

So, from a society of disorganization and fragmentation arises postmodernism – a conceptualization of reality, society, organization and self as fragmented. Central to postmodernism is the assumption that the world is formless, fragmented and intertextual: there is no hidden order. As befits its (dis)organizing theme, there is considerable variety within postmodernist theorizing. The following is a collage of some important themes.

Postmodernists challenge the modernist desire for unifying views with their belief that knowledge is fundamentally fragmented – knowledge is produced in so many different bits and pieces that there can be no reasonable expectation that it will ever add up to an integrated and singular view. Lyotard contemptuously labelled efforts at universal understanding as 'grand narratives'. He stated: 'I define postmodern as incredulity towards metanarratives' (quoted in Burrell, 2006: 159). The theorizing of Marx, Weber, Durkheim, Polanyi and some feminists lay out what postmodernists regard as grand narratives. There is no one truth that is knowable through the use of objective science. Rather, there are multiple ways of knowing and multiple 'truth claims'. Indeed, postmodernists suggest, analysts should be more concerned with examining *representations* of 'reality' rather than fruitlessly searching *for* 'reality'. Baudrillard (1994) argues that we live in societies where people respond to media images rather than to real people or places. The search to separate our reality from representation is fruitless when all that exists is 'hyper-reality' – the intertwining of the two.

Baudrillard and Bauman (2004) argue that our shifting identities are led by our patterns of consumption rather than our role as producers (workers). Moreover, the key aspect of what we consume is not the 'use-value' of goods and services, but rather their associated images, or their 'sign-value', which allow us to differentiate ourselves from others. In this signifying consumption, tastes are frequently eclectic, playful and transient, with an emphasis on style over substance. This emphasis on consumption and over production represents a major break from the critical modernist theories. As Burrell (2006: 158) puts it, 'the postmodern turn is less about economics, production and work than it is about philosophy, consumption and leisure'. One of the unifying aspects of Marx, Weber, Durkheim, Polanyi and strands of feminism is that they all point to the sphere of work as the key arena in which the vital aspects of societies and individuals' identities and experiences are structured. This is denied by postmodernism. So, for instance, Bauman (2004) argues that the key 'discontent' of postmodern times is felt by those underclass in contemporary societies who do not have the means to engage in the playful and eclectic consumption. For Baudrillard, the key discontent of societies lies in the inevitable and hollow failure of individuals' project of trying to differentiate themselves from others through the sign-value of what they consume.

These ideas from postmodernism pertain to the sociology of work in the negative sense of destabilizing the social theories (at work) that have been presented in this chapter so far. The writing of Foucault, however, has been used in a more positive sense within the sociology of work. Foucault's critique of modernist social theory went further than arguing counter to the key assumptions. He also argued that the whole process of the creation of various theoretical disciplines, not least that of social theory, was an integral part of the development of the 'disciplinary society'. Historically, Foucault argued that two modes of domination have characterized the Western world: the 'traditional' and the 'disciplinary'.

To contrast the two, in a startling beginning to *Discipline and Punish*, he describes two modes of punishment. First, he describes an execution in 1757:

> His flesh will be torn from his breasts, arms, thighs and calves with red-hot pincers, his right hand, holding the knife with which he committed the said parricide, burnt with sulphur and on those places where the flesh will be torn away, poured molten lead, boiling oil, burning resin, wax and sulphur melted together and then his body drawn and quartered by four horse and his limbs and body consumed by fire. (1977: 3)

Then he describes rules 'for the House of Young Prisoners in Paris' drawn up just some 80 years later:

> At half past seven in summer, half past eight in winter, the prisoners must be back in their cells after the washing of hands and the inspection of clothes in the courtyard: at the first drum-roll they must undress and at the second get into bed.

In this contrast between violent, public execution and timetable, we see examples of the shift from *traditional* to *disciplinary* modes of domination. Increasingly, punishment is directed at the soul and the will of the individual in austere organizational settings, with minute detail paid to every aspect of the individual's behaviour. This disciplinary approach comes to pervade all organizations, as Foucault outlines in one of his most famous quotes: 'prisons resemble factories, schools, barracks, hospitals, which all resemble prisons' (1977: 83). Just as the nature of state-sanctioned punishment changed dramatically, so the growth of factories represented a clear break from the past, with factories coming to be significant places for the disciplinary mode of domination. Disciplinary domination involves concentrating individuals in space, with a timetable for activity, manuals for the correct movement of the body and a precise, economical system of command. Individuals become 'cases' who are measured, described, evaluated, examined and compared. In this process, theoretical disciplines, apparently built out of 'objective knowledge', play a crucial part.

For Foucault, the panopticon was *the* metaphor for the disciplinary mode of domination. He found the idea of the panopticon in the writing of Jeremy Bentham, a 19th-century British political thinker. The panopticon was an architectural innovation that involved a circular building with a central observation tower from which inmates (or workers or prisoners) could be surveyed without being able to observe those who were observing them. The aim was, according to Foucault (1977: 201):

> to induce in the inmate a state of conscious and permanent visibility that assures the automatic functioning of power. So to arrange things that the surveillance is permanent in its effects, even if it is discontinuous in its action; that the perfection of power should tend to render its actual exercise unnecessary; that this architectural apparatus should be a machine for creating and sustaining a power relation independent of the person who exercises it; in short that the inmates should be caught up in a power situation of which they are themselves the bearers.

Under the field of the (potential) gaze of surveillance, a process of internalization occurs (Foucault, 1977: 202–203):

> He who is subjected to a field of visibility, and who knows it, assumes responsibility for the constraints of power; he makes them play spontaneously upon himself; he inscribes in himself the power relations in which he simultaneously plays both roles; he becomes the principle of his subjection.

As we will see, Foucault's wider ideas about the disciplinary society as played out within the arena of work and his more specific use of the metaphor of the panopticon have both been taken up by some sociologists of work.

Overview of social theories at work

The preceding section outlined six different understandings of the social world overall and specifically the social world related to work. Chapter 1 pointed to the importance of debate, and debates between these social theories at work are ongoing – sometimes

Table 2.1: Overview of social theories at work

School of social theory at work	Major problem or tension at work	Solution
Marx	Exploitation; class conflict; alienation	Working-class revolution to create communism
Weber	The iron cage of rationality within bureaucracy	Largely pessimistic; no solution
Durkheim	Anomie	Temporary phenomenon to be replaced by organic solidarity
Polanyi	Disembedding the economy (and therefore work) from society; labour commodification	Counter-movement to re-embed the economy in society
Feminism	Subordination of women; the relationship between domestic labour and paid employment	Empowerment of women
Foucault and Postmodernism	Withering of importance of work; disciplinary domination through the panopticon	Increased polyvocality in a fragmented social world

explicitly and sometimes implicitly, sometimes articulated at a broad level but more often played out in discussion of some specific aspect of the social world of work. To be presented with many different ways of viewing the nature of the social world in relation to work may be, and hopefully is, exciting. But it can also be a dizzying experience. This section should help to steady things a little. It offers an overview of these social theories at work; first, in terms of the key substantive differences between these schools of social theory, and then in terms of considering some abstract dimension of social theory against which we can locate the social theories.

Table 2.1 offers a broad-brush overview of the key problem or tension that each social theory's world-view highlights, and the related approach to resolve that problem. Each school of social theory has different core assumptions about the essential nature of the social world of work, and this leads to each school identifying different major problems or tensions in work. The logics of their world-views suggest different ways of resolving or addressing the highlighted problem. So, for instance, Marx points to exploitation and class conflict as essential features of work under capitalism, and, given the logic of his dialectical materialist world-view, the solution lies in a revolution towards a new economic system of communism, in which there is no exploitation of labour.

The table highlights differences between these schools of social theory, but we should not allow the summary to hide nuanced analysis that notes important areas of overlap and compatibility between some schools of social theory at work. Although these world-views are different, it does not follow that they are *necessarily* mutually incompatible. Many contemporary sociologists of work, for instance, position themselves as informed by *both* Marxist and Weberian social theory. Notably, this is the case for some writers who have developed a 'labour process theory' approach to the analysis of work (Thompson and Smith, 2009: 925). There is an ongoing debate on whether the 'unhappy marriage' of Marxism and feminist analysis can be sustained (Hartmann, 1979). Provocative, and curiously overlooked (Burrell, 2006; Hyman, 2006), is Marsden's (1999) argument for the compatibility, and indeed complementarity, of aspects of Foucault's writing and Marxist analysis. Marsden argues that, while Foucault brilliantly analyses the *processes* by which power is enacted, his theorizing fails to adequately account for *why* the processes of disciplinary domination unfold. Marsden argues that Marxist analysis can account for this – the imposition of disciplinary *domination* is informed by the logic of capital accumulation. Marsden argues (1999: 2) that 'ascending spirals of disciplinary technologies and capital accumulation, interweave … Foucault explains the "how" of power, Marx explains the "why"'.

Another way to look across social theories at work is to consider them in terms of important abstract dimensions of social theory (see, for instance, Burrell and Morgan, 1979; Hirschman, 1982; Grint, 1998; Korczynski et al, 2006; Reed and Burrell, 2019). One such dimension concerns agency and structure and their relative weights. The structure–agency debate is one of the key fault lines that runs through discussions of social theory. Layder (1994: 4) states that the debate 'concentrates on the question of how creativity [agency] and constraint [structure] are related through social activity – how can we explain their co-existence'. Those who prioritize agency focus on the social practices through which people create and reproduce the social world. Those located on the structure side stress the importance of the objectified external relations and patterns that shape the social world. A social structure might be an institution like a school or a firm, but it could also be something less tangible, more informal, like a form of masculinity, or norms related to a work role (such as prison guard – see the discussion of the Stanford prison experiment in Zimbardo, 2011).

It has been common to position some social theories as emphasizing structure over agency. Weber, especially when placed next to his arguments regarding the rise of formal rationality and bureaucracy, is often subject to such categorization. Marx has often been treated similarly, with regard to his emphasis on the structuring dynamic related to the economy, or materialism. By contrast, a key criticism of some postmodernist literature has been that, by highlighting the scope for creative agency, for instance in terms of identity creation, it loses sight of wider structuring forces of society. Such categorizations of social theories appear easy, but a careful analysis suggests that they may be given too hastily. Consider, for instance, a famous quotation from Marx (1859: 7): 'Men [sic] make their own history, but they do not make it as they please; they do not make it under circumstances of their own choosing, but under circumstances existing already, given and transmitted from the past.' This shows a clear acknowledgement by Marx of the structure–agency tension within social analysis: the agency of people to 'make their own history', but that the structure of that history is created 'under circumstances existing already, given and transmitted from the past'. Such an acknowledgement should make us pause before simply labelling Marxism as necessarily carrying an over-emphasis on the structures of society and work.

Overall, it appears that much of the social theory outlined in this chapter can be home to nuanced appreciations of both structure and agency. It is notable, indeed, that the many attempts to build a conceptual bridge across the structure–agency fault line appear in themselves quite compatible with a range of social theory. The concepts of structuration (Giddens, 1984), habitus and field (Bourdieu, 1984), micro and macro coupling and decoupling (Goffman, 1990) and the tactics and strategies of everyday life (de Certeau, 1984) have little that, intrinsically, stands in the way of their use by sociologists from a range of theoretical traditions.

It is important to be aware of the conceptual space for agency within social theories. Without that space, the picture summarized in Table 2.1 appears overwhelmingly negative. With the exception of Durkheim, and some postmodernist writing, there is a common landscape of structures that create systematic social problems and tensions within the world of work. The image can appear dark and heavy, with structures of exploitation, alienation, the iron cage of rationality, disembeddedness, commodification, patriarchy and the panopticon looming large. The social theories at work are brilliant in highlighting the dark side of the social world of work. This is a crucial role for social theory – not least because, as we will see later, it is one of the key roles of human resource management (HRM) departments in organizations to emphasize the positive nature of work and to marginalize and hide dark sides to working life.

Nevertheless, for all the importance of highlighting systematic dark patterns in the social world of work, there is a danger that the picture becomes too bleak: so bleak that it starts to lose correspondence with people's lived experience of working. As will become clear throughout the book, the image of people's working lives provided by research within the sociology of work is *not* one of overwhelming negativity. There are systematic negative patterns in people's working lives, but that story is not the only story. Often, there is a positive part of the story. This positive part often relates to the space for agency, not least in the active creation of meaning and community at work, and workers' often sociologically brilliant resistance to oppressive structures. One trap to be aware of in considering abstract social theory is that it can be too easy to be seduced by the beautiful logic of ideas used in showing the deep structures underpinning the social world of work. Abstract ideas about social structures are one thing, but everyday practices are often a very different thing. Compelling and internally coherent ideas about mutually supporting social structures may often end up some distance from the messiness, compromises and contradictions in the everyday practices within the social world of work. The best sociology of work holds to this – it understands that there can be powerful social structures at play that, to use Hirschman's (1982) term, can degrade us, and it also understands that even the most powerful social structures have cracks and imperfections in practice, and that we need to see and analytically celebrate the light that gets in through these cracks.

Towards postcolonial social theory at work?

Postcolonial sociological theory points to the foundational, and continuing, influence of colonialism, both on the contemporary social world *and* on contemporary sociology, particularly sociological theory as a form of knowledge. It is sociological theory (at work) *as a form of knowledge* that is particularly at issue here. A starting point is to consider social theory as Eurocentric. Thus, this chapter can be critiqued for its Eurocentrism as it focuses on the contribution of European theorists while overlooking the contribution of scholars from Asia, Africa and elsewhere in the world. More broadly, we can see that, historically, the discipline of sociology has itself been structured by colonialism. This is clear in the division that emerged between sociology – concerned primarily with studying modern, industrialized countries – and anthropology – concerned primarily with studying the non-European and non-modern world (Costa et al, 2010). There is more to the critique of Eurocentrism than merely pointing out the specific and partial geographic location of the social theorists, however. The next level of critique notes that these European social theorists presented pictures of universal patterns of social relations related to work. 'Universal' here is used in the sense of general patterns that can be expected to pertain regardless of location – think of Marx on capitalism, Weber on bureaucracy, Durkheim on the consequences of the growing division of labour. The critique is that, rather than being universal patterns, these may be Eurocentric patterns that are just assumed to be universal by the theorists.

There can be two ways forward in considering this challenge. The first is to take issue with the whole universalizing logic of the social theories per se (there are overlaps here with the postmodernist critique of grand narratives). An important strand of postcolonial theory critiques the universalizing ambition of some social theory as itself conditioned by a colonial mindset. Another way of putting this is that social theory is critiqued for its tendency towards seeking to generate *etic* knowledge. Etic forms of knowledge emphasize the role of the researcher as outside observer, and involve concepts and perspectives that are applicable across contexts. If this is the critique, the way forward is to focus on creating *emic* forms of knowledge that emphasize the importance of the researcher as an embedded insider and articulate deep contextualized understandings of different social milieux.

The second way forward is not to throw away the search for etic knowledge, but rather to seek to create better, postcolonial, etic knowledge. This needs to have at its heart a focus on how colonialism has influenced, and continues to influence, the social world of work. This is likely to be based on two key pillars. The first is that we can only move to a fuller understanding of the colonially influenced social world (of work) if we hear more voices of the people marginalized and silenced through colonialism. For instance, early postcolonial theorist C.L.R. James (1938), in his study of the Haitian revolution, showed that enslaved people, not the colonizers, made history by rising up in the construction of an independent state. The second pillar involves seeing the *relationalism* of people, as structured by colonialism. Go (2016) argues that, to properly understand the continuing influence of colonialism on the social world (of work), sociologists need to be attuned to relationalism. Thus, postcolonialist writing asks us not just to raise the voice of those marginalized by colonialism and its legacies, but also to consider how the position of those living and working in the colonizing countries (for example the UK and France) is related to those living and working in the colonized countries.

Some postcolonial writers argue that there needs to be a rethinking of the very foundations of sociology, and social theory. Bhambra (2014: 4), for instance, advocates for 'reconsidering what we previously thought we had known … [it is] an argument for the reconstruction of concepts and the reinterpretation of histories in light of that reconstruction'. Debates on this proposition are only just beginning. See, for instance, Pradella's (2016) defence of Marxist analysis against critiques by postcolonialist writers. Indeed, as we will see in the following chapter, Marx wrote extensively regarding the systematic interconnections between capitalism and imperialism.

Social theory and contemporary work

Hopefully, some of the social theories at work reviewed in this chapter have been eye-opening. There may still be a nagging doubt, however, regarding the *contemporary* relevance of these – often old – ideas. Can something Marx wrote in the 1840s really help us understand the social world of work in the 21st century? The answer is given by contemporary sociologists of work who frequently use these social theories in conducting illuminating studies of today's workplaces and today's workers. By way of illustration, the following sections briefly outline some key studies – inspired by different schools of social theory – that illuminate contemporary service work, platform work and knowledge work.

Social theory and service work

Weberian social theory and service work

George Ritzer's McDonaldization thesis (2011) derives from Weber's analysis of the rise of formal rationality and the bureaucratic organization in contemporary service work. Ritzer argues that the increasing pervasiveness of formal rationality, or the process of rationalization, can now best be captured in the concept of McDonaldization. He sees McDonald's as a clear and easily recognizable manifestation of how far rationalization has proceeded. McDonald's epitomizes the process of McDonaldization, but the process applies to many other aspects of life other than the fast-food chain. McDonaldization involves four aspects: efficiency, calculability, predictability and control. Although Weber did not use all of these concepts, they have strong overlaps with his thinking. Within McDonaldization, efficiency concerns 'the optimum method of getting from one point to another' (Ritzer, 2011: 9); calculability relates to an emphasis on measuring; predictability relates to repeated efficiency – formalization, routine, discipline and order – and control has an emphasis on technology determining the service worker's actions. Ritzer argues that the process of McDonaldization is leading to the creation of more and more McJobs which require little or no skill so that the worker is structured to act like a 'mechanical nut' (2011: 13) and a 'human robot' (1998: 60). Not only are service workers' actions controlled, their words too are controlled through the imposition of scripts to which they are expected to adhere when interacting with customers. Following through on Weber's pessimism regarding the iron cage of rationality, Ritzer argues that, although McJobs are highly dehumanizing, the resistance of workers against them tends to be low because, 'if most of one's life is spent in McDonaldized systems, then there is little or no basis for rebellion against one's McDonaldized job since one lacks a standard against which to compare and judge such a job' (1998: 67).

Ritzer's multi-edition *The McDonaldization of Society* is one of the biggest-selling sociology of work books. It offers an energetic application of Weber, with its clear focus on the logic of rationalization and control in contemporary service work. It has, however, also been widely criticized, not least for its over-emphasis on structure over agency, and for the failure of its strongest claims regarding McJobs to be grounded in research support (Smart, 1999; Korczynski, 2002). In Korczynski (2002 and 2009b), I developed a different way of applying Weberian analysis to service work. Going back to Weber's foundational question regarding key forms of authority in a society, I argue that the customer has become a key figure of authority, and that the customer orientation and formal rationality have become dual logics structuring the organization of service work. Overall, the organization of service work can be conceptualized against the theoretical type of the customer-oriented bureaucracy, rather than as a simple McDonaldized bureaucracy, as Ritzer argues. Within this structure, service workers often have contradictory experiences of work, enjoying working with customers, but also suffering from customer abuse, such that customers are often seen as 'our friend, the enemy' (Korczynski, 2009b). The updating of Weber is not a simple application of Weber's ideas; it is an approach that builds on Weber's ideas in the spirit of the quote at the start of this chapter from Galtung about how good theory offers space to develop further theorizing.

Feminism and service work

Feminist analysis has also made a key contribution in service work. Feminist analysis has shown how service jobs are often deeply gendered – in a number of ways. First, there is gendering in terms of who occupies service jobs. There is a very high density of females in most service jobs. While this might sound like a positive thing, when this is combined with knowledge that these service jobs tend to have poor pay and conditions and weak career paths (Korczynski, 2002; Perales, 2013), it becomes a systematic problem in the labour market. Women are more likely to be recruited into service jobs, partly because of the gendered expectations held both by management and customers (whom management seeks to please), and sometimes because these gendered expectations are internalized by the people applying for the jobs. Macdonald and Sirianni's observation from their pioneering book still pertains (1996: 14–15):

> Even though discrimination in hiring … exists in all labour markets … in no other area of wage labour are the personal characteristics of the workers so strongly associated with the nature of work. … Traits such as gender, race, age and sexuality serve a signalling function, indicating to the customer/employer important cues.

In addition, feminist analysis has shown that, once people are recruited into service jobs, how those jobs are experienced, enacted and controlled are also gendered processes. For instance, Hall (1993: 456) argues that the job of a waiter (in a café or restaurant) is systematically different for women and men. Women, more than men, must 'learn to humble' themselves each time they approach a table of customers. Taylor and Tyler (2000) studied a call centre and found that management expected women to hit the 'soft' targets of service quality, while the men were expected to focus on the 'hard' targets related to sales. The differences in the service job experience between women and men comes out most strongly with regard to sexual harassment, and the wider sexualization of service labour. A recent study of 'bikini baristas' quotes a worker in its title: 'Sexual harassment is my job' (Wozniak, 2022). Management actions can effectively condone and reproduce customer sexual harassment of women service workers. In a study of hospitality work in Ethiopia (Mefteh et al, 2022: 1612), a female waiter is quoted as saying:

> Four male customers, after using service, one of their friends asked me to be with him when I finish my work. And I said no, and they refuse to pay for the service they used. Then I went to the manager and told him to get the money from them. He said 'they will give your money if you say ok to their offer'. When he said this, I was angry and kick him with a Sprite glass and he fired me.

Social theory and platform work

Platform work has only emerged recently, but, already, it has been a site of collective labour mobilizations and challenges. Umney et al (2024) studied such collective labour challenges and argued that there are basically two core types of challenge: one is the sort that Polanyi's social theory would predict, and one is the type that Marxist social theory would predict.

Polanyi argued that a key contradiction at the heart of the capitalist market economy was that labour was treated as a fictitious commodity, and that there is a constant battle between disembedding the economy from society (where labour is treated more as a commodity), and re-embedding the economy in society (where the commodity status of labour is lessened, often through legal protection, regulation and workers' rights). Umney et al (2024) argue that one pattern of collective labour actions in platform work relates exactly to this issue of disembedding and fights to re-embed labour so that its commodity status is lessened. Platform work operates so that the platform firms tend to deny that the people offering services via the platform – such as Uber drivers or Deliveroo riders – are workers. Rather, platform firms seek to position these people as independent contractors who do not, therefore, qualify for legal rights for workers, such as the minimum wage (or living wage) and rights against discrimination. In Polanyian terms, the labour of the taxi drivers and the delivery riders is being disembedded, and the commodity status of labour is heightened. Umney et al argue that one pattern of collective labour challenge is about workers seeking to reassert their status as workers, and to re-embed their labour in existing legal regulation and protection. For instance, Ilsøe and Jesnes (2020) show how platforms in Norway threatened to disembed labour from comparatively strong employment and social protections, and that this led to a counter-movement from labour organizations to ensure that people providing services via platforms should be treated as workers in an employment relationship, and should, therefore, qualify for the strong social protection offered to workers in Norway.

The second type of challenge involves workers mobilizing for a greater return for their labour, primarily through higher pay. In Marxist terms, this is workers collectively challenging exploitation by fighting for a greater share of the surplus value that they produce through their labour. Studies by Tassinari and Maccarrone (2020) and Woodcock (2021) have shown that pay claims can be central to emerging solidarities and new forms of workers' organization among platform workers.

So, having set up two types of collective labour challenge relating to platform work, each of which, they argue, matches a different school of social theory, Umney et al (2024) seek to bring evidence to bear on the debate between Polanyi and Marx. They assemble media reports of platform-worker mobilizations and challenges and ask what this data reveals about labour mobilization in the context of platform-mediated work. They argue that the media reports show that collective labour challenges do tend to be *either* about challenging the commodity status of labour (following Polanyi) *or* about challenging levels of exploitation (following Marx). They also argue that Polanyi-type labour unrest was more likely to involve mainstream unions and was significantly more likely to involve methods such as legal challenge. These challenges tended to happen in countries where existing social protection and rights for workers are significant. By contrast, labour challenges involving battles over levels of exploitation more often involved new collectivities of workers, sometimes not even associated with a formal union, engaging in tactics such as strikes or log-offs and demonstrations. Such challenges tended to occur in countries where existing labour rights are low.

Social theory and knowledge work

Durkheim and knowledge work

Richard Sennett's book *The Corrosion of Character: The Personal Consequences of Work in the New Capitalism* (1999) has proved to be one of the most important pieces of writing in the sociology of work of recent decades. It focuses on a range of people, and considers how the nature of contemporary work affects their character, or their moral and social being. Most of the people in the book are in or have been in knowledge-work jobs. Although Sennett does not explicitly frame his book as influenced by Durkheim, there is a strong Durkheimian logic to his core argument (also see Fevre's reading, 2000). Sennett argues (1999: 27) that the new, flexible, short-term, team-based structures of (knowledge) work are leading to a breakdown in 'those qualities of character which bind human beings to one another and furnishes each with a sense of sustainable self'. This concern with the relationship between the structures of work and the qualities that bind people in society is exactly the core concern of Durkheim in *The Division of Labour in Society*. Where Durkheim argued that the temporary phenomenon of anomie, or normlessness and disconnection, would disappear with the increasing division of labour, leading to new social cohesion based on organic solidarity (a sense of mutual interdependence), Sennett effectively argues that there is a new, more persistent form of anomie that is related to short-termism, hyper-flexibility and fluid team structures at work.

It is worth considering Sennett's arguments regarding teamwork in knowledge-work settings in more detail. The history of the rise of teamwork in employment settings is linked to what is known as the human relations school of thought, which is intimately tied to Durkheimian thought. The human relations approach originated in studies of factories in the early part of the 20th century where there was a high degree of division of labour (recall Adam Smith's description of the pin factory). The Hawthorne studies, led by Elton Mayo, who was heavily influenced by Durkheim, argued that strong work-group relations in such settings could help both productivity and worker morale. In Durkheimian terms, this is an argument that structures of teams, or small work groups, could create social cohesion in a workplace despite de-skilled work created through the minute division of labour. The growth of the rhetoric around team structures within employment came on the back of this. In contemporary knowledge-work settings, teamwork often takes the form of project teams formed temporarily to undertake a specific task. One of Sennett's chapters focuses on Rosie, who finds herself lost and adrift in the structure of project teams. She has no meaningful social connection to her team members. The social relations are temporary, surface-level and superficial. 'People felt the lack of sustained human relations and durable purposes' (Sennett, 1999: 98) and 'teamwork exists in the realm of tragedy to enact human relations as a farce' (p 106), with its superficial management-speak and what Kunda (1992) calls the 'deep acting' of cooperation. Everybody knows that everybody is acting, but everyone continues to do it. In this context, people come to develop an ironic view of themselves, yet 'no society can cohere through irony' (Sennett, 1999: 116). Sennett's is a pessimistic updating of Durkheimian analysis, with particular resonance for contemporary knowledge-work settings.

Foucault and knowledge work

A number of studies have used Foucault's wider ideas about the disciplinary society and examined how they have played out within contemporary society. Nikolas Rose, for instance, in his 1990 book *Governing the Soul*, developed Foucault's ideas about how power increasingly operates through people's internalization, often through a process that can be analysed using Foucault's metaphor of the panopticon. Rose analyses 'technologies of the self' (often developed by psychiatrists) and how they have been used to create 'the productive subject' within the workplace. Note that Foucault and Foucauldians tend to use the term 'technology' to refer to the ways in which modern social and political systems control, supervise and manipulate people. It is one of those irritating terms of sociological jargon that confuse more than help. Barbara Townley (1994) also made an important Foucauldian contribution by analysing HRM as a discourse and set of practices that construct knowledge about the worker, who becomes 'calculable' and predictable through HRM technologies of discipline. One key technology Townley focuses on is 'the confession'. The individual worker comes to confess through such processes as the selection interview, mentoring and self-assessment in performance appraisals.

Townley's broad argument was carried forward and applied in the specific context of knowledge work by Covaleski et al (1998). They studied the processes by which large accounting firms in the US 'transform professionals into disciplined and self-disciplining organizational members whose work goals, language and lifestyle come to reflect the imperatives of the organization' (p 293). The authors describe (p 311) the way in which:

> power seeps into the very grain of individuals, reaches right into their bodies, permeates their gestures, their posture, what they say, how they learn to live and work with other people.

In these accounting firms, this process often occurred through the process of mentoring – in which junior new recruits are paired up with experienced senior people in the firm, to be guided by them.

The firms did have formal guidance documents on appearance, which listed as inappropriate 'rubber watches', and 'short socks/hairy legs', but people often came to internalize norms of appearance and style through informal conversations with their mentor. Further, mentors sought to mould mentees' work life *and* personal habits, and ultimately identity, to suit potential advancement within the organization. One senior mentor is quoted as saying, 'my challenge … is to try and develop in them a sense of awareness that this is not a job, this is you, it's a reflection of your own life' (Covaleski et al, 1998: 321). The authors conclude that 'mentoring was complicit in subjectivizing the protégé and transforming the protégé … [into] a businessperson and corporate clone, in the sense that mentoring involved tying the protégé's and mentor's identities to the firm and its norms' (p 322).

Sociological imagination – your turn

Consider your own job experience, if you have had some, or talk to your friends about their job experience. What were the key points of tension and conflict in your jobs? Were these points of tension the same for your work colleagues? Which of the social theories reviewed in this chapter help you make sense of these points of tension and conflict? Do any of the social theories help you understand the social structures of your job in a new way?

3

Structures of Power at Work

The sociology of work is attuned to analyse a wide range of structures that constrain and guide people's behaviour and thoughts at work. If you are a call-centre worker, for example, and your manager is pressuring you about not reaching performance targets (such as average length of call and number of sales), it may be tempting to see the individual personality and/or the management style of the specific manager as the key structure of power at work. However, we have seen the importance of thinking bigger than focusing just on immediate interactions and surface-level understandings. The imperative of the sociological imagination at work is to connect private troubles (your manager giving you a hard time) to wider social structures. So, we have to ask: what are the key structures that the call-centre manager, and the call-centre firm, inhabit?

This chapter focuses on some key social structures that influence how work is enacted and experienced. We saw in the previous chapter that social theorists have often pointed to important macro-level structures. This chapter looks at some of those most important macro-level structures – capitalism and its different forms, globalization and the international division of labour – before moving on to examine how they inform the nature of control within workplaces.

Capitalism

The core feature of capitalism is that it is an economic system in which production (whether in terms of manufacturing a car, running a call centre, designing software or making and delivering a pizza) is undertaken for a profit. Other important features are: the means of production (for example the car factory) are privately owned, in the form of firms; these firms operate within a market system; and production is enacted through a system of wage-labour. Economists are adept at characterizing the capitalist economic system in terms that seem to write out structure of power. Consider, for instance, Gregory and Stuart's abstract definition (2013: 41):

Capitalism is characterized by private ownership of the factors of production. Decision-making is decentralized and rests with the owners of the factors of production. Their decision-making is coordinated by the market, which provides the necessary information. Material incentives are used to motivate participants.

By contrast, sociologists – particularly those informed by Marx and Weber – tend to define capitalism in terms that point to the operation of key structures of power. Consider Thomas and Walsh's (1998: 372–373) outline of a Marxist-informed definition of capitalism:

> The capitalist mode of production entails the manufacture of commodities to be sold in a market for a profit which transforms production and products from use value to exchange value. But the basis of capitalist production is the use of labour as its major force of production, and it entails its commodification through the sale of labour by the labourer for a wage to the manufacturer who uses it to manufacture commodities for sale in the market. The surplus value extracted from the labour of the labourer in this process, in terms of the difference between the cost of labour and the value of the commodities produced by it, constitutes the basis of profit.

Following this approach, we can draw out some clear and important implications of the structure of capitalism for the nature of work.

Asymmetry of power

There is a structural asymmetry of power in the employment relationship in capitalism. Workers, who do not own the means of production, have only their labour power to sell and are compelled to seek an employer who will buy their labour power, or, in more everyday terms, will employ them and pay them a wage. Although workers may change employers (Smith, 2006), they are still compelled to sell their labour power to an employer. This is the core *structural* imbalance of power – an imbalance that underpins all employment relationships in capitalism. In addition, there can be important contextual factors that will affect the playing out of power relations in employment. Most notably, the nature of the labour market can play a significant role in impacting power relations at this level. So, when there is a shortage of workers in the labour market, workers will be in a stronger position to demand improvements in the terms at which they sell their labour power to an employer, for instance in terms of a wage rise. However, the waxing and waning of power relations in these terms should not be confused with the core structural asymmetry of power in the employment relationship in capitalism.

Indeterminate nature of the employment relationship

When workers enter an employment relationship with an employer, they enter into a contract regarding the terms for the capacity to work (known as labour power). As

Blyton and Turnbull (2004: 38–39) put it, 'the employment contract itself is open-ended [or indeterminate], in that the wage might be agreed in advance but effort is not and cannot be, specified explicitly or exactly ... it is labour time and not work itself that is purchased ... paid working time is not necessarily equivalent to time worked'.

The employer needs the delivery of work, rather than the capacity of work, and, to ensure the creation of profit, the employer sets up a system of hierarchy (supervisors, managers) within the firm to maximize the delivery of work from workers. Blyton and Turnbull (2004: 39) note that 'what the employer purchases in the labour market is the capacity of men and women to work (labour power), whereas what the employer is actually interested in is the performance of work'. Power enters again, therefore, for the employer's system of hierarchy seeks to maximize the delivery of labour, often in ways that workers may not want. For instance, in a call centre, employers may set a target that workers should take an average of 20 calls per hour, whereas workers may find this target unreasonable.

Coexistence of conflict and cooperation

The discussion of the necessary playing out of power within the employment relationship – in transforming labour power into labour – points to the systemic existence of conflict in the employment relationship within capitalism. Edwards (1986) argues that there is a 'structured antagonism' within the employment relationship. The employment relationship within capitalism is such that the employer will only employ the worker when they (the employers) are able to extract more value from the worker's labour than the wage that they pay the worker. This is a structural form of exploitation that creates a clash of interests between the worker and the employer. There is a systemic basis of conflict. However, cooperation is also present. First, employers cannot rely solely on coercion to maximize the delivery of labour: employers inevitably need workers' cooperation. Second, as we will see in Chapter 5, workers develop, create and find meaning in work, so 'there is likely to be at least a latent degree of co-operation with management' (Blyton and Turnbull, 2004: 41). The employment relationship is an inherently contradictory one in that it simultaneously generates conflict and cooperation. The employment relationship is, according to Edwards (1986: 6):

> the coming together of two sides in a relationship which is inherently contradictory: employers need workers' creative capacities, but cannot give them free rein because of the need to secure a surplus and to maintain a degree of general control; and workers, although subordinates, do not simply resist the application of managerial control.

Implications of competition

In capitalism, firms compete with each other, unless the firm is in a monopoly position in the product market. This has important implications for the operation of power at work. First, the structure of competition means that there are pressures for firms to lower the costs of production. This will not always be the strongest pressure in terms of competition from other firms, but often it will be, and it will always be present. Thompson and McHugh (1990: 40) note: 'There are constant pressures to cheapen the costs of production, notably labour. This may take place through deskilling, relocation of plant, work intensification or some other means.' At the same time, firms may face competitive pressures to improve the quality of their product or service. This may inform the employer seeking to develop the commitment, skills and creative capacities of the workers. So, these price-based and quality-based competitive pressures may occur simultaneously, exacerbating the contradictory nature of social relations within the firm.

Second, individual firms as employers are not islands that can autonomously set up patterns of social relations that function without regard to what other firms are doing. This means that there are significant limits to the ability of firms to set up long-term trust-based relations with their workforce. Even if firms want to offer job security to workers in order to foster their commitment, they may not be able to follow through on this intention (Thompson, 2003). There have been periods when large quasi-monopoly firms have been able to insulate themselves significantly from competitive pressures from other firms in the product market, but, as we will see, there is compelling evidence that such insulation is increasingly difficult, particularly in liberal-market forms of capitalism, as seen in the US and, increasingly, the UK. This point leads us on to consider different forms of capitalism.

Forms of capitalism

While there are significant implications regarding how capitalism, per se, structures the operation of power within employment, it is also the case that, if we want to understand employment in specific periods, countries, sectors or workplaces, we need to consider that there is a range of forms, or types, of capitalism. Scott and Marshall (2005: 52) note: 'The insights to be gained from describing both mid-Victorian and late 20th-century Britain as capitalist are limited. The same applies to its wide geographical and cultural scope. ... More precision can be gained by specifying types of capitalism.' The following section starts by considering attempts to characterize broad patterns across *all* capitalist economies before turning to examine approaches that point to *multiple types* of contemporary capitalism.

Fordist capitalism

The term Fordism has been used in a range of ways in sociological and political economy writing. Here, the focus is on Fordism as a characterization of an overarching type of capitalism that points to convergent, mutually supporting patterns in production systems, work organization, consumption, state regulation and welfare. The root of the term is Ford, the car manufacturing firm, and, in order to grasp the concept of Fordism, it is useful to briefly tell the story of the development of that firm by its founder, Henry Ford, in the early- to mid-20th century in the US. Ford aimed to own the first firm to mass-produce low-cost cars – the black model-T

Ford. He did this by using assembly-line production, where workers stand by a moving conveyor belt and complete their task on the product as it passes. Workers' jobs involved narrow, repetitive, low-skill tasks, undertaken intensively under close supervision and with strict targets (a system known as Taylorism – see Chapter 4). At the same time, however, Ford paid the workers a high wage, introducing the $5-day in 1914. The payment of high wages served two key purposes for Ford. It lowered labour turnover, and it meant that the workers who made the low-cost cars would themselves be able to buy the low-cost cars. Mass production and mass consumption were linked supportively.

In addition to the elements of Fordism that can be influenced or developed by the original firm, the concept of Fordism also relates to wider state action, such as macro-economic policies to support full employment and protective welfare policies. Between the end of the Second World War and 1980, it was nearly universal that Western countries had governments that adopted macro-economic policies with the fundamental aim of achieving full employment (and therefore minimizing unemployment). These policies followed the ideas of UK economist John Maynard Keynes and, hence, are known as Keynesian policies. So, not only firms, but also the state were aiming to support job security for workers. For those people who did fall, likely briefly, into unemployment, states introduced welfare benefits.

Fordism is a concept that uses the policies of the Ford car manufacturer as its starting point and then develops a theoretical pattern – known in sociology as an 'ideal type' – of a wider system of social relations and policies. Scholars have used the concept to characterize broad patterns in Western countries in the mid- to late-20th century. It can be thought of as pointing to a form of social contract between capital and labour, overseen by the state, in which employers create profits by paying high wages and offering job security for mass production of low-cost goods and services, and in which workers are subject to intense de-skilling in return for job security and the high wages that give them access to consume the goods and services mass-produced. It is a social contract that appears to be a mutually supporting system generating a win-win-win scenario for employers, workers and the state. At its heart, however, it has one key moment of power that is unspoken. In this social contract, there is a particular set of interests of workers that takes precedence over other important interests of workers. Essentially, the system prioritizes workers' extrinsic benefits of work – high wages and job security – over workers' intrinsic meanings and benefits relating to work – such as being trusted to undertake skilled work in a creative way. Rather than seeing Fordism as a convergent, mutually supporting pattern of relations, in which power appears to play little role, it may be more appropriate to consider it as an attempt to create a social compromise that has a hidden tension at its heart.

Scholars have also pointed to another important limitation in the concept of Fordism: that it is centred on a conception of work as that undertaken by full-time, permanent *male* workers. It is seen as hardly accidental that the industry on which the concept is centred – the car industry – was particularly male-dominated (Glucksmann, 1990). Pfau-Effinger (1993) argued that the Fordist compromise favoured male workers who were free from work in the domestic sphere, whereas women were given primary responsibility for domestic work and were therefore restricted in their ability to take part in paid employment.

There is a range of other debates that have grown up around the concept of Fordism. Perhaps the most important concerns the argument that, while Fordism appears clear and even elegant as a *theoretical* concept, this does not mean that it adequately characterizes empirical reality. Indeed, Jessop's (1992: 50) overview concludes that 'whatever the virtues of an ideal-typical ... Fordist regime, there is a yawning gap between ideal and reality'. Thompson (2003) also notes that, as scholars tried to apply the concept of Fordism to individual countries, they inevitably had to qualify the form of Fordism that was played in practice, using adjectives such as: flawed, blocked, delayed and peripheral (Boyer, 1996). Clarke (1990) argues that it is still useful to use the concept of Fordism as long as it is understood that there is a range of Fordist projects.

Post-Fordist capitalism and precarity

Theory suggested convergence in the pattern of relationships within Fordist projects, but, by the end of the 1970s, these interlocking relationships were breaking down. One of the crucial factors was the increasing internationalization of economies. It turned out that key elements of Fordism involved the dominance of a domestic, or national, economy. For instance, the link between mass production and mass consumption only holds if workers use their high wages to buy products made within the national economy (Ford cars made and bought in the US). The link becomes loose when workers start buying Japanese-manufactured cars instead. Similarly, states' attachment to Keynesian full-employment policies only functioned when the extra government spending to create jobs created jobs within the country. It made little sense for the UK government, for example, to increase government spending with the aim of keeping full employment in the UK when the jobs being created were in Germany because consumers were buying more German goods and services. In addition, many countries experienced increasing conflict within employment in the form of strikes and absences. This conflict, in part, informed many advanced economies experiencing both high inflation and rising levels of unemployment. Further, mass consumption began to break down as consumers began increasingly to seek customized products in niche markets rather than standardized products in mass markets.

With a breakdown in the mutually supporting patterns of relations that constituted Fordist capitalism, what type of capitalism was coming next? There have been a number of attempts to identify and characterize the nature of post-Fordism capitalism. The first serious attempt was Piore and Sabel's (1984) argument that a system of flexible specialization production was emerging to meet the demand for niche, customized products and services. In terms of the organization of work, they presented an optimistic argument for an emerging new form of craft production. Notably, there has been little evidence to suggest that such optimism has been realized.

Although not couched with explicit reference to post-Fordism, subsequently, there have been arguments of similar optimism concerning the rise of the knowledge economy (Hislop et al, 2013; Unger, 2019) populated by post-bureaucratic organizations. The central premise of this argument is that, in advanced economies, the key productive resource has become knowledge. Leadbetter (1999: vii) emphasizes how this is materially different from the Fordist period:

> Most of us [knowledge workers] make our money from thin air: we produce nothing that can be weighed, touched or easily measured. Our output is not stockpiled in harbours, stored in warehouses or shipped in railway cars. Most of us earn our living providing service, judgement, information and analysis. … We are all in the thin-air business.

This new centrality of knowledge is seen as necessitating the structures of the economy moving away from Fordism because Fordist bureaucracy and hierarchy are seen to stand in opposition to the creation of knowledge and the creative analysis of knowledge. Collaboration and cooperation, not hierarchy and control, are understood as necessary to the development of the knowledge economy (Sölvell and Zander, 1995). Structurally, this points to the rise of post-bureaucratic organizations, which may take a range of specific forms. Alvesson and Thompson (2005: 487) note that 'the paradigm of the post-bureaucratic organisation says that the decentralised, loosely coupled, flexible, nonhierarchical, and fluid organisation is, or will become, dominant'. Whatever specific organizational form, the key underpinning is the importance of collaboration and cooperation. Alvesson and Thompson provide an overview of the claims made regarding the rise of the post-bureaucratic organization in the context of the knowledge economy. They conclude that many organizational forms within knowledge-intensive sectors do differ significantly from bureaucracy, but that there is no evidence of the withering of bureaucracy outside knowledge-intensive sectors. Here, it is worth recalling, from Chapter 1, that Brinkley et al (2009) estimate that around 30 per cent of the labour force can be described as knowledge workers. Chapter 4 looks in more detail at the form of organization of knowledge work.

The scholarship on the rise of precarity can be interpreted as the most sustained attempt to delineate the key character of the post-Fordist era. This is a more pessimistic characterization of the essential nature of post-Fordism. As Kalleberg (2018) notes, there is an implicit normative critique in much of the literature on the rise of precarity. Broadly, precarity can be understood as involving forms of employment-related uncertainty and insecurity that are seen as having mainly negative implications for workers.

Kalleberg (2018: 15) points out that the scholarship related to precarity can be considered to have two streams. The first stream concerns more general theorizing by scholars who use precarity and related concepts 'to describe a new phase of capitalism, characterized by a lack of predictability or security'. Bourdieu (1998) originated this approach, and he argued that precarity was a state in which workers were forced to submit to their exploitation. Kalleberg also places Beck's theorizing as part of this stream. Beck (2000) argues that there is a new political economy of uncertainty, which he characterizes as 'the risk society'. He suggests that there is a wider logic of the individualization of risk, which, in the context of employment, means a shifting of risk on to individual workers. A concrete example of this rather abstract concept would be that an employer, rather than taking the risk of having to meet sustained demand from consumers by appointing workers on permanent contracts, passes on the risk to workers by only offering short-term, temporary employment contracts.

The idea of the importance of rising precarity was then popularized by Standing (2011) in his bestselling book *The Precariat: The New Dangerous Class*. Standing's core argument is that there is an important new class comprising casual workers, temporary workers and the working poor. He labels this class the 'precariat' – a term combining precarious and proletariat (the latter being Marx's name for the working class – see Chapter 2). Standing estimates that around a quarter of the working population can be placed as belonging to the precariat because they lack one or more of seven key forms of 'security'. He argues that neoliberal and globalization revolutions that have enhanced global competition and weakened the power of labour since the end of the 1970s have driven the rise of the precariat. Although Standing's claim for the precariat as a new class has not been taken up (Alberti et al, 2018), the resonance of the book's focus on precarity can be interpreted as its arguments chiming with the zeitgeist (a wider sense of the spirit of the times).

Table 3.1 provides a comparison of Fordism with post-Fordism, characterized as an era of precarity. The five key dimensions (on the left) are those against which Fordism tends to be defined. The middle column charts Fordism against those dimensions (following from the discussion of Fordism in the previous section). The column on the right charts post-Fordism-as-precarity against the same dimensions. That column is based on the overall logic of the theoretical arguments of Bourdieu, Beck and Standing. Where these theorists have not directly touched on a dimension, I have extrapolated from the logic of their arguments so that a clear comparison can be made between Fordism and post-Fordism across the same dimensions. For production, Fordism was based on mass production, while post-Fordism is based on temporal-specific systems, such as just-in-time production in manufacturing (Rainnie, 1991), project-based structures for knowledge work (Hislop et al, 2013) and customer management systems in service work (Korczynski, 2002). Regarding consumption, Fordism involved mass

Table 3.1: Comparison of Fordism and post-Fordism as precarity

Dimensions	Fordism	Post-Fordism as era of precarity
Production	Mass production	Temporal-specific production
Consumption	Mass consumption	Key principles of immediate temporal access and wide choice
Work organization	De-skilled, routine (Taylorist) work; high wages; job security; legitimacy of labour unions	Insecurity and uncertainty pervade work organization
State macro-economic policy	Keynesian policies for full employment	Growth to be generated by supply-side market reforms
State welfare policy	Welfare state with principle of universalism	Limiting of welfare further to valorization of exposure to insecurity

consumption, while, in post-Fordism, the defining characteristic of consumption is *immediate* access to a wide range of choices. The rise of Amazon, the world's largest retail company, is emblematic of this form of consumption. For the dimension of work organization, Fordism featured the core Fordist bargain of high wages, job security and legitimacy of labour unions in exchange for low-skilled, routine (Taylorist) work. In post-Fordism, uncertainty and insecurity pervade work organization. What this means in concrete terms is unpacked in more detail shortly. While the Fordist state's approach to macro-economic policies was a demand-side plan for sustaining full employment, in post-Fordism, the state focuses on generating economic growth through supply-side reforms that facilitate the running of the 'free market'. In Fordism, the state's approach to welfare was informed by the mass principle of universalism, whereas, in post-Fordism, states have moved away from universalism to limit welfare rights, partly as a reaction to globalization (and migration) and partly from a valorization of exposing people to uncertainty.

So, Table 3.1 offers a very abstract, theoretical way to consider post-Fordism as an era of precarity; one that is derived from the theoretical approaches to precarity that Kalleberg (2018) calls the first stream of relevant scholarship on precarity. The second stream of scholarship on precarity is based on empirical research into elements of work organization. Examining this stream enables a closer look at the dimension of work organization and what is meant by uncertainty and insecurity pervading work. This stream of scholarship examines types of precarious work arrangements that include temporary work, contract work (comprising both independent contractors and employees of contract companies), involuntary part-time work, irregular and casual employment and self-employment. Kalleberg (2018: 12) argues that these forms of work can usefully be pulled together under the label of precarity, but notes that, sometimes, other terms are used to describe these types of precarious work, such as 'contingent work; non-regular work; atypical work; market-mediated work arrangements; alternate work arrangements, non-traditional employment relations; flexible staffing arrangements or work practices'. Precarious work here is implicitly positioned as standing negatively against the picture of (usually male) workers in the Fordist era in a standard employment relationship, involving job security and a full-time job.

Limitations of space preclude an examination of all the types of precarious employment. Instead, I focus on what is arguably the core element at the heart of arguments about precarity: job insecurity. Job security is usually measured by average job tenure – the average length of time people spend in their jobs. A trend towards job insecurity is inferred when this average time falls. A puzzling finding from an important strand of research has tended to show, at least for the UK, overall *stability* in recent decades in job tenure (see review by St-Denis and Hollister, 2023). This runs counter to the expectations set by arguments concerning the rise of precarity. However, St-Denis and Hollister (2023) and Kalleberg (2018) argue that this *is* compatible with the picture of the present as an era of precarity. There are two stages to this argument.

First, they explain that, while there may be some overall stability in job tenure, this overall figure is informed by two countervailing trends. One trend *is* towards greater job instability, but, running against this, are demographic trends (in the make-up of who is in the labour market) that, on their own, will tend to lead to higher job stability (for instance, the overall workforce is becoming older, which is relevant because older workers tend to have longer job tenure than younger workers). Kalleberg shows that, for the male prime working age, full-time workers (who tended to have job security in the Fordist era), job tenure has, indeed, fallen.

The second stage to the argument is that we need to have a wider concept of precarity than just job (in)stability and departure from the standard employment relationship. Kalleberg (2018: 80) argues that whether an employment relationship is classed as standard or non-standard may be less relevant for defining it as precarious than the kinds of social and legal protection linked to it. He points out that, in liberal market economies such as the UK and the US (see the section 'Varieties of capitalism', later), social and legal protection afforded to workers tends to be lower than in social democratic and coordinated market economies. The OECD (Organization for Economic Cooperation and Development, comprising 38 high-income countries) has created an overall index of employment protection against individual and collective dismissals. For the latest available data (2019), the US is ranked at the bottom of levels of protection, and the UK as sixth from bottom.

Different elements of precarity can be demonstrated by considering distinctive ways in which precarity is manifest within knowledge work, service work and platform work. It is appropriate here to start with the latter as many commentators position platform work as a case that exemplifies the era of precarity (Umney et al, 2024). Within platform work, workers have no security regarding the amount of work they may be able to undertake in a given week. They have no security of employment. Indeed, platform operators seek to position workers as independent contractors rather than employees, or workers as such. So, they lack the rights and entitlements that flow legally to workers as workers (for instance regarding maternity leave). Platform work is precarious work *in extremis*. In knowledge-work occupations, precarity is more likely to be played out in moves towards project-based organization of work, which relies on the systematic use of knowledge workers as independent contractors (Apitzsch et al, 2022). Bulut's (2020) ethnographic study of video game developers in the US, titled *The Precarious Game*, makes the wider argument that, in many knowledge-work sectors, organizations are imbued with an overall culture of precarity. In service work, an important way in which precarity is played out is through the flexible scheduling of labour (Halpin, 2015; Wood, 2020). Employers increasingly use customer-demand management systems to create micro-predictions of different levels of customer activity and then use these to inform the scheduling of labour requirements – scheduling that is subject to frequent changes with little notice given. Harknett et al (2020: 3) state that 'the reality of work for millions of Americans, especially those in the retail and food service sectors, is of work schedules that vary from day-to-day and week-to-week, often with little advance notice'.

In the UK, the logic of the use of flexible scheduling can lead to the use of zero-hour contracts, which involve a contract of employment between a worker and an employer that lacks a guaranteed minimum number of hours. However, Koumenta and Williams (2019) note that zero-hour contracts are restricted to a small number of occupations (for instance, one in six zero-hour contracts occur among care assistants and home carers) and appear unlikely to become a pervasive feature of the service sector.

Financialized capitalism

The developing scholarship on financialized capitalism and shareholder-value capitalism argues that there is a clear emerging pattern in structures of contemporary capitalism – structures that are particularly strong in the US and the UK (and are becoming strong elsewhere). While there are distinct bodies of scholarship on financialized capitalism and shareholder-value capitalism, there are also significant overlaps between the main arguments developed in these areas (Fligstein and Goldstein, 2022). Here, I refer to both sets of scholarship under the aegis of 'financialized capitalism'. The starting point is that there has been a significant change in the nature of ownership of corporations from the end of the Fordist period. Kollmeyer and Peters (2019: 3) note: 'Previously, corporations were typically held by wealthy families and dispersed shareholders operating at the national level. Now, corporations are mainly held by financial firms and institutional investors such as mutual funds, pension funds, exchange-traded funds, and investment management corporations.'

In contrast to standard business practices of the Fordist period, it is argued, contemporary financialized firms operate under a 'shareholder model' of corporate governance, in which firms focus more heavily on returns to investors and often use their resources to purchase financial assets rather than reinvest in the productive capacity of the corporation (Appelbaum and Batt, 2014). Financialized capitalism leads executives to view their firm in narrow economic terms as a set of assets whose returns can be maximized through various strategies, including mergers, acquisitions, divestitures and downsizing. Furthermore, the pressure to give immediate returns to shareholders means that firms use shorter time frames to evaluate business investment decisions, making them less likely to put forward long-term plans, for instance to develop training, loyalty and citizenship among the workforce. Workers, who played a key role as an important stakeholder in the Fordist period (mainly through unions), now come to be seen more as an area where short-term cost-cutting can be enacted to boost shareholder returns.

The logic of financialized capitalism has been further strengthened by the internationalization and deregulation of the financial market that occurred in the 1980s and 1990s. In the Fordist period, financial markets tended to be subject to considerable state regulation (further to the financial crisis at the end of the 1920s), and there were significant barriers to international capital flows. From the 1980s onwards, however, numerous regulatory changes have occurred, such as abandoning capital controls on foreign exchange and derivatives trading, loosening restrictions on the international buying and selling of domestic equity, lowering bank liquidity ratios and legalizing hedge funds, so that financial firms and institutional investors now have significant freedom to operate outside their national borders. This leads to greater pressure to overturn long-established business practices of the Fordist era, notably in terms of a move away from the Fordist compromise of accepting the presence of unions and of seeing the workforce as an important and legitimate stakeholder within the firm.

In addition, rather than being owned by a local wealthy family, who would often operate implicitly within social norms of the area and country, large firms are more likely to be owned by globally disbursed shareholders and financial institutions who are subject to no such social norms and pressures. For instance, Boots, the major UK-based health and pharmacy firm, with its manufacturing centred in Nottingham, was founded in Nottingham and used to be owned by the local wealthy Boots family. It is currently owned by an international private equity firm. More generally, with the greater importance of financial assets in the generation of profit, the finance sector itself grows so that it becomes the dominant sector within financialized capitalism, and the logic of thinking in narrow instrumental financial terms comes to be adopted as the default business approach. Labour recedes, from being a strong stakeholder with legitimate interests within the Fordist period, to become a cost to be reduced.

Varieties of capitalism

While the literature on Fordism and post–Fordism and financialized capitalism tends to explore the issue of common patterns across all advanced capitalist economies, the scholarship on varieties of capitalism has considered whether it is more fruitful to look for key differences between advanced capitalist economies. Notably, Hall and Soskice (2001) have argued that it is appropriate to differentiate two main types of advanced capitalist economies: liberal market economies and coordinated market economies.

Liberal market economies are the six countries in the Anglo-American family: the UK, the US, Ireland, Canada, Australia and New Zealand. Broadly, liberal market economies are capitalist economies in which shareholders dominate other stakeholders in firms (such as workers, suppliers, consumers, citizens), that run along free-market principles, oriented to the short term, and in which the state plays a minor, arm's-length role. Liberal market economies are characterized by short-term orientated company finance, deregulated labour markets, general education and strong intercompany competition.

Hall and Soskice (2001) identify ten countries as coordinated market economies: Germany, Japan, Switzerland, the Netherlands, Belgium, Sweden, Norway, Denmark, Finland and Austria. In short, coordinated market economies are capitalist economies in which stakeholders in firms take priority over shareholders, in an economy in which economic behaviour is strategically coordinated, to an important extent, through non–market mechanisms, oriented to the long-term, and in which the state plays an important role. Examples of non–market mechanisms include business associations, trade unions and multi-employer collective bargaining, cross-shareholding (for instance through firms holding shares in their suppliers), industry–wide vocational training systems and worker-voice governance structures such as works councils and national consultation bodies. Coordinated market economies share the following characteristics: long-term industrial finance, cooperative industrial relations, high levels of vocational training, and cooperation in technology and standard–setting across companies. The movement towards Brexit in the UK can be understood in part as being informed by the tensions arising from the UK as a liberal market economy being linked to the European Union, which leans towards an approach more suited to a coordinated market economy.

Hall and Soskice (2001) not only point to two different models of advanced capitalist economy, they also argue that *both* approaches appear able to generate long-term economic growth. This fundamentally puts into question the broad assumption in UK and US political-economic discussions that markets are the most efficient method for an economy to be run on. Blyton and Turnbull (2004: 45) argue:

> The market might be efficient when it comes to impersonal forms of contractual exchange, where prices provide sufficient information for all parties. Yet many relationships in business and employee relations depend on co-operation rather than competition, trust rather than opportunism, equity as well as efficiency … reciprocity instead of indifference.

These different approaches have important implications for the organization and nature of work. Consider job security, for instance. When a company firm has a poor year in terms of sales in a liberal market economy like the US or the UK, there will be a tendency for firms to maintain high short-term returns to shareholders by cutting labour costs, perhaps through making some workers redundant. By contrast, for this same firm in a coordinated market economy like Germany, the pressure to keep high short-term returns to shareholders will be less intense, partly because of long-term, trust-based relations between firms and their financers. In addition, it would be much harder for the firm to make workers redundant because of worker-voice institutions within the governance of the firm, such as works councils, and because the nature of employment law makes such decisions much more difficult. Regarding the latter, according to the OECD's comparative employment protection index, it was around four times more difficult or costly to terminate a worker's job in Germany than in the US (Hipp, 2020).

The arguments for seeing varieties of capitalism are important, and there is real benefit in understanding that, despite frequent rhetoric to the contrary, free-market principles are not the only principles capable of informing functioning capitalist economies. Nevertheless, there have been a number of important points of critique raised regarding Hall and Soskice's arguments. One area of debate concerns the argument that there are *two* basic types of capitalism. Hall and Soskice (2001) have been criticized for only being able to say of the economies of France, Italy, Spain, Portugal, Greece and Turkey that they are 'ambiguously positioned' regarding the distinction between liberal market economy and coordinated market economy. In addition, other ways of considering different types of capitalism have been offered. Most notable is the characterization of China as a form of 'state capitalism' (Musacchio et al, 2015).

A more fundamental sociological critique of Hall and Soskice's argument is put forward by Streeck (2018). He agrees that it is important to analyse different patterns in how capitalist economies function. However, he characterizes Hall and Soskice's approach to this as a 'rationalist-functionalist' approach in which issues of power and tensions arising from key contradictions of capitalism are written out. He notes (p 25) that for Hall and Soskice, 'national models of capitalism are controlled by firms in search of efficient relations of production. The problems firms must solve are conceived as those identified by transaction cost economics and rational choice institutionalism'. Further, Streeck argues that the Hall and Soskice approach fails to show proper understanding of the social and political creation of the forms of capitalist economies that are labelled coordinated market economies. Streeck offers a more critical sociological overview. He notes that many scholars see the case of Japan through an analytical lens from Polanyi's concept of social embeddedness such that the nature of Japanese capitalism is related to the important degree to which 'traditional, pre-capitalist codes of social behaviour and norms of social control continue even under capitalism to moderate the egoistic pursuit of economic interests' (Streeck, 2018: 18). In addition, Streeck praises Korpi's (1983) analysis of Sweden as involving a 'power resource model' of understanding diversity across capitalist economies. In this approach, emphasis is given to seeing the importance of non-capitalist social solidarity in political-economic relations. Such solidarity is not analysed as being a residual of pre-capitalist traditions, but is seen as constructed by collective political action and redistributive politics. Here, social democratic politics and institutions, such as labour unions, are understood as replacing traditional institutions and norms that are weakened in the course of capitalist market expansion.

Globalization and the international division of labour

One final critique of the argument for the importance of two distinct varieties of capitalism is that variation in the form of national capitalism is less important than the fact that capitalism is increasingly functioning through international modes. Some argue that it is appropriate to think of capitalism as a predominantly globalized system (see Streeck, 2018). In this section, I consider arguments about what globalization means for developments in work. Particularly important here are considerations of the contemporary international division of labour configured through global supply chains.

Abstract discussions of globalization can be frustrating. Globalization as a concept can become so big that, by talking about everything, we seem to end up talking about nothing. Here, I am concerned with globalization primarily in terms of the playing out of globalized capitalism. This should allow for a much tighter and focused discussion. The idea of capitalism as having a global logic was raised by Marx and Engels as far back as 1848 (p 7):

> The need of a constantly expanding market for its products chases the bourgeoisie [the capitalist class] over the whole surface of the globe. … The bourgeoisie has through its exploitation of the world market given a cosmopolitan character to production and consumption in every country … it has drawn from under the feet of industry the national ground on which it stood.

In particular, Marx argued that this global imperative of the capitalist class was what centrally informed imperialism in the 19th century, led by the UK, at the time of his writing. In the late-20th century, Wallerstein (1979) sought to develop Marx's insights. He argues that there is a 'modern world system': one world economy in which all nations are connected by capitalist economic relationships. Wallerstein argues that imperialism and colonialism established economic relationships of dependency between the colonized countries and the colonizing countries that still pertain today. He explains that there is a system with a core of more-affluent countries and a semi-periphery and periphery of less-affluent countries. Although some countries may be able to shift positions within this hierarchy, a hierarchy of nations within the world economy itself is systemic and constant.

Wallerstein's scholarship can be seen as a key stepping stone towards the analysis of globalization of capitalism. Within the discussions regarding what constitutes globalization, there are a number of clearly important pillars. A first pillar is the growing liberalization – or opening up to wider competition – of markets that has occurred in recent decades. Consider the example of Europe. After the Second World War, there were significant barriers to open international markets, most notably through import taxes. At first, Germany and France and some smaller countries came together to establish free trade (no import taxes) in a small number of industries. This has subsequently grown to become the contemporary 27-nation European Union, in which a key principle is open markets to firms within member states (but there are significant barriers to firms from outside the EU from entering the EU markets). As this example indicates, although there has been significant movement towards the internationalization of markets, there is still some distance to go before we can say that there is a completely open global market.

Multinational corporations (MNCs) are a second pillar of capitalist globalization. MNCs are firms that operate in more than one country. Many of the biggest MNCs are names recognized in households in many countries across the globe, such as Amazon, Facebook, Apple, McDonald's and Nestlé. MNCs account for between two thirds and three quarters of all world trade (Kordos and Vojtovic, 2016). In some ways, MNCs have a greater economic status than many countries. In 2001, 500 MNCs had annual sales of over $10 billion. In that same year, only 75 countries had an economy (measured by Gross Domestic Product) larger than that. For instance, Ford's sales were greater than the size of the Slovakian economy, and ExxonMobil's sales were greater than the size of the Colombian economy (Foreign Policy, 2012). MNCs should be regarded as a central element in globalization not just because of their role in global production and sales but also because they have played key roles in the political processes of opening up markets to international competition. Frenkel (2006: 397) points specifically to the role of MNCs with their original base in the US. He argues that trade liberalization should be seen as a central element of a 'neoliberal project that has been vigorously pursued by US MNCs supported by the US government and key international agencies'. We do not need to take Frenkel's word for it. We can listen to an insider to these processes – Joseph Stiglitz, cabinet member during Clinton's US presidency, and chief economist at the World Bank 1997–2000 (2003: 204):

America pushed the ideology of the free market and tried hard to get access for US companies overseas. In doing so, we in the Clinton administration too often put aside the kind of principles for which we should have stood. We did not think about the impact of our policies on the poor in the developing countries, but on job creation in America. We believed in liberalising capital markets but didn't think about how it might lead to great global instability. ... While we talked about democracy, we did everything we could to maintain our control of the global economic system, and to make sure that it worked for ... financial and corporate interests.

A third pillar is the overall time–space compression (Harvey, 1989) that has occurred further to the development of information and communication technologies and international transport. Thus, it has become commonplace for consumers in one country to interact with call-centre workers situated in another country. What is commonplace now was unheard of only a few decades ago. Perhaps the overall international spread of capitalism itself can be thought of as the final pillar. Giles (2000: 182) argues that there has been an 'extension of the capitalist mode of production to virtually every corner of the planet'. Notably, former communist countries in Central and Eastern Europe have become home to capitalist economies, while state capitalism has developed in China. These four pillars of capitalist globalization mean that production of goods and services increasingly occurs in internationally interdependent networks in which MNCs play a major role.

A key debate in the sociology of work regards the implications of such capitalist globalization for the nature and experience of work. For the view that there are positive implications, there is the classic economic argument that the opening up of markets has the effect of rising economic activity, which will lead to a rise in incomes for workers, globally. Another argument pointing to the positive side of globalization for work is the idea that MNCs will be able to spread wider their 'best-practice' management techniques regarding work organization. Such techniques might take the form of, for instance, best-practice human resource management or Japanese-inspired manufacturing systems (Frenkel, 2006). Generally, however, claims of best-practice management techniques tend to be approached by sociologists with considerable scepticism. At best, these are claims of technical rational efficiency that implicitly seek to close off the space for an appropriate analysis of the social relations and forms of power within such management techniques. At worst, they can be glossy management-speak attempts to deny the existence of important coercive elements within the organization of work.

The main counter-argument in this debate – that the logic of globalization may have serious negative consequences for the nature of work – is that the opening up of markets, coupled with the dominant role of MNCs, leads to a greater power of capital over labour, globally, with overall negative consequences for workers. Beck (2000) and Castells (2000) argue that globalization alters power in the favour of capital because 'capital is global, work is local' (Beck, 2000: 27). Workers live and are embedded in specific places, whereas capital has no such embedded ties. The greater mobility of capital gives firms a stronger bargaining position in relation to (relatively) immobile workers. A further development of the logic here is that capitalist globalization at its core involves an 'international race to the bottom' with regard to labour costs and work conditions (Blyton and Turnbull, 2004: 51). The argument here is that countries will compete with each other in seeking to be the location for MNCs to situate their sites of production, and such competition involves stripping away labour rights and protection to make that country more attractive to MNCs. Thus, a logic of the global degradation of labour standards is set in motion, with governments effectively subservient to the more powerful MNCs (Silver, 2003).

MNCs can make use of the bargaining power that their greater mobility gives them in one of two ways. The more direct route is to actively locate their production sites in the lowest-cost settings across the globe. Cooke's (2003) analysis of investment behaviour by MNCs indicates that their investment decisions – to build production sites – are influenced by the search for lower labour costs and greater management freedom from laws and regulation regarding labour (p 82):

> MNCs have chosen to invest in countries whose industrial relations systems offer (1) greater net comparative unit labour cost advantages and (2) greater flexibility to either diffuse or create preferred Human Resource Management/Labour Relations practices. As such, host country industrial relations systems marked by lower compensation costs for skills sought, by less imposing government workplace regulation, and by less extensive union representation … attract greater foreign direct investment.

This process is most clearly manifest when MNCs cease production in a site with higher labour costs and relocate to where labour costs are lower. However, it may not have to come to this, for MNCs may simply use the *threat* of relocation to force through changes in work organization, leading to lower costs in their existing sites of production. Unions here are forced into what is known as 'concession bargaining'.

The indirect route for MNCs to gain from the greater power of capital further to globalization is simply to outsource production. For instance, the Etch A Sketch toy used to be manufactured by workers in Ohio, who earned $9 per hour. However, the firm outsourced these jobs to the Kim Ki Corporation. As Sweet and Meiskins (2008: 48) note, 'this toy, along with most other toys available to American consumers, is now manufactured in China by workers who earn 24 cents an hour and who are expected to work 12 hours a day, 7 days a week'. This process of transferring activities that used to be undertaken internally to be provided by an external supplier is known as outsourcing. Such outsourcing is now very common in the textile sector. Globalization and MNC outsourcing were the wider social structures informing the mass work-related deaths at Rana Plaza in Bangladesh. In 2013, the Rana Plaza building, which housed five textile factories, collapsed, killing over 1,100 textile workers. Despite clear indications that the building was unsafe (cracks were appearing, and other companies located in the building closed for business), the workers were ordered to continue working by the textile manufacturing firms who were under pressure to meet the conditions of the low-cost bids they had made to manufacture for MNCs (Chowdhury, 2017).

Naomi Klein, in her important 2001 book *No Logo*, pointed to the significance of this pattern of large MNCs, with major, commonly recognized brands not directly manufacturing anything – because of outsourcing. Klein argued that the process of creating meaning and attachment to brands among consumers has become the key value-creating activity of many corporations. In this logo-centred capitalism, the actual product to which the logo is attached becomes almost peripheral, meaning that MNCs have no significant concerns about quality when they outsource production contracts to the cheapest bidders. Klein puts forward Nike as the epitome of the new logo-centred capitalism. Nike does not own any factories. It is a 'product-free brand' (2001: 199). With the actual products relatively unimportant, Nike uses global sourcing to produce cheaply in poor labour conditions. Rather than human resources being central to competitive advantage, 'the people doing the work of production are likely to be treated like detritus – the stuff left behind' (p 197).

Klein's analysis points to a new *international division of labour* emerging in contemporary globalized capitalism. We can think of a hierarchy of three main forms of job in such logo-centred globalized capitalism – knowledge work linked to finance and the creation of meaning in marketing and advertising; service work, involving shop workers selling products directly to consumers; and manufacturing jobs, where the physical products are made to which the logo is attached. Klein (2001) argues that knowledge work and service jobs are mainly based in affluent countries. Knowledge work tends to be based in the MNC host country, underpinned by advanced education systems that foster creativity in knowledge work. As noted, the manufacturing jobs tend to be located in less-affluent, low-wage countries. After having outsourced the production of the goods in low-cost locations, the MNCs then ship the goods to the affluent countries, where consumers have money to pay the high prices that MNCs are able to charge because of consumers' brand loyalty to their logos. The shop workers selling the goods, therefore, are also located in affluent countries. Here, Klein is effectively putting forward an amended version of Wallerstein's (1979) core–periphery world-systems model.

A linked, but perhaps more nuanced, argument is that the international division of labour is best understood as emerging from *global supply chains*. The argument is that MNCs do not simply put products to be outsourced to one manufacturer (in low-cost countries) who complete the whole product; rather, MNCs outsource *parts* of the production process to a *network* of suppliers. Such networks are made up of production activities that form a tightly interlocked chain, from raw materials to the final consumer (Gereffi and Korzeniewicz, 1994). Such supply chains may be globally dispersed, but they are centrally coordinated and controlled by MNCs – a process facilitated by the speed and depth of information flows allowed by developments in information technology. It is hard to overstate the centrality of global supply chains to the global economy. Reinecke and Donaghey (2023) note that global supply chains accounted for 80 per cent of global trade and 60 per cent of global production in 2016.

Sociologists and geographers have analysed the implications of global supply chains for the international division of labour in a wide range of commodities, from clothing to electronics and automobiles (Raikes et al, 2000). Such analyses, although more nuanced than a simple core–periphery model, still point to significant tiers in the international division of labour. China and India are the key sites for dispersed production within global supply chains. Suwandi et al (2019) estimate that 43 per cent of total supply-chain employment is based in China, and 16 per cent in India.

So far, this section has outlined the core elements of capitalist globalization, and discussed the two sides of the debate concerning the implications of such globalization for the nature and experience of work. Overall, in considering the debate, it is reasonable to conclude that many workers in low-cost countries are subject to intensified labour conditions and tight systems of control. At the same time, it is clear that there are wage gains; for example, China's movement from a low-income country to a middle-income country is significantly informed by the role of Chinese labour in the international division of labour. Although this indicates an important form of gain from globalization, the sociological analyses of Wallerstein, Klein and global commodity-chain analysts clearly indicate that the international division of labour is structured by systemic imbalances. As Pocock (2008) puts it, international inequality is a continuing 'fault line of inequality'. Capitalist globalization tends to reproduce rather than challenge global inequality. This is examined further in Chapter 8.

Structures of control and authority in the workplace

Looking at the essential features of capitalism per se, then considering different forms of capitalism, before examining the international division of labour allows us an understanding of the macro-structures of power at work. This section turns to look at the structures of power relating to the workplace. These are the structures of power that most directly pertain to people's daily working lives. Recalling how the chapter started, so far the chapter has allowed us to analyse the macro-structures of power that structure the operation of the call centre. In this section, we turn to more workplace-based elements of power at work. This is best done by considering the operation of *control* in the workplace. Richard Edwards (1979: 17) defines management control as 'the ability of managers to obtain desired work behaviour from workers'.

There are many competing arguments from sociologists of work regarding the nature of control. It is useful to look at these by first stepping back to consider key abstract elements in the nature of control. Burawoy (1979) argues that forms of management control over workers can be located on a continuum between coercion/force and consent/legitimation (Wood, 2020). Friedman's analysis (1977) points in a similar direction. Friedman argues that there are two main abstract forms (or, in sociological jargon, 'ideal types') of control within capitalism: direct control and responsible autonomy. Central to direct control is the operation of coercion from management, such as through direct observation of workers, while central to responsible autonomy is the operation of consent among workers.

Such an approach that focuses only on the operation of coercion/hierarchy and consent/norms would be seen as limited by most economic sociologists. When economic sociologists consider how economic actions are directed, they tend to consider three main modes of direction: the market, power/hierarchy and norms (Beamish and Biggart, 2006). Following this lead, we will consider the operation of control of work in relation to each of the market, power/hierarchy and norms. In keeping with the focus of the book, important examples feature service work, knowledge work and platform work.

The market

There have been some significant periods and major economies in which the operation of work relations, including control, has been insulated from the market. We can think of arguments concerning the operation of Fordism and coordinated market economies as pointing to significant insulation of work relations within a firm from the operation of the external product market and the external labour market. For instance, when firms are in a quasi-monopoly position in the product market, that provides considerable insulation of the operation of the firm from shocks and competitive forces in the product market. A classic mode for work relations to be insulated from the external labour market is through the operation of collective bargaining between trade unions and employers to set wage rates and key employment conditions.

This insulation, perhaps, has been the main reason that abstract consideration of how control operates by sociologists of work has tended to overlook the role of the market. Such oversight about the role of the market in the operation of control, however, is becoming increasingly untenable. Cappelli et al (1997) make the strong case that, in the US, employment relations are increasingly 'marketized'. Increasingly, firms, rather than seeking to insulate the management of labour from the external product market and from the external labour market, are exposing the management of labour to these external markets. Grimshaw and Rubery (1998) make a similar argument for the UK. Although McGovern et al (2007) present a counter-argument that claims of marketization of employment relations tend to be overstated, the recent rise of platform-mediated work does point to the increasing exposure of the management of labour to external markets. Note that this is not a statement that the market is the dominant mode of directing employment relations. Rather it is a statement that its significance has increased. Further, in some sectors of liberal market economies, marketization of employment relations is an important phenomenon.

So, what does the rise of marketization imply specifically for the operation of control? Primarily, it means that workers are increasingly directed by market forces to act in ways that management desires. Often, increased exposure to the external product market brings increased exposure to the external labour market. To present a contemporary example, outsourcing tends to increase workers' exposure to product market forces. Indeed, Weil (2014) argues that, in the US, large corporations are increasingly shedding their role as direct employers in favour of outsourcing work to small companies who are in fierce (product) market competition with each other. This story echoes what was said earlier in the chapter regarding MNCs and global supply chains. As Weil notes, workers in such outsourced jobs tend to have precarious employment, the terms of which are set by direct consideration of labour market conditions, sometimes defined globally. In terms of the operation of control, this means that these workers will often feel keenly the disciplining effect of the market in ensuring that they comply with management directions. Burawoy's (1979) analysis of changes in the nature of workplace regimes of control in different periods of capitalism is partly underpinned by this logic. Notably, Burawoy's characterization of the first major form of capitalist workplace regime of control is that of 'market despotism', in which 'the disciplinary power of the market' (Purcell and Brook, 2022: 394) plays a key role.

The rise of platform-mediated work is perhaps the clearest symbol of the increasing importance of the operation of market forces in the operation of control. Chapter 1 stated that a central aspect of platform work is that the platform seeks to mediate a relationship between a worker (service-provider) and a client (service-user), and the platform seeks to do this in such a way that the work is undertaken outside an employment relationship with the platform company. This can be thought of as an extreme version of outsourcing, in which workers are not outsourced to smaller firms in competition with each other, but they are outsourced to a position where they are treated as individual, self-employed contractors. Further, this is a position in which the external product market and the external labour market are collapsed into one, and the workers either conform to the behaviour that the market directs or they have to exit this structure. In terms of the operation of control, management effectively devolves a considerable part of control to the operation of market forces.

If platform-mediated work is the most extreme form of the use of the market to control workers' actions, a less extreme form is the use of economic incentives by management. The market operates to direct behaviour by providing economic incentives to act in certain ways. Within the hierarchical structure of the employment relationship, management can attempt to set up an economic incentive structure to ensure workers act in the way that management desires. Bonus payments, payment-by-results schemes and commission-based pay in sales work are all examples of this approach (Korczynski, 2002; Bone, 2006).

Hierarchy

The second main mode for control is the operation of power within a hierarchy of the employment relationship. There may be a range of ways in which hierarchical power can inform control systems. Although Ouchi (1979) writes from a managerialist perspective, his analysis of management control is analytically useful in that it points to two key factors that influence the form of hierarchical control that can operate. The first is management's knowledge of the labour process, or, as he terms it, the 'transformation process'. When management has a precise knowledge of the labour processes within production, then control can operate through the stipulation and observation of workers' behaviours. Ouchi (1979: 843) explains – using a tin can factory as an example – that management can:

> achieve effective control simply by having someone observe the behaviour of the employees and the workings of the machines. If all behaviours and processes conform to [the] desired transformation steps then [management] know with certainty that proper tin cans are coming out the other end. By specifying the rules of behaviour and process, [management] could create an effective bureaucratic control mechanism in this case.

This form of control has close correspondence with Friedman's (1977) category of 'direct control', in which there are coercive threats and close supervision. It also corresponds to Edward's (1979) categories of 'simple/direct control' (direct observation) and 'technical control'. A classic example of technical control is the operation of the assembly line, where the operation of machines directs worker behaviour. Here, management structures the knowledge of the labour process within the processes of the machines.

Ouchi emphasizes that management's knowledge of the transformation or labour process cannot be assumed to be perfect (also see Littler, 1990). Indeed, even where management *thinks* they have a perfect knowledge, detailed sociological workplace research has pointed to the frequently enduring importance of workers' overlooked 'tacit' knowledge and skills (Lewis, 2012) in the production process. Ouchi (1979: 843) gives the example of customer-facing service work as an instance of management lacking key knowledge of, or being unable to prescribe in detail, the labour process. In a 'high fashion ... boutique [w]hat it takes to be a successful buyer or merchandiser is quite beyond [management's] understanding so [management] could not possibly hope to create a detailed set of rules, which, if followed by buyers, would assure success'. In such cases, Ouchi argues, for hierarchical control to operate effectively, management needs a high ability to measure outputs. Management's ability to measure outputs is the second key factor that Ouchi's analysis points to as affecting the operation of control through hierarchy. Where management lacks key knowledge of the labour process, but has a high ability to measure outputs, control will centre on the measurement of outputs of the labour process, for instance, the number of sales achieved. Ouchi's analysis also allows us to see that control through hierarchy will be at its tightest when management has *both* high knowledge of the labour process *and* a high ability to measure outputs. Notably, as will be outlined in Chapter 4, these conditions will exist when management follows a Taylorist design of production process (that is, where there are repeated, easily measured and monitored, low-skill tasks to be performed).

Ouchi's approach helps us to understand the operation of control through hierarchy, but it is important to be aware that his managerialist assumptions and starting point mean that issues of conflict and resistance tend to dissolve away in the search for technical solutions to what is actually a sociological problem of control. For instance, for Ouchi, the problem of control appears to be solved if management has a high ability to measure outputs. However, a critical sociological approach would suggest that this merely points us analytically to where key issues of power will be played out within the workplace. Notably, there is a tradition of ethnographic research that points to the ongoing battles between management and workers regarding what constitutes acceptable output *targets* (Roy, 1954; Beynon, 1975; Korczynski, 2014). Such struggles occur further to, and are not resolved by, management's ability to measure outputs.

So far in this discussion of control through hierarchy, there has been a broad assumption that management is *the direct* agent that is observing, directing and/or measuring. However, sociology of work research points to other important agents and processes that management can call upon – most notably, technology, customers (Fuller and Smith, 1991; Gamble, 2007) and peers (Barker, 1993). Here, we focus on technology. Zuboff (1988) points to the importance of the monitoring capacity of information technology (IT). IT does not just automate activities, it also 'informates' in that it provides information on how it is being used. Zuboff presciently argued that management would use this informating capacity of IT to monitor workers' behaviour. IT, as well as being a tool for workers in undertaking many jobs, also becomes a way in which management can easily monitor workers' behaviour. The direct overlooking of behaviour by supervisors can be replaced by IT-based monitoring. In this way, IT comes to play a key role in management control. Indeed, in the context of call-centre work, research has pointed to the pervasiveness of monitoring facilitated by IT. For instance, one call-centre worker, in a study by Frenkel et al (1999: 140), remarked that 'you get measured on how many times you scratch your shoulder'. Fernie and Metcalf (1998) go so far as to argue that IT monitoring constitutes a contemporary-workplace form of the panopticon in action. The panopticon, discussed in Chapter 2 regarding Foucault (via Bentham), involves a system of power and observation in which a person is pervasively observed such that they internalize the sense of being observed and act in the way that the observer desires. Fernie and Metcalf (1998: 1) argue with regard to the monitoring of workers, 'for call centres Jeremy Bentham's 1791 Panopticon was truly the vision of the future'. While IT does play a key role in monitoring in call centres as part of management control systems, Bain and Taylor (2000) are correct to caution against the simplistic use of the metaphor of the panopticon at work. The use of the metaphor of the panopticon here assumes that complete and perfect information is provided by IT monitoring and that workers are simply passive in this system of control. Neither of these assumptions is appropriate.

Norms

As Weber argued, power is often more effective when it is taken as legitimate – seen as acceptable and appropriate – by those whose actions are being directed. In terms of the analysis of management control of workers, this leads us to consider the key norms held by workers that can legitimate power, that can lead them to work in the way that management desires. Ouchi (1979) accedes that, when management lacks detailed knowledge of the labour process, and lacks a high ability to measure outputs, control systems must rely on norms.

As discussed in Chapter 2, Weber (1904, 1921) argued that a key form of authority, or legitimate power, in capitalism is rational-legal authority, where power is legitimate because it is part of an efficient structure for attaining an end, and where that structure follows accordingly systematic rules. This abstract argument has not been directly followed through in research in the sociology of work. However, research on unitarism and organizational commitment can be interpreted as, in part, speaking to Weber's arguments. Unitarism and its close cousin, organizational commitment, are perhaps the most important norms that management often propose and seek to develop within the workforce. Unitarism is a system of thought in which the organization is regarded as a team 'unified by a common purpose' (Fox, 1966: 2). There is a harmony of interests in achieving the success of the organization. Metaphors in which the organization is portrayed as a family, or a team, and phrases such as 'we are all in this together' and the repeated use of the collective 'we' and 'us' to refer to the organization are typical ways in which management promotes unitarism. Human resource management departments in organizations can be analysed as key promoters of unitarism in the workplace (Legge, 2005). Where workers accept the unitarist perspective, they will tend to develop organizational commitment: an acceptance of organizational goals and a willingness to exert effort on behalf of the organization (Miller and Lee, 2001).

Management also aims to develop organizational commitment by seeking to develop an overall organizational culture in which togetherness and joint striving are emphasized. Kunda (1992) conducted an important ethnographic study of normative control through the development of a corporate culture at a computer engineering firm in the US. In this culture, the firm's founder is presented as a heroic figure in stories and in film. The firm seeks to develop a culture of belonging in and to the firm, and an overall sense of family, informality, creativity and fun. The firm very carefully seeks to design, or engineer, the culture, with structures from senior 'internal ideologists' (Kunda, 1992: 218), who enthusiastically cheerlead the culture, to 'boot camps' of presentations and activities, to a 'culture manual' that shows how things are at the firm. Casey's (1995) analysis of the careful development of corporate culture at a technology firm in the US paints a similar picture regarding the approach and strategies of management to develop normative control: 'team and family are promoted … [to achieve] greater levels of employee involvement and attitudinal change in the pursuit of excellence and dedication to total customer satisfaction' (p 98). These approaches to develop organizational cultures often involve the promotion of substantive values within these organizations. In that sense, these approaches are becoming quite distinct from Weber's value-free concept of rational-legal authority. These firms go out of their way to present themselves as something much more than just an efficient means to an end linked to a set of systematic rules.

Although these insightful studies were undertaken in tech firms, it should not be assumed that the management of corporate culture for control is a new phenomenon. Some scholars have analysed this in terms of the historical promotion of paternalist cultures (Jacoby, 1998). Given that the Latin word *pater* (meaning father) is the etymological root of this term, it can be readily seen that, again, there is an emphasis on the metaphor of the family, with the company positioned as the provider of care, protection and security to its dependent children. One of the most extreme examples of the development of organizational culture in tandem with paternalist policies (such as supporting job security and provision of good benefits), at least in a Western country, took place at IBM in the middle of the 20th century. The promotion of the organizational culture involved the use of the IBM Songbook (El-Sawad and Korczynski, 2007). Sales workers frequently sang songs that promoted sales as a strong work ethic and IBM as paternalist protector – songs such as 'Ever Onward, IBM' (El-Sawad and Korczynski, 2007: 79):

> Ever onward! Ever onward!
> That's the spirit that has brought us fame.
> We're big but bigger we will be,
> We can't fail for all can see,
> That to serve humanity has been our aim.
> Our products now are known

In every zone.
… ever onward IBM.

If Weber's arguments about rational-legal authority constituting a key form of legitimate power within modern capitalism has limited direct research support, this does not invalidate Weber's wider sociological search for key forms of authority that operate across societies and workplaces. Using Weber's search as a starting point, as noted in Chapter 2, I argue (Korczynski, 2002) that *the customer* has become a key figure of authority in a society that is increasingly characterized as a consumer society. Following this, Korczynski et al (2000) show how management draws on the figure of the customer to attempt to develop normative control, where norms relate to serving the customer. This was operationalized in the frequent management statement that workers should put themselves 'in the customer's shoes'. Training sessions often involved role plays where workers had to take on the role of the customer. Indeed, this normative role of the customer was a key part of the culture examined by Casey (1995: 98), with its dedication to 'total customer satisfaction'.

Still taking Weber as a starting point, it is appropriate to consider *democracy* as perhaps the most powerful contemporary way to legitimate power in society as a whole. Crucially, democracy is a form of authority that management in most capitalist firms conspicuously seeks to avoid. It is the elephant in the room in contemporary management systems of control. The power of the shareholder, and of management, is clearly threatened by the operation of democracy within workplaces, so management avoids referencing democracy. There are some exceptions in those social market economies where the labour movement has pushed to enact some (limited) formal worker decision-making power within firms. For instance, in German firms, there are legally prescribed worker representatives who sit on the boards. Broadly speaking, however, management is unable to call upon democratic authority in the development of normative control.

Overview

There is a broad consensus that management control systems tend to utilize multiple elements. It is not just the market that operates to direct worker behaviour; it is not just management monitoring behaviour and/or measuring outputs and setting targets that disciplines and directs worker behaviour; it is not just the operation of norms through corporate culture that leads workers themselves to act in ways that management wishes. Often, elements of all of these are present in a workplace. Furthermore, they will tend to be co-present in contradictory ways. Blyton and Turnbull (2004: 109) argue that 'instead of a choice between alternative strategies – direct control versus responsible autonomy … direct supervision or self-managed teams – many organizations are faced with the tensions, and at times outright contradictions, of applying different systems of control to the same workers'. Fox's (1974) classic book on trust in the context of the employment relationship shows that management's rhetoric of valuing and trusting workers is frequently undermined by establishing close monitoring of their behaviour and outputs, for the latter practices effectively demonstrate that the workers are *not* trusted.

Given that multiple elements of management-control efforts coexist in contradictory ways, sociologists of work explore patterns in this situation of contradictory coexistence. Both Frenkel et al (1995) and Fleming and Sturdy (2011) point to ways in which management control systems both have coexisting contradictory elements and operate in ways that seek to obscure that contradiction. Frenkel et al argue that info–normative control is increasingly important in both service work and knowledge work. Info–normative control is 'control based on data objectification (performance indicators) and employee accommodation or commitment to performance standards' (Frenkel et al, 1995: 774). There is both hierarchy – measurement of behaviour and/or outputs – and a normative element present. Info–normative control involves management actively combining these elements by seeking to generate the normative commitment to the targets linked to the hierarchical measurement. The quarterly or six-monthly performance appraisal meeting between manager and worker is the social structure in which info–normative control is enacted, for, typically, a key element in an appraisal is the worker's normative agreement to hit performance targets in the coming period. Fleming and Sturdy's (2011) study of control in a call centre argues that the management promotion of a normative culture of fun and 'being yourself' serves to distract workers from, and obscure the operation of, the hierarchical measuring control processes that are typical of call centres.

A final point to note in this overview analysis of management control as a key structure of power in the workplace is that this discussion has not yet considered the central importance of worker agency and resistance in respect to systems of control. That is examined in Chapters 5 and 6.

Sociological imagination – your turn

Think about your job experience or talk to a friend about their job experience. What were the main forms of control that were in place? In terms of norms, did your manager/supervisor try to develop a unitarist culture, with reference to 'we', 'us', 'team', 'all in this together' and so on? How did they do this? If so, how did you and your work colleagues react? In terms of hierarchy, did your manager/supervisor observe your work and/or measure your outputs? How did you and your work colleagues react? Did the market play any role in the system of control?

4

The Organization of Work

At the heart of the sociology of work is the analysis of how work is organized. This is the core focus of this chapter. Key dimensions of work organization are outlined. This allows us to build up to consider different overall types of work organization. Debates are examined regarding how best to characterize work organization in service work, knowledge work and platform work.

Work organization – key dimensions

What do people talk about when they are comparing one job with another? What do people look at when comparing, for instance, the job of a platform worker delivering pizza and the job of a call-centre operator in an insurance firm? One of the first things would probably be pay. But what if the salaries of the jobs are similar – what else is important in thinking about whether you prefer one job over the other? Perhaps the security of employment might feature as important, and perhaps the degree of independence there is in the role. Beyond these features, many people might struggle to get to grips with this issue. Given that jobs are a fundamentally important aspect of most people's lives, this is not a trivial issue. Gladly, sociologists of work have given the question of comparing jobs – particularly regarding how work is organized – systematic thought. This chapter draws upon this scholarship.

The organization of work, in principle, can be broken down into very many sub-dimensions. For some purposes, it might make sense to do that. But for our central purpose – to lay out the main rooms in the architecture of work organization – it is enough to concentrate on the most important abstract dimensions. Note that different social theories often emphasize the importance of different dimensions of work organization. For instance, scholars following a Marxist approach tend to focus on the labour process, while scholars oriented by Durkheimian thought will focus more on the nature of peer relations.

The following sections lay out four key dimensions: the basis of division of labour, the labour process (skill and work intensity), peer relations and individual job mobility.

Note that control is also a key dimension of work organization. Control and authority relations were discussed in detail in the previous chapter. It made sense to discuss control as part of the focus in Chapter 3 on structures of power at work, but it also deserves its place in this chapter. Control explicitly reappears in this chapter when we turn to consider overall patterns in work organization.

Division of labour

A fundamental question that sociologists ask is: 'What is the basis by which a "job" comes to exist?' Take some contemporary examples of typical jobs – a call-centre operator in an insurance firm, a software programme developer in a management consultancy, an operative in a food-processing factory. How is it that such 'jobs' have come to be? How is it that those groups of tasks come to be bundled together into these things we call jobs? Jobs come about socially, through human framings, actions and interactions. And the key question arising from this simple observation becomes: what is the basis for the decision-making that leads to a certain group of tasks to be bundled together into a job rather than a different group of tasks? Or, to put it more sociologically, *what is the basis for the division of labour?*

Across time periods and across work settings, there have been several different bases for the division of labour. Perhaps the most important change in these bases was caused by the advent of industrial capitalism in the industrial revolution (which first occurred in the UK across the 18th and 19th centuries). In the pre-industrialized period, jobs tended to centre on occupations, often linked to a clear product, with jobs entailing a holistic grouping of tasks necessary for production. A carpenter, for instance, would be able to produce a range of wooden materials, from tables to chairs to shelves and doors, and the job of the carpenter would entail all the tasks from the sourcing of the wood to the design of the table to the execution of the tasks to create the table. Tradition also implicitly had a role within this division of labour: a carpenter's job was like that because it had always been like that. 'Custom' was an important word informing the fabric of pre-industrial work and society (Thompson, 1991).

Moving on from the *customary social* division of labour involving wide, traditional occupations, the industrial revolution led to the primary basis for the division of labour becoming the aim of *maximizing task efficiency*. This led to the detailed division of labour (involving narrow, specialized jobs) that Adam Smith described as operating in a pin factory (quoted in Chapter 1), and which occupied Emile Durkheim in *The Division of Labour in Society* (discussed in Chapter 2).

Another key point in the development of specialization and a detailed division of labour was the birth of 'scientific management' associated with Frederick Taylor in the early decades of the 20th century in the US. Important here was the principle that there should be *a separation of the conception (planning, design) of a task from its execution*. Taylor proposed that tasks involving conception should be constituents of managerial jobs, and the role of executing tasks should become the default job description of the production operative. This scientific management principle, or Taylorist principle, was a vital element in the organization of work associated with Fordist capitalism (discussed in Chapter 3). One of the reactions against the principles of maximizing task efficiency and separating conception from execution was the movement towards more human-centred, alternative forms of job design (Kelly, 1982), often linked to an approach known as a socio-technical system approach. The aim – rarely realized in practice – was to put forward *the principle of meaningful work* as the basis for the division of labour, and for the design of technology (Berggren, 1993).

There are other important bases for the division of labour. In service work, where the key part of the job involves interacting with a service recipient, the principle of the *creation and maintenance of a relationship with the service recipient* (patient/guest/diner/customer) can play an important role in the division of labour (Korczynski, 2002). For instance, in nursing in the UK NHS, this is manifest in the principle of care, which is 'patient-centred rather than task-centred, and is characterized by each patient having a single, identified, qualified nurse who is responsible for their care during the entire period of their hospital stay' (Wicks, 1998: 186). In professional work, the basis of the division of labour often revolves around the professional association that identifies professional jobs with a *discreet, systematic body of knowledge and expertise* (Abbott, 1988). There is also an important stream of sociology scholarship that shows how the division of labour can be, and often is, *gendered*. The core argument here is that the bundling of tasks into distinct jobs, and the allocation of types (gender) of people to those distinct jobs, do not occur separately but are interrelated. There is a bundling of 'masculine'-linked tasks into jobs to be occupied mainly by men, and there is a bundling of 'feminine'-linked tasks into jobs to be occupied mainly by women (Abbott et al, 2005).

Labour process – skill and work intensity
Skill

The core of work organization is the enactment of workers' labouring, something that many sociologists refer to as the labour process. The term 'labour process' has origins in Marx's ideas about the core of the capitalist economy involving the transformation of the potential to labour (labour power) into actual labouring. Skill is a key element of the labour process. There is a large literature in the sociology of work regarding what is meant by 'skill' (Spenner, 1990; Green, 2013). Here, we follow Spenner (1990) in focusing on two central elements within the concept of skill: the complexity of the task and discretion. The complexity of a task refers to whether the nature of the task is simple and easily accomplished, with little learning required (associated with jobs labelled as 'low skilled'), or whether it is intricate and complicated and would usually require a long period of learning for it to be accomplished well (associated with jobs labelled 'high skilled'). The second element in Spenner's concept of skill, discretion, refers to the degree and scope of decision-making given to the job-holder. Jobs with higher discretion are seen as higher skilled than those with lower discretion (everything else being equal). So, making a burger in McDonald's is seen as a low-skill job in large part because the job has been designed such that there is almost no discretion for the worker regarding how to accomplish it – the worker just follows a set structure of processes linked to specifically designed technology used to make the burger (Leidner, 1993). By contrast, a chef making a burger in a mid-range restaurant is likely to have very high levels of discretion, around both the recipe and the processes of mixing and cooking the burger, and such a job tends to be seen as high skilled.

It is important to note that sociologists have studied how and when certain jobs are labelled skilled or unskilled and have concluded that this process should be understood as a political one. It has often been a deeply gendered political process: when men undertake a given task, the task is more likely to be labelled as skilled than when women undertake similar tasks (noted in Chapter 2).

Note that jobs involving high discretion often involve the worker having both execution and design tasks to undertake – compare this with the job design approach of Taylorism. Indeed, the jobs that sprang from the application of the principles of Taylor's scientific management were narrow, low-skill jobs. When such principles were allied to the technology of the assembly line, the nature of work appeared as a seemingly endless and intense cycle of executing monotonous tasks.

Work intensity

The second element of the labour process focused on here refers to the amount of labour to be enacted in a work period. Green (2001: 56) formally defines work intensity as 'the rate of physical and/or mental input to work tasks performed during the working day'. Work intensity comprises several aspects, including the rate of task performance; the intensity of those tasks in terms of physical, mental and emotional demands; and the gaps between tasks (Green et al, 2022: 460). A key element in sociological research in recent decades has concerned whether there has been an increase in work intensity. Recalling the discussion in Chapter 3 of the important distinction between labour power (the potential to labour) and actual labour enacted, a concentration on work intensity focuses exactly on a core struggle at the heart of the employment relationship. Ethnographic studies of workplaces (where the researcher becomes part of the workforce for an extended period) often highlight that a significant point of conflict between management and workers concerns the degree of work intensity. I undertook an ethnographic study of work in a factory manufacturing window blinds. The following workers' quotes from that study demonstrate conflict about the intensity of work (Korczynski, 2014: 142–143):

> Pauline [a worker in the factory] says, 'They [management] want us to work 150 per cent. For that wage, there's no way we're going to do that.' ... Molly said, 'We don't work any faster if there are absences, but they want us to. I'm not going to cover two machines. If I do it once, they'll expect it all the time.'

In January 2023, the BBC reported that the first strike by Amazon workers was occurring in the UK, at the Coventry warehouse (Jordan and Conway, 2023). Striking workers who were interviewed pointed out that the work intensity was so high that toilet breaks were tightly policed by supervisors, and that supervisors focused heavily on minimizing 'idle time' (when workers were not digitally logged as undertaking measured productive tasks).

Green et al (2022) present a comprehensive study of work intensification in Britain in the first decades of this century based on data from the Skills and Employment Survey, a consistent series of nationally representative sample surveys of employed people in Britain. They write that 'the story from 2001 on [until 2017] is one of renewed work intensification' (p 468). The authors saw a consistent rise in the proportion of workers reporting that their job requires them to work very hard, includes high-speed work and involves working to tight deadlines. They also note (p 478) that this intensification is 'far from an isolated episode, [as] the rise follows an earlier period of work intensification in the 1980s'. In addition, they point out that the work intensification in the 21st century has *not* been one associated with an ongoing de-skilling and simplification of work. They argue that the key factor underlying this work intensification has been the increasing power of employers over workers. Chapter 3 pointed to a number of significant developments in the strengthening of employer power over workers. Green et al (2022: 480) go on to say that 'because of the declining power of both organized and unorganized labour to resist pressures from employers in Britain's liberal market economy, technical and organizational changes have been harnessed in combination to intensify work'. Not all jobs feature high work intensity – Green et al position around 60 per cent of workers in 2017 as occupying jobs with high work intensity. (The second half of this chapter analyses specific forms of work organization with regard to openness to or barriers to work intensification.) Finally, note that, although Marx argued that there was an inevitable logic within capitalism for work to become more intensified, Green et al (2022: 481) argue that 'getting people to work harder is inherently self-limiting as a growth strategy' because there are physical limits regarding how hard people can work. They point out that there are other, less limiting strategies to achieve profits and growth, such as 'investing in their human capabilities or new capital'.

Co-worker relations

Another important dimension of work organization is that of lateral, or horizontal, relations: the relations between workers at a similar level in the hierarchy. This dimension is perhaps the most overlooked of the ones covered here. Hodson (2001: 202) notes that there has been a 'relative inattention to work groups, and co-worker relations'.

Marx points to two fundamental logics in co-worker relations – logics that push in different directions. There is the logic of competition between wage-labourers in the labour market. Such competition pushes workers apart from each other. Hodson's (2001) overview of workplace ethnographies notes that co-worker conflict such as (racialized and gendered) back-biting, bullying and malicious gossip often grows in the context of organizational chaos, where work is not so much organized as disorganized. However, Marx also pointed to a stronger logic of association through mutual cooperation within the labour process and workers' shared position in the employment relationship. Marx (1848: 27) saw great potential for the emergence of class solidarity from the latter: 'Wage-labour rests exclusively on competition between the labourers. The advance of industry, whose involuntary promoter is the bourgeoisie, replaces the isolation of the labourers, due to competition, by the revolutionary combination, due to association.' Ethnographic studies show that workers frequently enact a range of cooperative practices in and around the labour process, and that such practices are often underpinned by norms of solidarity and reciprocation. For instance, consider this excerpt from Santino's (1991: 70) ethnography of the work of railway porters in the US: '[Porters] aided each other – for example, covering a fellow porter's car while the man stole a few hours' sleep, warning each other if somebody learned that a spotter was on board, and teaching new porters the tricks of the trade.'

Informal group solidarity is often played out through gestures of kindness. Cavendish (1982: 67) describes a shop-floor-wide culture of mutual care and sharing. She was struck by the generosity of the poorly paid women with whom she was working:

[After returning from a two-week unpaid sick leave] I was talking to Anna when she stuffed a £10 note in my trouser pocket so quickly I wasn't even really sure what it was. She was giving it to me because I would be short, having lost two weeks' wages ... I was quite overwhelmed by her generosity; the gift was completely genuine, and she really didn't want the money back.

We should not assume that such cultures are a thing of the past, overtaken by rising individualism in recent decades. My more recent ethnography (Korczynski, 2014: 42) outlines the everyday enacted community among workers in a blinds factory:

On my second day at McTells, Rachel came over to the work table to pick up a batch of roller blinds. ... She picked up an armful and turned to carry them back to her stitching table, but in so doing, she caught one of the blinds on a trolley, and all the blinds spilled on the floor. Almost before she could say 'oh, bugger', there were already four people crouching down, helping her to pick the blinds up. 'Don't worry, they'll be fine', said Sheila, handing back three of the blinds to Rachel.

The study goes on to report that these workers undertook much of the same informal collective practices as the railway porters noted by Santino. Korczynski and Wittel (2020) argue that we can usefully think about such co-worker cooperation as a form of 'workplace commoning': a set of cooperative practices and values that are shared among workers, often underlain with an ethic of solidarity and mutual care. The idea of commoning (De Angelis, 2017) derives from political economic scholarship on the commons – basically an analysis of how best to look after and reproduce things that are held in common, without specific ownership (such as the air, seas, the environment). One strong tendency within capitalism is for capital to enclose the commons, to take the commons into private ownership or control (Hardin, 1968). Notably, in Britain between the 17th and 19th centuries, land that had been held in common, known as the commons, was systematically enclosed and taken into private ownership and control. This is relevant because Korczynski and Wittel (2020) argue that management's widespread drive for teamwork within the organization of work can be analysed as an attempt to *enclose* informal workplace cooperation and commoning – to take it into management's control and to mould it to management's will.

The move to formal teamwork stands as one of the most important management developments with regard to work organization over the last century – since the Hawthorne studies highlighted to management the importance of informal work groups and their norms (noted in the discussion of Durkheim in Chapter 2). Such management-initiated teamwork structures tend to be underpinned by a hierarchical threat against non-participation by workers. Further, such management-initiated teamwork seeks to ensure that *all* of the cooperation that occurs contributes to the core management aim of profit creation. So, for instance, management-initiated teamwork structures among porters would involve learning the most efficient way to do the job (rather than the 'tricks of the trade'), and would *not* involve such practices as covering each other's cars to allow sleep or helping each other with the knowledge of management spotters. Existing research on teamwork has highlighted extreme cases of management-framed 'concertive control' (Barker, 1993) where teams become forums in which workers discipline each other, but, in the UK context, a more common finding is the incompleteness of management's attempts to enclose informal workplace cultures of co-worker commoning and cooperation within formal teamwork structures (for example Findlay et al, 2000).

Mobility of individuals

So far, the dimensions we have focused upon relate to the social structure of how work is organized, and they predominantly link to a static, cross-sectional snapshot of an organization. The dimension of the mobility of individuals within and between organizations, by contrast, focuses upon the importance of understanding the dynamic element across time of the patterns that people make in their journeys across job roles. Often this is discussed in terms of patterns of careers, but, because the concept of career is rarely applied to significant sections of the people in low-skilled and low-paying jobs, here, the term 'mobility of individuals' is used. A good sociology should feature not just a static analysis of the social structures that face people, and which people enact, but also a dynamic analysis of how people create journeys through such structures.

There is a greater focus on the agency of individual workers in this dimension, but it is also crucial to see that there are important social structures that pattern the mobility of individuals across job roles. A key first distinction that scholars make in thinking about these social structures is between the internal labour market and the external labour market. The internal labour market refers to a firm's internal job structures, wages, training and promotions policies that are developed as largely shielded from the wider external labour market (Doeringer and Piore, 1970). The external labour market covers jobs and wages set in the wider, open market. The relative importance of the internal or external labour market is a crucial element in the social structures that pattern individual job mobility. Table 4.1 lays out the main patterns of mobility

Table 4.1: Mobility of individuals across jobs

Main mode of mobility of individuals	Main mobility pattern	Key structuring agent
Internal labour market	Within organization, vertical	Organization
External labour market – occupation	Within occupation (between organizations), horizontal and vertical	Professional association
External labour market – employability	Between organizations and sectors, mainly horizontal	Individual workers positioned as responsible; employers and state bodies as enablers
External labour market – the hustle	High short-term mobility across forms of employment, horizontal	Employer assumes no responsibility for employability training, leaving worker in short-term search for job gigs

of individuals across jobs. The first row pertains to situations where the internal labour market plays the central role.

When there is an emphasis on the internal labour market, the individual is more likely to be linked to a single organization. The organization plays the key structuring role. Jacoby (1998) writes that many of the large corporations of advanced industrialization put considerable emphasis on the internal labour market and the 'career job system'. Corporations organize their jobs into ladders or hierarchies and set out clear criteria by which individual workers could move internally up these ladders. Edwards (1979: 21) puts it thus: 'Work becomes highly stratified; each job is given its distinct title and descriptions; and impersonal rules govern promotion. "Stick with the corporation" the worker is told, "and you can ascend up the ladder".' The company promises the worker a *career*.

Baruch (2004) characterizes the organizational career 'deal' of advanced industrialization in the middle decades of the 20th century as involving a long-term commitment from organization and workers to each other, in which a job mobility pattern of gradual advancement is linked to length of job tenure. Although aggregate job tenure data has not indicated a strong shift away from the importance of internal labour markets, qualitative studies tend to paint a picture of increasing precarity and the increasing salience of the external labour market over the internal labour market as the key structures for job mobility (St-Denis and Hollister, 2023, discussed in Chapter 3).

The subsequent three rows in Table 4.1 concern situations where the external labour market is dominant. There can be important differences in how the external labour market plays a role. The second row relates to situations where the external labour market is structured for mobility within occupations, and between organizations. Here the main structuring agent tends to be a professional association. Consider how Devine et al's definition of a profession (2000: 522) involves a key role of the professional association in the structuring of jobs. The professions are:

a range of exclusive occupational groups with special skills and knowledge – have long been known to occupy positions of power and privilege in the labour market. Their power derives from authorised knowledge and, consequently, professions have been careful to protect their expertise via the activities of associations who control the recruitment and training of new entrants and the conduct and standards of work by individual professionals.

Doctors, lawyers and accountants are examples of such professions, in which professional associations play key roles in structuring the external labour market in which individuals can be mobile. The percentage of jobs that are professional, in the sense of Devine et al's definition, has grown in recent decades. According to the UK government's occupational classification, the proportion of the labour force in professional occupations rose from 19.5 per cent in 2012 to 25.7 per cent in 2021 (GOV.UK, 2022).

The penultimate row in Table 4.1 concerns job mobility through the external labour market where *employability* is becoming the dominant structure. The importance of employability is signalled by the widespread renaming of career advice services offered at schools, colleges and universities as 'career and employability' advice. Employability structures are designed to promote training and learning among people in and entering the labour market that equips them to find employment – to be strong candidates for jobs in the external labour market. In broad government policy terms, there has been a significant shift away from seeking to generate full, and relatively stable, employment (see the discussion of Keynesian policies as part of Fordism in Chapter 3) towards promoting the capacity of people to keep finding jobs in an increasingly unstable economy. As Forrier and Sels (2003: 641) put it, '"lifetime employability" is often put forward as an alternative to lifetime employment with the same employer'. The structures that support and promote employability often feature a mix of individual employers, employer associations, colleges and other state bodies (Dill and Morgan, 2017). Within these structures, there has been a key shift towards pushing on to the individual worker the responsibility for their continued employability, with employers and state bodies positioned as 'enablers' for individuals to sustain their own employability (Chertkovskaya et al, 2013). Research on varieties of capitalism (see Chapter 3) show that this shift has been much more pronounced in liberal market economies, such as the UK, Ireland and the US (Jackson and Deeg, 2006). Training and learning for employability often feature broad, general skills that are considered transferable between occupations and sectors.

A positive take on employability emphasizes the opening up of individual choice, the freeing up of career horizons for the individual worker, sometimes characterized as the creation of 'boundaryless' careers. Sweet and Meiskins (2008: 138) note that the 'optimistic view envisions a mobile workforce charting boundaryless careers, engaging in transient relationships between different employers and thereby expanding a variety of portable skills'. An emblematic positive example of this is the software programmer in Silicon Valley who rotates through companies, expanding innovation, knowledge and their own financial rewards (Saxenian, 1996). However, there are also critical voices regarding the rise of employability as a key structure for the mobility of individuals between jobs. One point of criticism is that transferable skills for employability can become so generic that they become almost empty of substantive meaning (Chertkovskaya et al, 2013), such that, for low-paid workers, learning linked to employability can offer few positive outcomes (Dill and Morgan, 2017).

A more profound sociological critique flows from an analysis of the social relations and power relations within the structures of employability. Chertkovskaya et al (2013) argue that employability promotes a social relationship in the labour market in which the individual worker is positioned as a form of entrepreneur increasingly freed from constraints linked to the old economy and its limited forms of job mobility. For these authors, such a positioning is damaging because the individual worker with limited substantive skills is, in reality, a weak rather than empowered figure in the job market. Moreover, the idea within the structures of employability that individuals are responsible for their own careers inevitably leads to a structure where individuals come to internalize a lack of career success as a sign of their own moral failure, despite the fact that much larger social structures, such as the international division of labour (see Chapter 3), may place major constraints on the possibility of upward job mobility (Shildrick et al, 2012). Furthermore, the more the individual worker is positioned as the empowered entrepreneur, the more hidden become the deep power imbalances in the nature of the employment relationship and within the structures of the job market. This is the social structure that leads to unpaid internships becoming, apparently, more acceptable (Discenna, 2016). Chertkovskaya et al (2013) also take issue with the unrelenting positivity with which the idea of employability is promoted, even by universities, which should be institutions that hold power to account and should not become cheerleaders for social structures that have significant negative implications.

The waxing of employability against the waning of organizational careers constitutes a significant shift in the social contract around work. Employers move from an implied obligation to promote career paths within their organization to an implied obligation to promote jobs and learning opportunities that support workers' wider employability. All this assumes that employers follow the path of implied obligation, but we must also consider the nature of individual job mobility when employers do not even meet the more limited obligation of supporting employability. Employers who rely on platform-mediated labour are exhibit number one here as they deny that they are employers and thereby seek to step away from obligations as an employer (Ravenelle, 2019).

In this context, where the term boundaryless career is an 'oxymoron' (Kost et al, 2020), job mobility centres on 'the hustle' (as in the final row of Table 4.1). The hustle involves individual workers who have limited training, who face conditions of high employment insecurity and no support for wider training and who respond to that context with practices that support their short-term access to a range of forms of employment. The hustle often involves a blurring of the formal and informal, and perhaps a blurring of the licit and the illicit (Thieme, 2018). The hustle may, for instance, involve a worker undertaking a number of part-time jobs simultaneously, while trying to become an influencer on social media (Cottom, 2020), while also developing a network of contacts that can give a lead into the next short-term employment opportunity. Rooted in immediate necessity, these practices promote a short-term job-mobility-entrepreneurialism. As Thieme (2018: 530) puts it, the hustle 'both normalises and affirms conditions of uncertainty'. It can be seen as part of a focus on the immediate present forced by conditions of uncertainty and precarity – what Desmond (2023) calls a 'feverish present-mindedness'. Ens' (2021: 1) study of influencers, or Seller Stylists, on the social media marketplace Poshmark, argues that 'hustling, in the way Seller Stylists celebrate it, re-routes precarity into fulfilment, [while] individualizing systemic problems such as student debt, and lack of maternal benefits'. Cottom (2020: 19) concurs, noting that the hustle is a response to situations where 'risk has shifted from states and employers to workers'.

Work organization – the contrast between craft work and Taylorism

Here, we move from looking at the individual dimensions of work organization to consider how these individual dimensions cohere into overall patterns in work organization. A key contrast drawn in overall work organization is that between work organization according to craft principles and work organization according to Frederick Taylor's principles of 'scientific management' (that is, Taylorism). Table 4.2 plots these two contrasting forms of work organization against the dimensions covered earlier (along with the dimension of control discussed in Chapter 3).

Work organization – craft principles

Although craft work is largely associated with historical forms of skilled manual labour, if looked at abstractly, craft can be and has been applied to a wide range of contemporary jobs, from software engineers and laboratory technicians to academic work (Kroezen et al, 2021). Therefore, rather than rely on either historical forms of craft work or on examples of what is painted as a contemporary resurgence of craft work (Bell et al, 2018), it is more useful – in terms of drawing a contrast to

Table 4.2: Craft and Taylorist work organization

Dimension of work organization	Work organization – craft principle	Work organization – Taylorism
Basis of division of labour	Unity of conception and execution	Task efficiency through separation of conception and execution, and task fragmentation
Labour process	High skill, limited intensity	Low skill, potential for high intensity
Control	Adherence to occupational norms	Hierarchical measurement of output, and observation of labour process
Peer relations	Strong principle of peer respect, some hierarchies regarding expertise	Weak principle, highly individualized jobs created
Individual mobility	Within occupation	Potential for limited progression through job hierarchies

Taylorism – to look at the core abstract principles informing craft work. Or, to use the sociological jargon, it is more useful to consider an ideal type of craft work organization. A core to craft work is a unity of conception/design and execution. This is the principle for the division of labour. For Braverman (who laid out a foundational contrast between craft work and Taylorism), the unity of hand and brain work was fundamental to (manual) craft work (1974: 76), as 'the [craft] worker combined, in mind and body, the concepts and physical dexterities of the specialty'. The craft worker sees the whole, understands how to make the whole (or at least a contribution to it) and is able to enact that making. Kroezen et al (2021) label this the 'all-roundedness' of craft work. Within the labour process, craft work is high skill, as it involves both great complexity of task (understanding the design and the relationship between design and execution, and the complexity within the execution itself), and high discretion in the completion of the task. Regarding discretion, Mills (1956: 222) writes of a model of craft in which the craft worker 'is free to begin his [sic] own plan, and during the activity by which it is shaped, he is free to modify its form and the manner of its creation'. There is an implied limited intensity of the labour process within Mills' and Braverman's pictures of craft work. The primary form of control is that of occupationally created norms around what constitutes 'good work'. Sennett (2008: 1) gets at the importance of this in his definition: to do craft work is 'to do something well for its own sake'. These norms of good work are collectively created, shared and discussed by the craft workers themselves. Thus, peer relations – among the craft workers – play a key role in work organization according to craft principles. An important historical institutional example of this was the guild, which was composed of the craft workers in a locale and which set clear guidelines for the appropriate enactment of the craft. Kroezen et al (2021) discuss these peer relations in terms of the operating principle of 'communality' within a craft. Informal and sometimes formal hierarchies pertain in these peer relations, largely related to different levels of expertise and experience within the craft, from apprentice to master. Within an environment of workers being socialized into a strong internalized commitment to the craft itself, and where workers hold deep, substantively specific skills (how to blow glass, how to programme a particular form of software), individual mobility is within the craft occupation. This mobility is, therefore, limited. Griffin (2013) shows that, historically, such a lack of individual mobility (even horizontal mobility in becoming an apprentice to another master) sometimes could be experienced as deeply constraining.

Taylorist work organization

Frederick Taylor's scientific management, which he developed in the US in the early decades of the 20th century, was fundamentally about increasing efficiency through undermining the strong form of worker power within craft work organization. Taylor's (1948: 128) picture of such worker power within the steel industry showed that, 'as was usual then, and in fact is still usual in most shops [workrooms] in this country, the shop was really run by the workmen and not the bosses'. Fundamental to the reversal of these power relations was that the division of labour should be informed by a focus on increasing task efficiency to be achieved by separating design/conception away from execution. Crucially, the design/conception was to be held by management, and execution (and *only* execution) was the domain of workers. Further, task efficiency could be improved by designing jobs so that workers had to undertake only a simple array of narrow tasks. Skill within the labour process is low as task complexity is low, and, further, workers' discretion is minimal as they are positioned in a structure in which they are to follow management instructions. The potential for heightened labour intensity is clear. The logic of Taylorist work organization is one in which control can become pervasive, involving *both* output measurement *and* close observation of tightly prescribed activities. And the logic of Taylorism did lead to a tight prescription of the worker's body in enacting the labour process. At the most extreme, techniques were developed that involved attaching light bulbs to a worker's body to allow the clear tracing of its movements. Lundemo (2011: 3) paints the following picture:

> Taylor's time efficiency studies were invested with a chronophotographic complement when the American engineer Frank Bunker Gilbreth developed his 'micro-motion method' to make work processes more efficient … Gilbreth patented the Chronocyclograph in 1913, a camera coupled to a large number of small light bulbs. These lights could be distributed on a body performing a movement, most often a work process, in order to chart the successive positions of a movement. … Through the study of these instants of a gesture, the irrational movements wasting time and energy (and in capitalist production, money) could be identified and eliminated.

In addition, the development of Taylor's scientific management had potentially important implications for relations of authority. Scientific management means that technical knowledge relating to production is held exclusively by management. Managers become the experts and can gain authority from this expertise.

Moving to consider the dimension of peer relations, the key aspect to note is the strong logic in the Taylorist approach towards the individualization of job roles because workers are positioned as undertaking narrow, repeated and measurable tasks beside each other, with management overseeing control of the overall flow of production. This picture suggests little productive need for cooperative teamwork within Taylorism. Indeed, Adler (1997) wrote an article with the revealing title 'Work organization: *From Taylorism to teamwork*' (emphasis added). As such, peer relations have a very limited role within an ideal type of Taylorist work organization, although, in practice, teamwork structures have been applied to Taylorist settings (Baldry et al, 1998). It is fair to say that Taylor had little thought for the implications of individual job mobility for the workers occupying the roles set up along his 'scientific management' principles. Littler (1978: 185) argues that the logic of Taylorist work organization is devoid of any consideration of job mobility structures: 'Taylorism represents an organizational form without any notion of a career-structure … Taylorism does not involve, nor imply, a career system.' Edwards (1979) argued that, in practice, large firms in the mid–20th century accommodated Taylorism through a seniority career structure, in which workers could move up a ladder of many rungs with small gaps between them within an organization, where the rungs constituted Taylorist jobs (in which there may be a slight change in task complexity).

A sporting analogy may help in understanding the contrast between craft work organization and Taylorist work organization. We can say that the relationship between a craft worker and a production worker in a Taylorized job is akin to the relationship between a soccer (association football) player and an American football (gridiron) player. The job of soccer player (and the craft worker) has both conception and execution. At any given moment in the game, the players (working broadly within the remit set by their coach) must be able to execute a task and must also be able to design, or conceive of, the task: for example, should they play a square pass to the unmarked right back, or float a long diagonal pass to the left winger who is making a quick run? There are exceptions at the set plays of free kicks and corners, when the expectation is primarily to execute a role already designed by the manager, but, overall, a considerable proportion of the role involves both conception and execution. The job of the American football player (and the Taylorized job), by contrast, centres primarily on execution. With the breakdown of plays every few seconds, the primary task of the player comes to be executing a role in the plays that are pre-designed by the coach. Furthermore, American football mirrors Taylorism in having a very narrow specialization of roles, which is possible because there are unlimited substitutions permitted during the game. So, in current professional American football, there are distinct sets of 11 players for an offence situation, for a defence situation and for different 'special teams' where the team is kicking or lining up against a kick. Some players in special teams may come on and perform their role for only a few seconds each game. In American football, the coach is the Taylorist supervisor or manager, and the players are the workers in the Taylorized jobs. Hoch (1972: 9) brings out this analogy between American football and Taylorism:

> Every pattern of movement on the field is increasingly being brought under the control of a group of non-playing managerial technocrats who sit in the stands (literally above the players) with their headphones and dictate offences, defences, special plays, substitutions and so forth to their players below. It's no longer a game. It's a business and there is too much at stake to leave this business to the players.

Perhaps it is no accident that such an implicitly Taylorized sport as American football became popular in the US just as the organization of the jobs in its economy were increasingly designed along Taylorist principles.

The discussion in Chapter 3 of the rise of outsourcing and the new international division of labour linked to global value chains would suggest that the Taylorized manual jobs in manufacturing are predominantly located now in lower-wage economies such as China, India and Bangladesh. Silver (2003), for instance, outlines how the sites of car production (a highly Taylorized industry) have moved from high-wage economies to lower-wage economies across the globe. It is difficult to conduct independent, critical sociology of work studies in factories in China. Yu's (2008) study of a factory in southern China manufacturing for Reebok, the sportswear MNC, is, therefore, important. It shows 'Tayloristic production process, coercive labor disciplines and rampant labor rights violations' (p 517). Sandoval's (2013: 337) overview of manufacturing in the electronics sector, based on international watchdog reports, indicates that work is, indeed, highly Taylorized:

> Low skilled assembly line labour and uniform work procedures … dominate work in electronics factories. … Workflows are fragmented and repetitive. One worker told China Labour Watch: 'We finish one step in every 7 seconds, which requires us to concentrate and keep working and working. We work faster even than the machines' (worker quoted by China Labour Watch, 2010).

Further, this is often Taylorism imposed with the same iron discipline that existed on the Taylorized assembly lines at Ford in the US in the 1920s and 1930s. Sandoval (2013: 337) reports that at Foxcom (a manufacture-contractor for Apple), workers 'had to collectively reply "Fine! Very fine! Very, very fine!" whenever they were asked [by a supervisor] how they felt'.

The contrast between work organized along craft principles and work organized according to Taylorist principles stands as one of the analytical touchstones within the sociology of work. It was central to Braverman's (1974) highly influential and widely debated argument that the logic of capitalism leads to the replacement of craft work by work organized according to Taylorist principles. Noon and Blyton (2013) give a skilful overview of the debate on Braverman's argument (a narrower version of the argument is referred to as Braverman's de-skilling thesis). A key element of Noon and Blyton's approach is that Braverman's argument is too blunt. For the analytical touchstone of the craft-Taylorism contrast to be useful, it is important that we break down the issue into smaller parts – it is important we disaggregate the question. In that spirit, the rest of this section involves looking at debates on the nature of the organization *not* of all work as one block, but of specific types of work. Continuing the thread of the book, the focus is upon service work, knowledge work and platform work.

Overall work organization in service, knowledge and platform work
The organization of service work

When service work is examined, it is important to be aware of three specific aspects of that work overlooked within the broad craft–Taylorist contrast. The first relates to the meaning, status and role of the customer. Note that the customer is absent from the management–worker dyad that informs the craft–Taylorism contrast outlined in the previous section. In Korczynski (2013), I argue (p 1) that 'customers play a key part in the working experience of a significant proportion of the working class in contemporary service work'. That article points to different ways in which sociologists approach the analytical status of the customer – from downplaying any meaningful role for the customer, via seeing the customer affecting a small part of work organization, to seeing the customer's role as potentially important throughout work organization. Emotional labour and aesthetic labour are the other two important specific aspects of service work overlooked within the craft–Taylorism contrast. They both relate to what is distinct in the enactment of labour by *service* workers. The analysis of emotional labour began with Hochschild's groundbreaking book, *The Managed Heart* (1983). There are small differences in emphasis regarding how sociologists define emotional labour, but most see emotional labour as occurring when service workers manage feelings and behavioural displays associated with feelings in interactions with service recipients (for example customers or patients). In Korczynski (2002), it is put sharply (p 139): 'Car workers are not expected to smile at cars, computer programmers are not expected to behave empathetically towards software, but for many front-line workers expectations related to emotions are central to their job.' Think of the nurse's care, the flight attendant's smile and the barrista's light-hearted chat. Aesthetic labour (Warhurst and Nickson, 2020) relates to how service workers appear – through their body, clothes and movements – and sound to customers. While Hochschild concentrates on the *internal* management regarding emotional labour, the concept of aesthetic labour highlights the importance of the outward – visual and aural – display of service workers. Nickson et al (2001: 2) define aesthetic labour as:

> a supply of embodied capacities and attributes possessed by workers at the point of entry into employment. Employers then mobilise, develop and commodify these capacities and attributes through processes … transforming them into competencies and skills which are then aesthetically geared toward producing a style of service encounter intended to appeal to the sense of customers.

With an understanding established of distinct elements of work organization within service work, the analysis can move on to consider debates regarding how service work is organized. The discussion in Chapter 2 on how to apply Weberian theory to understand service work has already introduced the key debate here. Ritzer's (1998, 2011) arguments that service work is made up of de-skilled McJobs in McDonaldized structures have strong (and sometimes explicit) overlaps with the wider argument that (all) work is becoming Taylorized. Indeed, mapping Ritzer's arguments regarding service work on to the dimensions of work organization outlined in this chapter involves simply reproducing the Taylorist model of work organization with an add-on sub-dimension of the labour process regarding emotional labour (see the middle column of Table 4.3). Regarding emotional labour, Ritzer follows Hochschild's foundational argument, which itself can be interpreted, in part, as an application of Braverman's ideas to the emotional labour process. Hochschild (1983) makes the chilling case that employers are increasingly commodifying, taking control of, measuring and shaping service workers' emotions. Hochschild contrasts people's discretion in managing emotions in the private sphere, outside employment, with the control that employers impose on service workers' emotions within the structure of the employment relationship, saying that (p 198) 'when the product – the thing to be engineered, mass-produced, and subjected to speed-up and slowdown – is a smile, a mood, a feeling, or a relationship, it comes to belong more to the organization, and less to the self'. Hochschild further argues, mainly on the basis of her study of flight attendants, that management wants to manage service workers' *hearts*; that it wants them to internalize the feelings that management want presented to customers (hence the title of her book, *The Managed Heart*). Overall, she argues that management's control over emotional labour can have deeply harmful effects for service workers. In following Hochschild's analysis regarding emotional labour, Ritzer also follows the Braverman line of argument regarding the almost inevitable imposition of Taylorism in previous areas of craft discretion. He argues that this leads to service workers delivering a fake, 'have a good day' form of emotional labour.

The main broad counter made in Korczynski (2002, 2009b) to the McDonaldization thesis, however, is far from being simply a statement that craft principles continue to pertain in service work organization. Rather, the argument rests on the case that service firms do not compete simply by low cost and efficiency; they also compete on the basis of customer orientation: enchanting the customer through individualization and attempts to make them feel special and appreciated. Korczynski and Ott (2004) argue that the presence of customer orientation for the labour of service workers means a presentation of the enchanting myth of customer sovereignty. Competing on both efficiency/price basis and customer-orientation basis is the material underpinning, in Weberian terms, that the customer, as well as rational-legal authority, is a key basis of authority within organizations. Therefore, service work organization can be understood as a customer-oriented bureaucracy – see the third column of Table 4.3. Here, the logic of Taylorist/McDonaldized bureaucracy is joined by the logic of customer orientation.

In terms of the dimensions of work organization, for the basis of the division of labour, the emphasis on task efficiency is joined by the requirement to create relationships with customers and enchant them. We noted earlier in this chapter that,

Table 4.3: Service work organization – McDonaldized vs customer-oriented bureaucracy

Dimension of work organization	McDonaldization	Customer-oriented bureaucracy
Basis of division of labour	Task efficiency through separation of conception and execution, and task fragmentation	Task efficiency *and* customer relationship and enchantment
Labour process	Low skill, fake emotional labour, potential for high intensity	Low to medium skill (discretion in navigating competing logics); potential for intensification
Control	Hierarchical measurement of output, and observation of labour process	(Limited) hierarchical measurement *and* customer-related norms
Peer relations	Weak principle, highly individualized jobs created	Move from individualization towards cooperation among service workers
Individual mobility	Potential for limited progression through job hierarchies	Limited – structured through employability

in nursing, the importance of creating relationships with patients (service recipients) has become an important principle in the allocation of roles, expressed in the term 'primary care'. In restaurants, although it may lead to greater task efficiency for waiters to bring out meals to any available table, as diners, we hear instead, 'My name is Marek, and I will be your server this evening', as the firm tries to create a relationship with customers. Much of service work can be characterized as medium to low skill. In the labour process, service workers are constantly faced with dual logics of trying to act efficiently and to make customers feel that they are important and are being individually attended to. This gives service workers some important discretion (a key part of skill) in how they navigate these often-competing logics. In Korczynski (2002) the argument is made that the dual imperatives within a customer-oriented bureaucracy create spaces that are absent within a McDonaldized work organization. Hampson and Junor (2005) analyse these spaces in terms of 'articulation work' undertaken by service workers, 'the often unacknowledged management of awkward intersections among the social worlds of people, technology and organisations'. These same spaces provide a barrier to work intensification, but this barrier is becoming increasingly porous because of two linked developments. First, customer information management systems are providing increasingly accurate predictions of the peaks and troughs of customer activity (whether in shops, cafés, restaurants or call centres). Second, particularly in liberal market economies like the UK, Ireland and the US, employers are making increasing use of contractual arrangements in which they have the power to send away workers (during a trough of customer activity) or, alternatively, call on workers (during a peak) at extremely short notice. Here, service workers' hours are 'subject to change without notice' (Halpin, 2015). The combination of real-time customer information systems predictions with employer power to alter workers' working time at short notice suggests a strong potential for the intensification of a large segment of service work (Vargas, 2021).

Regarding control, Chapter 3 highlighted that, in much service work, it is difficult for management to gather comprehensive, meaningful measures of output and behaviour. Notably, service quality is a key output of the service encounter, and to access such data, management seeks to generate customer feedback on interactions, and to use mystery shoppers, who are employed by service firms to pose as customers in order to assess the standards of service and behaviour of the staff (Fuller and Smith, 1991). Despite these efforts, measurement data often have significant gaps, so management seeks to use customer-oriented norms as a normative supplement for hierarchical control. Thus, service workers tend to be recruited on whether they hold customer-oriented norms, and employers seek to develop such norms in training sessions (Korczynski, 2009b). Regarding peer relations, the analytical ideal type of the customer-oriented bureaucracy suggests a movement away from the highly individualized jobs of Taylorism and McDonaldization because the creation of a sense of relationship and enchantment among customers suggests the importance of information flows and cooperation among service workers. Although, Mathews (1994) suggested that teamwork based on building relationships with customers would sweep through service work organization, there is little evidence that this has occurred. Finally, on individual mobility, although it is suggested (Korczynski, 2002) that service work structured as a customer-oriented bureaucracy would tend to create a trap for service workers, it is also the case that there can be some limited mobility linked to employability, in which transferable skills often involve being customer-focused.

The debate between whether service work tends to be organized in a Taylorized, McDonaldized manner, or as a customer-oriented bureaucracy is an important one for understanding the nature of around a third of contemporary work. One of the most startling and powerful phrases regarding service work from sociology of work scholarship characterized call-centre work (an important part of service work) as involving 'an assembly line in the head' (Taylor and Bain, 1999). This imagery points to the dominance of Taylorism. Even in call centres, much research shows the presence of some elements of Taylorism, but not that work organization is effectively Taylorized. For instance, Sallaz (2015) shows that, in many ways, the work in the call centre he studied was not as Taylorized as images such as Taylor and Bain's suggest. More widely, Herzenberg et al (1998) and Vidal (2013) undertook overviews of patterns of work organization in the US economy. Both studies position very few service jobs in the Taylorism-like category of 'tightly constrained' work organization. Indeed, Vidal places only 6–7 per cent of the whole labour force in that category. Rather, the studies position most front-line service jobs within the 'semi-autonomous' and 'unrationalized labour intensive' categories. These are categories that have significant overlaps with a customer-oriented bureaucracy form of work organization.

The organization of knowledge work

As noted in Chapter 1, traditionally, sociologists focused their analyses on professional work. An important stream of research on professional work emphasized the power obtained by professions through the creation of a closed monopoly over credentialed knowledge (MacDonald, 2006). This research also pointed to the important gendered and racialized exclusions in professional work (Witz, 1992). However, this assumption of privilege, power and autonomy was challenged by the Bravermanesque argument that many professions were subject to de-skilling by the increasing dominance of bureaucratic structures over professional work, the effect of the introduction of IT and the growth of paraprofessional roles leading to de-professionalization (Friedson, 2001; MacDonald, 2006). The argument that there is systematic de-skilling and de-professionalizing of professional work has not gained widespread support (MacDonald, 2006).

The wider focus on knowledge work allows us to see professional work as a specific subtype of knowledge work – one where there is a closed monopoly of credentialed knowledge by a profession. A key starting point to analyse the nature of the organization of knowledge work is to note that recent discussions of craft work often reference knowledge work jobs as examples of craft work, from laboratory technicians to academics to software developers (Kroezen et al, 2021). This suggests that there are many shared elements in the organization of craft work and the organization of knowledge work. Both share a unity of conception and execution as the core basis of the division of labour. Whereas, for craft work, this has been traditionally understood in terms of a unity of mind (conception) and manual skill (execution), for knowledge work, both conception and execution occur with reference to forms of knowledge. Knowledge work, like craft work, is high-skill work. Abbott's (1988) astute analysis of the high task complexity within professional work can be usefully applied to the wider category of knowledge work (Frenkel et al, 1999). Abbott's argument is that central to the labour process of knowledge work is classifying a problem (to diagnose), reasoning about it (to infer) and taking action on it (to treat). These abstract processes are central to the knowledge-work labour process, whether it is enacted by a doctor, statistician, computer programmer or any other knowledge-work occupation. Knowledge workers also tend to have high levels of discretion and autonomy when undertaking these processes (Herzenberg et al, 1998; Vidal, 2013). The knowledge base and autonomy of knowledge work tend to create a barrier against labour intensification. However, with the advent of hyper-connectivity through digital technology, Mazmanian et al (2013) argue that an 'autonomy paradox' can occur, in which there is a self-authored tendency towards an intensified labour process. Mazmanian and colleagues studied a range of 'knowledge professionals' (such as lawyers and investment bankers), who had a high usage of connective technologies (mobile email devices) in their work. The authors argue that the knowledge workers were (p 1291):

> enacting a norm of continual connectivity and accessibility that produced a number of contradictory outcomes. Although individual use of mobile email devices offered these professionals flexibility, peace of mind, and control over interactions in the short term, it also intensified collective expectations of their availability, escalating their engagement and thus reducing their ability to disconnect from work. Choosing to use their mobile email devices to work anywhere/anytime – actions they framed as evidence of their personal autonomy – the professionals were ending up using it everywhere/all the time.

Hierarchical/vertical relations tend to be less important than horizontal/peer relations in knowledge work. Because of the depth of specialized knowledge in knowledge work, it is difficult for management to unambiguously measure outputs or meaningfully observe behaviour. Therefore, following the logic of Ouchi (1979) (see Chapter 3), control tends to operate through peer norms and peer review of work undertaken. The central importance of collegial, cooperative relations among peers for knowledge work is primarily explored through the concept of communities of practice. A community of practice is an informal 'group of people who have a particular activity in common, and as a consequence have some common knowledge, a sense of community, identity and some element of a shared language and overlapping values' (Hislop et al, 2013: 196, following Lave and Wenger, 1991). Such communities of practice tend to play out in informal networks of relations rather than in the hierarchical structure of the formal organizations. Indeed, Brown and Duguid's (1991) analysis positions communities of practice as improvising new knowledge in a group that forms outside formal structures, partly in resistance to management (Cox, 2005). Individual mobility tends to be through professional and knowledge (rather than organizational) hierarchies, as well as being structured by communities of practice.

Table 4.4: The organization of knowledge work (as intellectual craft work)

Dimension of work organization	Organization of knowledge work
Basis of division of labour	Bodies of knowledge informing unity of conception and execution
Labour process	High skill; barriers to intensification, but possible autonomy paradox
Control	Occupational norms, peer review
Peer relations	Core principle, importance of communities of practice
Individual mobility	Upward progression through profession and movement within communities of practice

Table 4.4 summarizes the overview of an implicitly craft-based understanding of the organization of knowledge work. There is currently no credible argument that Taylorism is being applied in a wholesale way to de-skill knowledge work (although the implications of AI may change things – see the discussion in Chapter 9). Indeed, Vidal's (2013) overview of forms of work organization in the US economy points to a rise in the size of high-skill autonomous work from around 30 per cent of the labour force in 1960 to around 38 per cent in 2005. However, Adler (2015) presents a nuanced Marxist understanding of how a simple analogy of knowledge work to an intellectual form of craft work fails to consider systematic pressures that run counter to this craft analogy. Adler's focus is primarily upon innovative, creative knowledge work. He argues that, while there is a craft-like collaborative logic in creative knowledge work, there is also a capitalist logic of control and creation of profit through exploiting labour. The logic of control and profit exists in constant pressure against the collaborative logic. As Adler puts it (2015: 450), 'the stability and cohesion of this collective [knowledge] worker community is constantly challenged by the divisive and demotivating effects of the valorization process – the profit imperative'. Adler applies this theoretical argument to a detailed study of software development – an archetypal knowledge-work occupation. He shows that, although management knows the importance of collaboration and communities of practice for innovation and quality, it finds itself undermining processes to support such communities because it is under pressure to show short-term profits to shareholders.

The organization of platform work

As outlined in Chapter 1, there are several different types of platform work. Again, we concentrate on the taxi, delivery and courier forms of platform work here. Vallas and Schor's (2020) insightful overview of the emerging scholarship on platform work notes that a range of interpretations has been put forward regarding the key nature of such platform-mediated work. The authors label the interpretation that highlights positive aspects as picturing platform work as 'incubators of entrepreneurialism'. This is a neoliberal view of the pure market as freedom, and the rise of platforms as a move to that pure market. Vallas and Schor (2020: 277) characterize this view thus:

> Many of the rigidities of the corporate economy are destined to recede in favor of a more egalitarian form of crowd-based capitalism in which corporate hierarchies no longer represent the dominant structure of economic activity. Crucially, the employment relation itself loses its predominance in the wake of 'an emerging networked society of microentrepreneurs'.

By contrast, there is the view of platform work as a 'digital cage'. This is a 21st-century updating of Weber's famous pessimism regarding work organization as a form of iron cage of rationality in which platform firms are the architects. Here, there is an emphasis of platform firms being at the leading edge of the 'surveillance society' (Zuboff, 2019), using the capacity of digital technology to micro-observe and measure the activities of workers, and platform firms harnessing power through their access to much greater information than is granted to (individualized) workers – often labelled as information asymmetry.

A useful way to navigate through this debate on the nature of platform work is to consider work organization dimension by dimension. Fundamental to the capacity of platforms to operate is the ability to identify bundles of tasks with a clear, measurable output. This is the core basis of the division of labour in platform work. Platform firms enlist labour through identifying a measurable output from a set of tasks and then setting up a digital architecture in which clients call upon the achievement of this measurable output (for instance, delivery of pizza, a taxi ride from A to B) from worker–contractors. As noted in Table 4.5, within the labour process, skill levels can be regarded as medium (recall the earlier definition of skill as involving task complexity and discretion). While task complexity may not be high, discretion over many elements of the labour process in platform work is high. Vallas and Schor (2020: 282) note that 'the platform firm retains authority over important functions – the allocation of tasks, collection of data, pricing of services, and of course collection of revenues – but it cedes control over others, such as the specification of work methods, control over work schedules, and the labor of performance evaluation'.

Table 4.5: The organization of platform work

Dimension of work organization	Organization of platform work
Basis of division of labour	Bundling of tasks with clear measurable output
Labour process	Medium skill (high discretion, but lower complexity), high potential for intensification through gamification, and structure of workers' weak labour market position
Control	Direct exposure to the market, payment linked to output measurement, customer evaluation
Peer relations	Individualized roles, structure of competition between 'contractors'
Individual mobility	The hustle

High discretion over many aspects of the labour process is a key aspect that many platform workers value about their jobs. Purcell and Brook (2022) highlight that the notion of 'at least, I'm my own boss' is central to the generation of worker consent in platform work, and, indeed, this notion is mobilized in recruitment marketing by platform firms. However, sociologists of work also point out that this construction of an idea of being your own boss is often situated in a gamified structure of the platform – where worker discretion is led in clear patterns by such features as price-boosting in certain locations and at certain times, so as to match customer demand. Gamification, involving the platform manipulating incentives to pattern worker behaviour, tied to the often very weak labour market position of many platform workers points to a high potential for a high intensity of work. Many platform workers are migrant people (see Chapter 8), whose skills and credentials from their home country often go unrecognized, and who are often denied forms of labour market protection, such as unemployment benefit (Van Doorn and Vijay, 2021). Of course, the weak labour market position of many platform workers is considerably exacerbated by the platform model of treating the taxi drivers, couriers and delivery people not as workers in an employment relationship but as independent contractors. As such, these workers do not have any right to employment protection and benefits, such as sick pay. The structurally weak position of many workers may, therefore, push them to keep working through periods of sickness.

With regard to control, Chapter 3 noted that platform work is directly exposed to the operation of the external market, and this, rather than a hierarchical supervisor – absent in platform work – is the key disciplining device. Some platforms also bring in hierarchy here by setting standards regarding elements such as percentage of gigs accepted and number of hours worked (also thereby eroding areas of worker discretion), such that, if workers do not meet these standards, they are 'deactivated' from the platform, which is the equivalent to being fired by an employer. Central to the discipline of direct exposure to the market is the clear measurable output linked to the completion of tasks. Failure to achieve that output means payment is withheld. Further, customers are enlisted in the operation of control through eliciting and monitoring of customer evaluation of the delivery of the output (Rahman, 2018). Within the organization of platform work, one interpretation could be that peer relations are formally absent in the sense that each gig is a discrete task to be undertaken by one worker-contractor, without any need to communicate or cooperate with another worker-contractor. A more accurate characterization is that not only are individualized jobs created, but, in addition, the platform puts the people who undertake gigs in a competitive social relationship with each other, in the sense that they directly compete to click 'accept' quicker than other worker-contractors and so secure the gig. Finally, the social structure set by platforms for individual job mobility is the hustle, as discussed earlier in the chapter. Platform firms step back from any responsibility as an employer and thus they avoid even the reduced responsibility of supporting job mobility through employability. Workers, often in weak labour market positions, are left with little option but to hustle.

From this overview of the organization of platform work, it is clear that Vallas and Schor (2020) are correct to say that neither the argument for celebrating platforms for creating micro-entrepreneurs nor the argument painting gig work as a digital cage are useful characterizations. It is also notable that the overview of gig work organization departs considerably from the expectations set by the craft vs Taylorism axis that has dominated sociology of work scholarship for a century. This is neither craft nor Taylorized work. Indeed, Kornberger et al (2017: 79) argue that work organization here exhibits a new geometry in which 'control is radically distributed, while power remains centralized'. Following this lead, Vallas and Schor (2020: 273) characterize platforms as 'permissive potentates that externalize responsibility and control over economic transactions while still exercising concentrated power'. Another way to think about the organization of platform work is to identify what kind of 'bargain' or social contract of work is implicit within it. The rise of Fordism – in which Taylorism triumphed over craft work – involved the central bargain of increased wages and consumption in exchange for de-skilled, alienating work (Gabriel and Lang, 2015). The rise of gig work involves the bargain of gaining (structured) self-determination for the loss of the rights and obligations tied to the employment relationship. The terms '(structured) self-determination' and 'subordinated agency' (Wood and Lehdonvirta, 2021) refer to the coexistence of increased scope for discretion and agency with a clearly defined and controlled structure of power in which that discretion and agency operates. While the Fordist social contract proved to have some stability and longevity, the dynamic and skewed political economy informing the gig-work bargain suggests that there may not be such stability in this bargain.

Sociological imagination – your turn

What do people talk about when they are comparing one job with another? In addition to salary, which of the dimensions of work organization considered in this chapter is the most important for you? The chapter has considered the main broad dimensions of work organizations, but are there other dimensions of work organization, not covered in this chapter, that you consider important? Overall, has this chapter been helpful for you in thinking about the characteristics of a job you want to do?

5

The Agency and Voice of Workers (1)

This chapter and the following one focus on the agency and voice of workers. The previous two chapters outlined and examined the key structures in which workers are embedded – from abstract macro-level structures, such as forms of capitalism, to more concrete structures, like forms of work organization linked to specific types of work. It is crucial to be aware of these structures. It is also important, however, that we understand that workers are not passive agents who simply occupy and work in given structures. Workers have agency to act within these structures, and to try to act upon these structures. Of all the academic disciplines applied to the analysis of work, it is the sociology of work that has been able to dig deepest in unearthing and understanding the voice and agency of workers. Specifically, these two chapters draw on and celebrate the tradition of ethnographies of work – where sociologists go into workplaces for extended periods of time to try to understand the nature of people's lived experiences at work. As Tope et al (2005) have shown, researchers generate much richer insights from 'being there', where the work happens.

Dimensions of agency and voice

This brief section outlines the way in which worker agency and voice are mapped in this and the following chapter. This mapping uses two dimensions. The first relates to form of agency – ranging from (informal) meanings, norms or beliefs via informal practice to formal practices. This is the horizontal axis in Figure 5.1. This chapter begins with a discussion of worker agency in the creation of meaning before turning to look at informal practices. Then, Chapter 6 is devoted to examining formal practices, for instance, in terms of the activities of labour unions.

The second dimension relates to the ends to which the agency is applied – whether it is agency that is mainly resistive to the employer or whether it is agency that is supportive of (at least some elements of) employer aims. This is the vertical axis in Figure 5.1. This is an unusual dimension to use in a sociology of work text. It is noted in, for example, Ackroyd and Thompson (1999), but then the upper half of the axis is overlooked. As such, the vertical axis requires further consideration.

Sociologists of work have tended to focus very heavily on resistive agency – the lower part of the vertical axis. Indeed, finding and analysing the subterranean forms of workplace resistance became almost the specialist focus among sociologists of work for some decades, from Roy's (1954) study of output restriction by work groups on the factory floor through to Burawoy's (1979) rather different analysis of similar practices in the same factory some decades later. Perhaps this focus of sociologists of work is a product of having been so heavily influenced by social theory at work and its emphasis on strong, oppressive structures to be *resisted* (for instance Marx on the alienating and exploitative structures of capitalism and Weber on the iron cage of rationality within the bureaucratic organization).

By contrast, scholars within the discipline known as organizational behaviour have tended to focus heavily on supportive agency – the upper part of the vertical axis. Organizational behaviour (OB) scholars tend to discuss such agency in terms of motivation, organizational commitment and organizational citizenship. The focus on this form of agency comes because scholars in OB often tend to see employing organizations in ways that marginalize issues of power and oppression. Indeed, this much is suggested by the adoption of the metaphor of organizational *citizenship* (Schnake, 1991) to label forms of worker behaviour. Citizens are empowered decision-makers with clear rights and obligations. Structures of power quickly become overlooked when this becomes the metaphorical frame of understanding. Note also that a significant managerialist-functionalism within OB is indicated by some OB scholarship referring to resistance as 'dysfunctional' behaviour by workers. Chapter 9 extends this discussion of the limitations of some OB scholarship.

There is no good reason to continue with the pattern of sociologists of work and OB scholars focusing on different parts of the vertical axis in Figure 5.1. The limitations of OB are too profound to leave the upper part of the axis in their hands. A good sociology of work should be able to find and analyse forms of resistance as well as being able to see and understand supportive forms of worker agency. This was a strong motivating approach within the widely admired scholarship of the great American sociologist of work, Randy Hodson. In his groundbreaking book, *Dignity at Work* (2001), Hodson points to the importance of *both* resistance *and* citizenship as forms of worker agency that are crucial in the establishment and defence of dignity at work. There is not just conflict within the social relations of the workplace, there is also cooperation. Indeed, both are often simultaneously present. As Edwards et al (2006: 129) put it, 'conflict and cooperation ... are both evident in any situation, as "two sides of the same coin"'. This was also a key part of the argument regarding the structure of the employment relationship in capitalism, discussed in Chapter 3. Therefore, when travelling along the horizontal axis in these two chapters – from meanings to formal organized practices – we will examine not only resistive agency but also supportive agency. Note also that these chapters involve *analytical* mappings of agency and voice in the sense that the chapters do not just describe key practices; they locate them in the macro-structures and work organization structures outlined in Chapters 3 and 4.

Figure 5.1: Dimensions of agency and voice

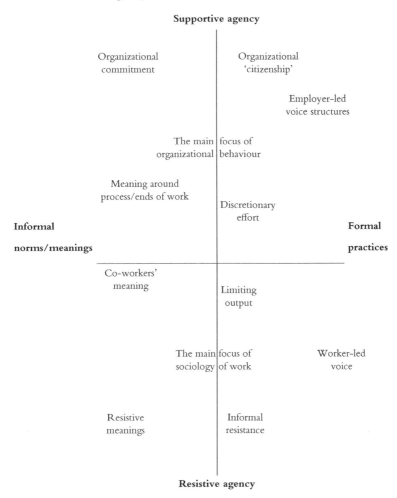

Creation of meaning

Work structures, on their own, do not carry meaning. It is people who create meaning in and around work structures. For Laaser and Karlsson (2022: 799), 'meaningful work is created, experienced and defended at the agency level, but shaped, constrained or denied by wider dynamics of the employment and workplace level'. The importance of the meaning of work to people is apparent when we consider research that shows that people who lack work, who are unemployed, frequently come to experience a sense of meaninglessness in their lives (Boland and Griffin, 2015). For many people, work is a key arena of meaning in their lives. Sometimes, people orient their lives in relation to work, and we orient our understanding of people partly in terms of the work they do. One of the earliest questions we ask when we want to find out about each other is: 'What do you do?' or 'What job do you have?' Other people, however, approach work instrumentally – its only meaning to them is that it provides a pay cheque. Psychologists tend to consider that individuals, per se, have different orientations to work, and they create typologies of people's different orientations and create measures so that they can place people within these typologies. Sociologists of work have a different approach. They do not see someone's orientations to work as an immutable part of an individual's character. They look for an understanding of how patterns of meanings are socially created. They look for the key social context in which meanings are created in relation to work – most notably, the workplace. Humans have the capacity to create meanings, to act for reasons, and Hodson (2001) identifies workers' pursuit of meaning as a fundamental way in which workers seek to attain dignity at work.

An important distinction to make when looking at the meanings that workers create in relation to work is that between intrinsic and extrinsic focuses. When workers create meaning intrinsic to work, there is something *within* the nature of the work that is the focus of meaning. Most of this section examines such intrinsic meanings. When workers have extrinsic meaning in relation to work, the focus of the meaning is something *outside* the work. The most important source of extrinsic meaning of work is the wage that it brings – wages that allow basic subsistence needs to be met and for the worker to be able to buy and consume goods and services, for themselves, or for their family. Goldthorpe et al's (1969) classic study of industrial workers in Luton offers a case of workers having an extrinsic focus. The researchers found that most of the workers had what they termed an 'instrumental orientation' to their jobs: the jobs were secure and provided a decent wage, and these aspects, and only these aspects, were sources of meaning for workers from their work. The obvious corollary of extrinsic meaning and instrumental orientation is that it points to a loud absence of meaning in those 35-plus hours that are spent in that factory, in that call centre, in that software design office or in that taxi. Such an absence of meaning can be interpreted as holding an *implicit* critique of work structures. Radical punk singer and writer Patti Smith sang about having only extrinsic meaning in relation to a job she had in a New Jersey factory (Shaw, 2008). There is also critique of the structure that drives her to only holding extrinsic meanings (the song is called 'Piss Factory').

More critical contemporary references that also point to an absence of meaning in relation to work come from Graeber's (2018) arguments that the contemporary workplace is populated with very many 'bullshit' – or useless and pointless – jobs, and from Frayne's (2015) argument that we should 'refuse' work essentially because work offers no meaning. However, although the extrinsic meaning of work is important for most people, for obvious reasons, the main pattern of research findings suggests that intrinsic meanings are also important for very many people. For instance, Soffia et al (2022) used the European Working Conditions Survey to examine some of the propositions of Graeber's 'bullshit' jobs thesis. They found that 'the proportion of employees describing their jobs as useless is low and declining and bears little relationship to Graeber's predictions' (p 816). Specifically, in 2015 only 5 per cent of EU workers responded that they did not have the feeling of doing useful work. Further, Noon and Blyton (2013) point to data from the Meaning of Work survey that show workers holding similar strengths of attachment to extrinsic *and* intrinsic meanings in relation to work.

Given that meaning in relation to work is partly conditioned by roles outside paid employment, it is important also to consider the role of gender. Because there remains a strong gendering of roles outside paid employment, with more domestic and childcare work responsibilities falling to women, it means that there are specific tensions for many women in their creation of meaning in relation to work. Catherine Hakim (2000) is a central figure in debates on the issue of how far women's position here is an outcome of structures or of agency and choice. Hakim emphasizes agency and choice. She argues that there are three main groups of women: home-centred women (15–30 per cent of women), whose main priority is children and family; adaptive women (40–80 per cent), covering women who want to combine work and family, and those who want to have paid employment but are not committed to a career; and work-centred women (10–30 per cent), whose main priority is their career. Hakim articulates a 'preference theory', arguing that women are now in the position to be able to choose whether to pursue a career or not. The majority of women who combine domestic and childcare roles with part-time jobs, according to Hakim, choose to seek part-time work even though they know that such work often has poorer conditions and fewer career opportunities. Ginn et al (1996), by contrast, make the case that the choices made by women are often severely constrained ones, so that the satisfaction they may express should be understood in the context of the lack of alternatives available, given the pressure that women face in the domestic sphere (see also Kan, 2007).

The first half of this chapter aims to dignify how workers create meanings by first examining workers' broadly supportive meanings in relation to the processes of work, the ends of work and job mobility, and in relation to the employer. Following the logic of the vertical axis in Figure 5.1, the section then considers more neutral and partly resistive meanings in relation to co-workers. The section ends with an examination of more directly resistive meanings.

(Partly) supportive meanings

Creating meaning in and through work processes

Scholarship on meaningful work is primarily concerned with examining and identifying those aspects of work that are supportive of positive meaning creation by workers. It is logical to look to work organization along craft principles as a structure where work processes are supportive of workers creating positive meanings. Notably, craft work as meaningful work is implicit in Sennett's (2008: 9) understanding of craft work as 'an enduring basic impulse, the desire to do a job well for its own sake'. Mills' (1956) ideal of craft work portrays a deep vein of meaning in this work for workers such that unity of conception and execution within the craft gives rise to a unity of meaning of work and life – meaningful work becomes central to a meaningful life. Meaning is also written deep when Kroezen et al (2021: 17) note that 'craft work … is often described as a "labour of love"'. The strongest statement of meaning within the work process comes from the application of Csikszentmihalhi's (2020) concept of 'flow' to work. The state of flow is one in which the person is completely engaged in the task at hand. The task is a challenging one that requires the full enactment of a person's skill, and, in the process of undertaking the task, the person (worker) becomes so absorbed in the task that they lose sense of time and even of self. Meaning is purely in the process of the moment. Given the discussion in Chapter 4 of elements of craft work within contemporary knowledge work, it is not surprising to see that studies have examined the playing out of flow within knowledge work (Quinn, 2005). There is an echo of the experience of flow in this reflection from a knowledge worker (a biochemist) on a highly meaningful part of his working life (Rabinow, 1996: 90):

> I was very interested in the job. It was really fun to learn how to synthesize DNA. ... It was the heyday of biotechnology. There were all kind of bold ideas floating around all the time ... and there was absolutely no constraint on the imagination ... [We] were right in the middle of something that was a red-hot kind of an area.

However, the ending of this reflection points to limits of such intense meaning in knowledge work – limits that come when the business imperative under capitalism (systemically) comes to knock louder: 'It got worse after about three years. It got more into the business side of stuff, but it was really fun at first' (Rabinow, 1996: 90).

Laaser and Karlsson's (2022) skilful discussion of meaningful work focuses primarily on three work processes rather than on overall craft work principles. They argue that work processes supportive of autonomy, recognition and dignity will also be supportive of workers creating positive meanings in relation to work. The argument regarding autonomy is similar to that of craft work as meaningful work. However, Laaser and Karlsson's (2022) arguments about dignity and recognition do not simply reproduce the craft-as-meaningful argument. They argue (p 804) that meaningful work will have work structures supportive of dignity, 'conceptualized as organizational policies and management practices and ... interactions between workers ... that uphold workers' dignity by meeting norms of respect and civility, while enhancing workers' self-respect'. They also point to the importance of work processes that are supportive of workers being recognized as people of equal value who have equal rights to participate in decision-making.

Creation of meaning in relation to the ends of work

Implicit in much of the sociology of work scholarship on the creation of meaning by workers is a focus on the processes of work rather than ends of work – the outcome of the work processes. The social theories examined in Chapter 2 point to good reasons why work processes may be an arena more open to meaning creation than the arena of the ends of work. Weber's understanding of organizations as bureaucracies points to the dominance of means over ends. Further, Marx's analysis of capitalism points to the creation of profit as the essential end of the capitalist firm. A firm may propound a wider mission statement such as Ford's: 'To help build a better world, where every person is free to move and pursue their dreams', but its material aim is to create profit.

Making profit for the shareholder appears to be an unlikely arena in which workers can create meaning (Silver, 2023). However, although there are important limits to, and structures against, meanings in relation to ends, there are still some spaces for workers to create significant meanings in relation to the ends of work.

Scholarship based on humanities (rather than sociology) on meaningful work does indeed point to the importance of the ends of work, often in terms of meaning lying in a transcendent aim beyond the self, such as serving others (Bailey and Madden, 2017). In service work, the process of emotional labour is central to the playing out of meaning in relation to the service recipient (customer, patient, client, passenger and so on). Baines (2016: 128) notes that, although emotional labour is increasingly subject to management control (see the discussion of Hochschild, 1983 in Chapter 4), it is also 'the main source of meaning and satisfaction for [service] workers'. The idea of helping, serving or caring for others is at its strongest in healthcare work. One of the most eloquent expositions of this is given in Stacey's 2011 book *The Caring Self*, which is an ethnographic study of the work of home-care aides in the US. Stacey shows that, despite the poor conditions tied to these jobs, there is still much that is deeply rewarding in their jobs for home-care aides. Central to this is how home-care aides create an identity of 'the caring self'. They emphasize the ethic of care and service to others, and they mark boundaries between themselves and 'non-caring' others. It is through the process of creating the sense of the caring self that aides are able to find meaning in their work, particularly in terms of their ability to create meaningful relationships with clients. Stacey's findings are echoed by Baines' (2016: 129) international study of care work, as exemplified by one care worker commenting on the low wages and benefits: 'If you haven't got meaning in these jobs, what else have you got?' In a Chinese context, Yan and Luo (2023) find that care workers called on the concept of *liangxin* as the key framework for creating meaning in their work. Liangxin is (p 1) 'a ubiquitous Chinese moral notion emphasizing the unity of feeling, thought, and action'. Comparing the care workers in Stacey's study and in Yan and Luo's study, it is clear that 'the caring self' and liangxin play similar roles and have overlapping meanings.

Tallberg and Jordan's (2022) sensitive ethnography of workers at an animal shelter charity implicitly shows the meaning that workers attach to giving care and protection to neglected animals. This meaning that workers have in relation to the ends of their work is the frame for the broken heart at the centre of the study: the pain that workers experience when they are placed in the position of having to end the lives of animals for which the organization does not have resources. 'Killing them softly' (the title of the study) is a profound sadness precisely because of the meaning workers attach to the ends of their work, the animals (Tallberg and Jordan, 2022: 864):

> The dog stiffened as we approached the kill-room. Fear flooded his big brown eyes and his hind legs started trembling while he sniffed the air. I forced him through the door [this is my job after all] and choked down my feelings at seeing his distress [overriding my instincts to stop]. I chained him to a wall with worn-down hooks from the countless others who had come before ... I found a frozen bone for him, actively ignoring body-bags crowding the freezer. 'My'

dog looked sadly at the bone (not touching it), then at me, betrayed, wordlessly pleading for me to help him, while he shivered on the cold concrete floor. Some would soil themselves in fear, but most got very still like they knew what was coming. I wish I could take him home, make him feel wanted, that he mattered … and not all humans wanted him gone. My colleague … got the fluorescent syringe ready as I looked away, holding my dog still for the injection. A perfect paw in my hand, vein filling with poison.

In Weberian terms, the workers' substantive meaning (and rationality) here clashes with the formally rational bureaucratic logic of the organization.

What sociologists call 'dirty work' is one of the most challenging arenas for the creation of meaning. Deery et al (2019: 631) explain that '"dirty work" refers to tasks and occupations that are perceived as disgusting, distasteful or degrading'. Jobs are regarded as dirty in the sense that they carry negative associations or social stigma. Dirt here can relate to physical dirt (for instance in sanitation work) and metaphorically to dirt as social taint (prison guard), emotional taint (suicide helpline worker) and moral taint (debt collector). How can workers create positive meanings in dirty work, or as Cath, interviewed in McMurray and Ward's (2014: 1139) study of suicide helpline workers, puts it, 'why would you want to do that?': 'Cath noted that friends and acquaintances often comment "why would you want to do that?" or "oh no, I couldn't do that!" when they discover the kind of emotional labour that being a Samaritan involves.'

Ethnographic studies tend to show that workers in dirty-work occupations create positive meanings in relation to their work through bottom–up rituals, through autonomously created values of peer respect and through referencing the ends of work – the social good that is done through their work. At the Samaritans helpline, workers expressed a strong meaning in the good that their work entails, often expressed through articulating a sense of privilege in being there to take the call (McMurray and Ward, 2014: 1136):

As Samaritan Steve concludes an encounter, with someone in the process of committing suicide, it appears as if the call is written on his face. It is written in terms of an empathetic concern and wonder at the emotional pain, loneliness and despair of the other. But there is also a sense of privilege at having been able and available to take their call – 'it was a real privilege to be there for them – they kept thanking me, and I would say "don't thank me, it's what I'm here for"'.

Creation of meaning in relation to job mobility

The meaning workers ascribe to individual job mobility is mainly analysed in terms of *career*. Studies position career as having two elements, relating, on the one hand, to the meanings individuals make of their career situations and, on the other, to institutional forms of career participation (Barley, 1989). It is useful to think of workers' subjective sense of career as 'unfolding from recurrent acts of sense-making that allow individuals to assign meaning to their employment biographies' (Baldry et al, 2007: 120). Once again, it is in the excavation of meaning that sociologists of work excel, with, for instance, Cohen and Mallon (2001: 48) showing how people's stories 'illuminate the ways in which individuals make sense of their careers as they unfold through time and space, attending to both the holistic nature of career as well as to specific career transitions'. As Weick (1995: 128) puts it, 'when people punctuate their own living into stories, they impose a formal coherence on what is otherwise a flowing soup'. Although self-authored stories may tend to favour an emphasis on the agency of the worker, many of these stories also reference important social structures that constrain and enable agency (recall the discussion in Chapter 4 of the structuring of careers and job mobility). This can come across particularly clearly in women's stories, as in this description of social structure as constraint: 'I was told that as a working class girl I could be three things: a teacher, a nurse, or a secretary. I didn't want to work with children and I hated blood, so I went to secretarial college' (Cohen and Mallon, 2001: 63). Cohen and Mallon (p 64) interpret another woman's story as linked to the societal change of greater opportunities for women:

> A participant ... reflected on how she had justified her decision to leave her job: 'At the time, I said it was for the children. The children were my excuse, and that was an acceptable excuse. No one questioned it. Now, though, I see that it wasn't the children at all. It was about me, and about my growth and development. I can say that now, but I couldn't.'

Such insightful studies tend to be based on analysing the career meanings among knowledge workers, including professionals. One of the key concepts in these studies is that of workers pursuing a *calling*, which Dobrow and Tosti-Kharas (2011: 1001) define as 'a consuming, meaningful passion people experience toward a domain'. Calling has been used to understand career meanings among such knowledge-work occupations as doctors, teachers, musicians, priests, academics and pilots (Lysova and Khapova, 2019). Lysova and Khapova note that the domain to which the consuming meaningful passion is applied is usually the occupation/profession. However, in conducting a study on a new emerging knowledge-work occupation – digital games development – the authors argue that the domain of meaning is as much the process of creativity itself as about the specific occupation in which the creativity is enacted, as expressed by one of the game developers interviewed (Lysova and Khapova, 2019: 37):

> This [being creative] is just something that I basically need to do. If we think about what creativity is and who creative people are – is a creative person somebody who is just really good in creating something or needs to create something even if it is crap? You know, I tend to believe more in the sort of second definition, where I think I am very creative person. I am constantly compelled to create things. I just get bored if I do not create stuff.

In enacting their career calling, these games developers found their drive for creativity to be in frequent tension with commercial imperatives (Lysova and Khapova, 2019: 39):

It is like a debate between sort of more artistic-oriented game studios and the more, I ... would say, professional, commercial-oriented studios who are making games to make money and are really focused on getting ... the most cash or the most effective way of earning money from it. Whereas the more artistic-oriented or those who view making a game more from an artistic-oriented perspective you see really a lot of these projects fail actually because they are not ... commercially viable but people who make them are really passionate. And I think that I count myself in that category rather ... than the other domain.

This tension – also noted in relation to flow and meaning in knowledge-work processes – follows the logic of Adler's (2015) analysis of the nature of knowledge work organization (see Chapter 4). Cohen et al (2019) also chart a telling story of how calling tied to public service ideals, for instance within local government social services, came into severe tension with centralized bureaucratic control and from large-scale reconfiguring, if not quite dismantling, of the founding ideals of state welfare. They movingly describe this process as 'losing the faith'. People in working-class jobs are much less likely than knowledge workers to view individual job mobility as a form of *career*. The following is an excerpt from Erickson's ethnography of working at The Hungry Cowboy, a neighbourhood restaurant in the US, in which the foreignness of considering waitressing as a career comes out strongly (2009: 33):

> Patricia [a waitress] was disturbed when a little girl described waitressing as her career. 'Like one night a couple weeks ago, I had this table and a little girl was looking at her cowpoke menu, and ... the little girl was like, "Look, ma'am, I found your career." And I'm thinking, this isn't my career. Waitress? That's a little scary.'

Some scholars see this as an almost inevitable adaptation by people to structural constraints on upward job mobility for those with limited skills and educational qualifications (see Kessler et al, 2019). Key constraints here involve limited possibilities for deep substantive skill development, particularly in liberal market economies, and the organization of work by employers featuring low-skilled jobs, with no clear career path out of these jobs. Despite such strong structural constraints, Li et al (2002) identified a residual core – albeit a minority – of working-class workers who perceived themselves as developing careers. Kessler et al (2019) skilfully follow up the implications with their detailed study of career aspirations among healthcare support workers. A quarter of these healthcare support workers perceive themselves as on, or aiming to be on, a career journey to become a nurse (see also Baldry et al's 2007 study of career aims of call-centre workers). The search for career meaning in job mobility and the barriers against that appear to be a key area for further research. This is also true for platform workers, especially as they are placed in a position of highly constrained job mobility in which the hustle appears as a dominant mode of adaptation (see Chapter 4). Adaptation is profoundly different from preference, however, and here it is appropriate to note that emerging research points to a search for career meaning among platform workers (Kost et al, 2018).

Creation of meaning in relation to employers

Organizational commitment is a major topic of study in organizational behaviour and HRM (human resource management) scholarships (Legge, 2005). Here, the key search is for the factors that increase workers' organizational commitment and their discretionary effort. One way in which sociologists have examined significant meaning of the employer to workers has been in terms of the development of organizational culture (outlined in the discussion in Chapter 3 of control through norms). Such organizational meaning and commitment have been most significant when the employer is able to establish long-lasting, stable, paternalist policies. This can be analysed as the employer establishing a durable social contract of work (Korczynski, 2023) in which there is deep mutuality and reciprocity: in exchange for the employer establishing supportive, positive work conditions and wider benefits, the workers give organizational commitment and discretionary effort. Strangleman's (2015) study of the paternalism at the Guinness brewery in London shows that the firm actively sought to create a sense of 'Guinness citizenship' among the workforce.

However, such paternalist, long-term, strong, social contracts of work are the exception rather than the rule. As Legge (2005) argues, firms may be adept at delivering a *rhetoric* of supportive HRM, but the *reality* tends to be a different matter. We saw in Chapter 3 that an analysis of the nature of the capitalist firm and the competitive context in which it operates allows us to understand this. Particularly in liberal market economies (for instance the UK, the US and Ireland), firms have to meet the short-term demands of return to shareholders ahead of trying to match the longer-term HRM rhetoric they give to people who work for them (Thompson, 2003). The stream of research on psychological contract breach – where the employer is perceived by workers as violating the implicit exchange of mutuality and obligations in the employment relationship – shows that such a breach has strongly negative effects on organizational commitment (Topa et al, 2022).

Despite the wider political economic structures offering a fragile basis for employers to attempt to build commitment from workers, Chapter 4 has pointed to more employers trying to develop cultures of commitment to the organization, in order to solve problems of control, particularly in knowledge work. Few studies find that such employer attempts lead to a deep sense of commitment that is widespread among workers. The more common finding is that there tend to be forms of resistance by workers to attempts to create organizational culture and commitment (Richards and Marks, 2007). Cushen's (2009) study of a hi-tech knowledge-work firm in Ireland is a case in point as it shows an employer operating from a fragile basis for commitment and not succeeding in developing widespread worker commitment. Despite the firm having recently made a large number of workers redundant, the HR department decided to launch an organizational culture programme, called Brand Essence, aimed at making the workers align themselves with the company goals. Through training sessions, workers were asked to be 'on brand', 'passionate, reliable, and innovative'. Many workers resisted this attempt at culture management. One pointed to the gap between rhetoric (Brand Essence) and practice (mass redundancies) (Cushen, 2009: 109): 'It's very hard to swallow, extremely hard, they're telling you one day how important you are to them and the next day they're making more redundant. ... It's just hypocrisy after hypocrisy.' Another knowledge worker simply objected to being subject to such clear attempts at culture manipulation per se (p 110):

> For professionals like me ... it really is insulting ... massively negative, it's like 'where is my school uniform?' when I'm getting up in the morning. I'm a professional you know, I've been to college and I've done all these things and I've qualified and you know there's people even more qualified than me and they're suffering this.

This is echoed by a worker quoted in a study of a culture change programme in a railway company (Huzell, 2009: 177): 'You know, I felt that they were trying to brainwash me! It felt like we were in a religious revival meeting. 400 people and a management consultant with three of his disciples and ... I can tell you, we laughed. But seriously, it was scary.' Thompson's (2016) overview of employer attempts to develop worker commitment through organizational culture initiatives argues that, while surface compliance by workers may be common, it is also the case (p 114) that workers' 'disengagement from corporate values and practices is a systemic feature of new managerial regimes [through organizational culture]'.

Sociologists also point to the *limits* in workers holding positive meanings with regard to their employer in the sense of the greater salience of other areas of work-related meaning. Baldry et al (2007) examined commitment to organization, co-workers, customers and occupation among call-centre and software workers. The call-centre workers rated commitment to co-workers and customers much higher than commitment to the organization. The software workers had a strong commitment to the occupation, to co-workers and to customers, and a much weaker sense of organizational commitment. Tam et al (2005) also note the limits that strong occupational commitment puts on organizational commitment among knowledge workers.

Neutral meanings

Creating meaning in relation to co-workers

The positive aspect of having meaningful relations with co-workers is one of the most significant areas of workers' creation of meanings. Analytically, there are two key structural elements that support the development of meaningful relations with co-workers. First, there is the fact that co-workers are located in the same position in the same social structure (employment by the same organization, in a specific position within the international division of labour, within a specific form of capitalism). Second, as Hodson (2001) intimates, most labour processes require cooperation and collaboration between workers for the work to be accomplished successfully. It is these elements of the shared position within a social structure and the daily ongoing cooperation and collaboration that support the involvement with, and attachment to, co-workers.

Meaningful co-worker relations are often a particularly strong feature for workers where the organization of work is Taylorized. Although pure Taylorism creates individualized jobs with the need for labour process cooperation minimized, it also creates a stark social structure in which people tend to recognize their shared social position. With opportunities for meaning in relation to work per se severely constrained, workers turn to each other. A worker in a Taylorized blinds factory describes exactly that situation as she explains why she is quitting her job after many years: 'The people here are great, I love the people and I'm going to miss them but then the job is awful, there's no variety' (Korczynski, 2014: 114). In service work, recognition of a shared social position can occur in relation to customers. In an ethnography of work in a cocktail bar, Spradley and Mann (1975: 49) outline how waitresses show frequent mutual support. An example comes when a potentially disruptive group of young men from the college football team enter the bar: 'Sue glances at Denise and catches her eye, an instant message of sympathy hidden to everyone else. Sue nods her head at the clock and Denise shakes her ahead in agreement: "it's a long time until closing".' In knowledge work, meaningful co-worker relations tend to be linked to the deep nature of cooperation among peers in the labour process (Baldry et al, 2007) (discussed as collaborative communities of practice in Chapter 4).

Overall, then, the sense of community related to work is often a strong one. In times of claims of a diminishing wider sense of community in society (Putnam, 2000), perhaps workplace communities may become an increasingly important space against fragmentation and individualism. Barnard et al (2023) find that LGBT workers in the construction industry experienced the workplace as a 'safe space' for negotiating LGBT identities. In the specific context of migrant workers, the sense of work-related community may operate as a refuge against being negatively positioned as outsiders in the wider society. Couloigner (2022) studied the effect of the UK Brexit vote on the experience of French knowledge workers living and working in the UK. There was a pattern of workers experiencing some hostility outside the workplace; for example, one man reported (p 143): 'Since Brexit, six times! Six times … [people] asked me some questions like: "but what are you still doing here?" … "[why] haven't you packed already?"' At the same time, these French knowledge workers continued to experience their workplaces as inclusive international spaces. Further, studies show that having inter-ethnic work colleagues is associated positively with inter-ethnic relations outside work (Kokkonen et al, 2015) and reduces wider anti-foreigner sentiments (Sønderskov and Thomsen, 2015). Klein et al's study (2019) finds that workplace contact between Israeli Jews and Arabs was significantly correlated with the willingness to meet Arabs in and outside the workplace and to perceive Arabs in a less threatening way.

The form of work organization that is most antithetical to the development of communities among co-workers is that of platform work, where workers are positioned as independent contractors in competitive relations with each other (see Chapter 4). Glavin et al's study (2021) reveals a strong and statistically significant relationship such that platform workers are more likely to suffer loneliness than other types of worker. Although structured as isolated, and in competitive relations with each other, it is not uncommon for gig workers to recognize each other as fellow workers with common interests, particularly when they congregate at hubs for work. An Uber driver speaks about the formation of community based on labour process cooperation in terms of sharing knowledge and experience and in terms of shared ethnic backgrounds (Kearsey, 2023: 176):

> When you go airports, Heathrow airport, we're waiting for other jobs, so there (they) have coffee, food, toilet, you know? And we pay one pound per hour. So, we wait there for other jobs from airport, and there is like a thousand, thousand drivers. So, we are getting experience, some of them (are from) my back home, some have been different country … European and Turkish and Asian, a lot of people. So, we after exchange the number and we know each other. I say: 'I'm from Barking', 'oh I'm living near Barking', 'oh you're from Walthamstow, I'm near there'. Then after I'm talking, say this happened to me, so you share experience.

Sociological analysis of community, as well as showing the meaning of community for people inside that community, needs to be analytically aware that the creation of community also positions people *outside* that community. Research has pointed to significant ways in which co-worker communities can have a strong gendered element. Perhaps the most illuminating example of this is Cockburn's (1983) classic feminist analysis of the masculine culture within the strong community of male printing workers. Here, Cockburn shows how this co-worker community infused with masculinity effectively served to block women from entering that occupation. Given that gendered job segregation continues to be significant – many jobs are done either mostly by men or mostly by women (see Chapter 8) – the exclusionary potential of gendered co-workers communities is a non-trivial issue.

Resistive meanings

I argued earlier in this chapter that the process of workers adapting to work structures that are antithetical to meaning (such as Taylorism) by developing extrinsic orientations to work can be understood as involving an *implicit* critique of those work structures. Ethnographies in Taylorized workplaces tend to reveal that workers actually create a more explicitly critical and resistive set of meanings within the workplace. Ethnographic studies across decades reveal that workers have a critical understanding of these jobs as boring, as demeaning, as brain-numbing:

> 'It's the most boring job in the world. It's the same thing over and over again. There's no change in it, it wears you out. It makes you awful tired. It slows your thinking right down. There's no need to think. … You just endure it for the money. That's what we're paid for – to endure the boredom of it.' (Beynon, 1975: 118)

> 'You're doing something that's basically unpleasant. … Most jobs are monotony and repetition. It can drive you nuts.' (Greenberg, 1986: 82)

> 'Yeah, it's brain-dead,' Jo says … 'That's it. Brain-dead. … You'd commit suicide if there wasn't something on in the background to sing along to.' (Korczynski, 2014: 73)

In *Songs of the Factory* (Korczynski, 2014), I unearthed the resistive meanings workers held about the Taylorized factory where they worked by asking them if there was a song that spoke to them about their working lives. The overwhelming majority of songs nominated were heavily critical in tone, as can be seen from titles of songs chosen, such as 'The Only Way Is Up' by Yaz, 'I Will Survive' by Gloria Gaynor, 'Things Can Only Get Better' by D:Ream, 'Stayin' Alive' by The Bee Gees, 'I Want to Break Free' by Queen and 'Killing Me Softly' by The Fugees. Overall, the main song that spoke to workers about their working lives was the Animals' 'We've Gotta Get Out of This Place' (Korczynski, 2014: 125): "'I know," says Margaret straightaway, "I don't have to think about it, 'We've Got to Get out of Here'" – she means 'We've Gotta Get Out Of This Place' by the Animals. "Everyone sings it – we all sing along with that when it comes on, we all do," she says.' But perhaps the most critical song was one written by one of the workers, Adam, who had had enough of the factory after only a few weeks there. Before he left, knowing I was interested in the musical aspects of factory life, he wrote a song for me about his leaving (Korczynski, 2014: 126):

> Working for the shark,
> Dodging his back when the sky goes dark,
> Bobbing and weaving for the time it will take
> Cos our minds are rocks and they will not break.
> Same old jazz, day in and day out,
> Will make us run, and scream and shout.
> The sixth week of boredom slowly it's passed
> When the clock strikes one, they can kiss my ass.

Beyond the oppressive structures of Taylorized workplaces, research shows that workers can develop critical understandings of the employer when employer policies block off important areas of meaning for workers, either in terms of the processes of or the ends of work. In service work, policies that block or hinder pro-customer behaviours can lead to workers' antagonism towards the employer. Baines (2016) makes this point in her study of care workers in non-profit organizations in the US and Canada. When these workers analysed employer policies as failing to deliver meaningful care to clients, they became directly critical of the employers. The earlier discussion of knowledge workers resisting employers' attempts at developing organizational culture is also relevant here. Some of these management initiatives backfired so profoundly – leading to workers developing critical understandings of the employer – because they clearly challenged the autonomy that is so strongly pursued by knowledge workers.

Perhaps workers develop the strongest forms of resistive meanings regarding the employer in relation to the exploitation of their labour for the employer's profit. For instance, the ethnography in Korczynski (2014) offers a number of points when workers articulated clear grievances that it was fundamentally their low-paid work that was building the wealth of the owners and senior managers of the firm (p 167):

> Kathleen and Rose are talking animatedly about the founder of the company.
> 'He sold this bloody company for millions, for millions, it was. And who made

those millions for him? We did, that's who,' says Kathleen. 'And you know what,' answers Rose, 'and us making the blinds, we're the ones who get treated like dirt, that's the thing'.

Similar comments are reported in other ethnographies where the workers are low-paid. Friedland (1971: 155) reports a worker saying to a supervisor: 'You know you've got it, you're loaded. You make a fortune off poor people.' In Pollert's ethnography of a tobacco factory, workers make fun of a manager's attempt to shake off the importance of inequality and exploitation (1981: 152–153):

Ivy:	Where are you off for your holidays this year, Mr. Dowling [a senior manager]?
Mr. Dowling:	I'm not going anywhere. I can't afford it. I have bought the wife a car, and I've spent our money. Honestly.
Ivy:	Have you? Ah! What a shame. Can you sell some of your shares then?
Mr. Dowling:	No, can't do that.
Ivy:	Come on, just a few. This produced laughter all round, the manager and his attempt at being 'just one of the workers' exposed to ridicule.

In platform work, Kearsey's (2023: 203) ethnography shows an instance of the widespread Uber workers' critical knowledge of inequality and exploitation:

[Uber] know that a single driver will not take them to the court because for me to take them to the court I have to spend £5,000 before I take them to the court. For them it's nothing ... they make £5,000 in an hour you know, maybe even half an hour, but I don't make it in whole six months.

Informal practices

This chapter's mapping of worker agency and voice continues to move rightwards on the horizontal axis of Figure 5.1, with the focus now moving on to informal practices. So, there is a shift to examining actions (rather than meanings and norms), and actions that are not the direct outcome of a formal organizational process. First, there is an overview of the important forms of practice that are broadly supportive of the employer, then a focus on practices that are about coping and surviving, before consideration of informal practices of resistance.

Supportive practices

Within organizational behaviour (OB) scholarship, two key concepts are discretionary effort and organizational citizenship. Discretionary effort is defined as effort above that required or expected of workers by management. In HRM and OB scholarship, discretionary effort is a key focus in research on 'high-performance work systems'.

Research here focuses on trying to identify employment practices, such as training, flexibility, teamwork and job security, that can generate high performance, often through the delivery of discretionary effort by workers (Kaufman, 2020). Kaufman (p 62) criticizes a tendency in this input–output approach for research to lose sight of the agency of workers:

> Employees in the HPWS [high performance work system] model are called human resources but more resemble horse resources ... which employer–masters select, train, compensate, form into teams, strategise how to get the most value from, direct with orders and commands, motivate and align with carrot/stick inducements to get the most acres ploughed and crops delivered to market.

Despite the managerialist appropriation of the concept of discretionary effort within this research approach, discretionary effort is still an important concept. If, as Chapter 3 argued, the employment relationship is considered as an incomplete contract in which employers seek the extraction of labour from the potential labour power of a worker, the presence or absence of discretionary work effort should be seen as a key part of the social relations of the workplace. In service work, given, as noted earlier, that service recipients are often a key source of meaning for workers, it is not surprising that studies find it common for workers to enact discretionary effort for service recipients (Frenkel et al, 1999; Baines, 2016). This often comes out in service workers' enactment of emotional labour. Bolton (2005) makes the convincing argument that, despite management efforts to apply control to the emotional labour process, there remains important scope for service workers' discretion to offer 'gifts' of philanthropic emotional labour to service recipients. Let us return to Erickson's ethnography of working at The Hungry Cowboy (2009: 38):

> Emotional labor operates as an incentive in a job that offers few structural rewards for working hard. ... What [Julie] does not say in the interview is just how remarkably good she is at waiting on tables, pouring a drink while she tells a story, getting a customer who is down on his luck to utter a laugh. ... She is fiery and brilliant, hilarious and sometimes very angry. She brings all of those moods, performances and passions to work with her. Julia offers up her substantial emotional resources repeatedly even though the pay structure does not reward her for her effort ... Julia and many other servers emotionally 'show up' night after night, recognising their customers' needs, remembering their favorites, livening up their evening, or listening to a story or memory. Servers describe the emotional labour they perform as both exhausting and rewarding. In fact, servers seek out emotional high points ... when they feel they have 'made someone's night.' Servers report that the emotional high points of the job motivate them and inspire their commitment to the work.

Ethnographies of knowledge work also often show knowledge workers engaging in discretionary effort. Rogers and Larsen (1984: 138) include this example from a study of Silicon Valley research scientists and engineers: 'We set the pace ourselves.

If the wheel was running at 100 percent, we would spin it up to 120 every morning. Nothing's happening unless you're a little frantic. I've often seen design groups induce this frantic feeling themselves in order to get their juices flowing.' Hodson (2001) finds that professional workers offer much greater discretionary effort, in the sense of overcoming challenges, than workers in bureaucratic/Taylorized settings. He notes that this often occurs in the context of professional workers seeking to develop their careers.

While discretionary effort concerns workers' agency in the enactment of the core tasks that are part of their work role, OB scholars understand organizational citizenship behaviour as workers' voluntary behaviour outside the core tasks of the work role. Organ (1988: 4) defines organizational citizenship behaviour as 'the behaviour that is discretionary, not directly or explicitly recognised by the formal reward system and that in the aggregate promotes the effective functioning of the organisation'. Examples of such citizenship behaviour include offering discretionary help to co-workers, managers and clients, volunteering for wider tasks and promoting the good name of the organization. As noted earlier, the metaphor of 'citizenship' is unhelpful as part of the name of the concept: it is a useful concept with an unhelpful name. A more appropriate, sociological term for the concept might be 'discretionary social labour'. Unfortunately, the managerialist and psychological/individualist domain of research in which this concept has been embedded has led to such focuses as how individual personality traits influence this discretionary behaviour and how 'transformational leadership' influences it (Khaola and Rambe, 2021). However, rather more telling sociological research was undertaken by Hodson (2001), who looked at patterns of citizenship across different types of work organization based on analysing book-length workplace ethnographies. He finds (p 152): 'Professional and craft workers typically exhibit extremely high levels of citizenship in their work. This ... contrasts sharply with below average levels of citizenship in bureaucratic settings and in work settings that rely on supervisory fiat.'

Practices for surviving and coping

Some informal practices are about surviving and coping in given work structures. In terms of the vertical axis of Figure 5.1, they can be plotted at the halfway point: they are forms of agency that are neither directly supportive nor directly resistive, although they may often be informed by resistive meanings. Another way to think of these practices is to see them as an example of what Katz (2004) termed 'resilience practices' that people undertake to survive oppressive conditions.

Given the picture in Chapter 4 of Taylorist work organization as an oppressive structure, it is no accident that many of the examples of practices and cultures of survival come from research in Taylorist settings. Many of these practices can be understood as a fight against workers experiencing an acute sense of boredom, as a worker in a plywood factory intimates (Greenberg, 1986: 82): 'The work? It's boring, I mean, that's the first thing that pops into anybody's mind that works there. That's the worst fight down there is fighting not to get bored.' Examples of such practices include people working ahead of their targets in the early part of the day or week, and then enjoying the less-intense labour needed in the later part of the day or week (Hodson, 2001: 121). Overall here, workers hit the production target, but they do so in a way that *they* have chosen. In addition, workers establish rituals in part of the day to create forms of autonomous meaning to punctuate the meaningless labour that they enact. Roy's (1959: 162) pioneering ethnography of highly Taylorized work noted that the work group broke up the day by having 'coffee time, peach time, banana time, fish time, coke time, and, of course, lunch time. Other interruptions, which formed part of the series but were not verbally recognized as times, were window time [and] pickup time'.

I conceptualize such practices (Korczynski, 2014) as workers fighting against *sensing alienation*, and apply this to analyse the 'Stayin' Alive' workplace culture observed on the McTells factory floor (p 68):

> I want to reclaim the usefulness of the concept of alienation … as a way of understanding the lived experience of labour as a social process. In particular, I argue for the importance of understanding how workers sense alienation. The idea of workers sensing alienation was everywhere at McTells. It was there in the very frequent way that workers discussed 'mood' on the shopfloor. 'It's been a terrible morning. There's an awful mood' was a statement that workers were palpably feeling that their senses were being overwhelmed by alienation, sometimes in terms of powerlessness, and sometimes in terms of meaninglessness and monotony. It was there in how their heard the soundscape of the factory. It was there in how they experienced time passing. It was there in their fabric of experience after they had just been subject to a public humiliation by a supervisor. Workers sensing alienation was also a social process in the sense that they constantly fought back against their senses being dominated by alienation. They erected their whole *Stayin' Alive* culture as a way of holding back the waves of alienation. This is what surviving at work at McTells meant.

Humour and music – the joke and the song – were central to workers' 'Stayin' Alive' culture in this particular Taylorized factory.

Another important type of informal practice of surviving in the contemporary workplace is the creation of *communities of coping* by service workers (Korczynski, 2003; Doerflinger, 2022). The point at which service work is at its most oppressive is in the social positioning of service workers as recipients of abuse and sometimes violence from customers. Although it is the organization that seeks to enchant customers through a myth of customer sovereignty, and it is the organization that systematically puncture holes in this myth (Korczynski and Ott, 2004), it is the service workers who are expected to put up with any direct customer anger that arises. Leidner's (1993: 130–133) ethnography of work at McDonalds draws out exactly what it feels like to be in a service position where you are de facto expected to put up with customer abuse. One worker, Traci, put it: 'We're sort of at their [the customers'] mercy.' Another worker, Lori, explained that 'you have to take their crap'. In these circumstances, with management tending to de facto expect service workers to put up with abuse, service workers tend to socialize the costs of such abuse by creating informal but dense communities of coping in which they offer support to each other. Korczynski (2003) describes (p 66) communities of coping operating in call centres:

> One worker at INSCO said that: 'Sometimes the customer is rude, they will say "fuck off" if you've given them a high quote. These comments are rare but they stick … they rebound round the whole team. One person will tell the person next to them and the word soon goes around the team.' A [worker] at US-BANK noted that: 'We discuss the calls. It's good to get it off your chest. "That guy was such a jerk" sort of thing.'

A large number of studies have highlighted the importance of such communities of coping across a range of service occupations (including Simms, 2005; Schneider et al, 2022). Cohen and Richards (2015) discussed collective coping by workers facilitated by social media.

In understanding these overall practices of surviving and coping in oppressive structures, it is useful to consider their direct outcomes and the longer-term implications for workplace relations. The practices of survival in Taylorist settings, and communities of coping in service work, do nothing to directly support or directly resist the oppressive workplace structures. They are neither supportive nor resistive. Yet, crucially, both forms of practice are informed by workers holding critical understandings of the structures facing them and the employer's role in creating them. In that sense, the practices are underpinned by resistive meanings. As Scott's important book, *Domination and the Arts of Resistance* (1990), argues, resistive meanings constitute the necessary architecture for the *potential* development of resistive practices.

Informal practices of resistance

With the precipitous falling away since the 1980s of strikes, it may be tempting to think that other forms of worker resistance are also withering (Thompson and Ackroyd, 1995). Chapter 3 outlined the structures of power that people inhabit at work, and Chapters 3 and 4 discussed how these macro-structures come to inform the nature of work organization, including patterns and techniques of control. To some observers, these structures of power and techniques of control may appear formidable enough to nullify and block off any significant informal practices of resistance by workers. Notably, there has been a movement towards the greater exposure of the employment relationship to external market forces. Resistance against market fiat may be much more problematic than resistance against hierarchical systems of control enacted by managers and supervisors. In addition, it may be assumed that new technologies of control and surveillance, linked to algorithmic control in platform work and the potential panopticon-like qualities of ICT, can effectively close off the possibilities of resistance (Woodcock, 2020; Joyce and Stuart, 2021). More generally, the shift in power towards employers over workers through globalization, the international division of labour and the weakening of unions may also serve to lessen resistance.

Sociology of work research indicates, however, that informal practices of resistance continue to have a significant presence in contemporary workplaces (Thompson,

2016; Mumby et al, 2017; Edwards and Hodder, 2022). I follow Edwards and Hodder (2022: 221) in defining informal practices of resistance as informal practices that are directed to 'alter the terms of the reward–effort bargain' at the heart of the employment relationship in workers' favour. A useful way to think about resistance is to see it played out at the frontier of control – a line relating to whether managers or workers decide on issues such as the pace of work, the observation of work, how and by whom the quality of work is defined, the allocation of jobs, discipline and recruitment, as well as reward (Goodrich, 1921). When the nature of the power relations between workers and employers shifts, there are likely to be new struggles enacted at the frontier of control. Crucially, informal practices of resistance at the frontier of control tend to be collective and social acts by workers. Notably, Ackroyd and Thompson (2022: 59) maintain that 'organizational misbehaviour' is predominantly a group phenomenon. Even when resistance takes the form of the apparently individual action of absenteeism, sociological research indicates that patterns of absenteeism tend to be set socially, often through collective norms established informally by workers among themselves (Edwards and Whitston, 1993; Miraglia and Johns, 2021).

Workers enact practices of resistance to a significant degree in reaction to the forms of control and overall work organization in which their labour is embedded (Hodson, 1995; Ackroyd and Thompson, 2022). Indeed, control and resistance can be seen to be in a dynamic, dialectical relationship. For instance, Anteby and Chan (2018) outline such a dynamic in their analysis of increased surveillance at an airport. They argue that workers tend to understand increased surveillance as a coercive controlling practice by management. Workers react then by engaging in what the authors call 'invisibility practices' in order to go unseen by management, customers and surveillance technology. Such invisibility practices include extending breaks, slowing down between the changeover of tasks, keeping a low profile and being inconspicuous in plain sight not only of management but also of customers – for instance, workers deliberately downplayed their emotions in front of passengers to have passengers pay less attention to them. Anteby and Chan (2018: 247) note that 'management, in turn, interprets these attempts as justification for more surveillance, which encourages workers to engage in even more invisibility practices, thus creating a ... cycle of coercive surveillance [and resistance]'.

With these overview points made regarding informal practices of resistance, we turn to outline the two main categories of such practices, illustrating with examples from service work, knowledge work and platform work where possible.

Restricting work intensity by limiting effort and time

Early studies by sociologists unearthed informal and sometimes clandestine practices by work groups to limit the intensity of work by limiting effort (sometimes called 'soldiering' by US sociologists) and limiting time spent enacting labour (for example by extending breaks) (Hodson, 2001). Given the potential for Taylorist work organization and control to drive high intensity of work, it is no surprise that practices to restrict work intensity have been commonly found in Taylorized work settings (Hodson, 1995). A key management technique in the operation of Taylorism is to allocate a time to a specific task, and then to measure and discipline workers in relation to this set time. Studies show that work groups became adept at making sure that set times were not based on intensive labour. Roy's (1954: 257) pioneering study noted that 'one cardinal principle of operator [task]-timing was that cutting tools be run at lower speeds and "feeds" than the maximum possible on subsequent production'. More recently, my study of a Taylorized factory (Korczynski, 2014: 143) found workers collectively and deliberately limiting effort and output:

> There was a joke about the slower pace of Linda's walk on the shopfloor compared to that outside which highlighted the consistent restriction of effort by workers:
>   We talk about Linda being a much faster walker outside of the factory than inside it. Inside she shuffles about and there's a joke that you should have seen her running to the car yesterday to get out, 'she's faster than blinking Zola Budd [an Olympic runner] she is.' And she said, 'oh, I was only getting out of here wasn't I?'

Hochschild's (1983) study of emotional labour among flight attendants gives an example of these service workers limiting the intensity of the emotional labour demanded of them. The flight attendants recount the story among themselves of a passenger complaining to one of the flight attendants that she was not smiling. The flight attendant challenged the customer (p 127): 'I'll tell you what. You smile first, then I'll smile.' The passenger smiled. 'Good' said the flight attendant, 'now freeze and hold that for fifteen hours'. She picked up her tray and walked away.

An extreme way to limit effort is to sabotage the production system and the products being made. Hamper (1991: 206) describes a work group's reaction of subtle sabotage to a new strict supervisor who aimed to increase work intensity: 'After three nights of this imposed bullyism, the boys had had their fill. Frames began sliding down the line minus parts. Rivets became cross-eyed. Guns mysteriously broke down. The repairmen began shipping the majority of the defects, unable to keep up with the repair load.' Prasad and Prasad (2000, 2001) found equivalent sabotage practices in a white-collar setting (a medical insurance firm). Similarly, Karlsson (2012: 39) notes the resistance of 'careful carelessness':

> Coffee cups and cans of soft drinks often stood right beside keyboards and someone could easily have knocked them over. People forgot to shut down their computers at night, and to save important documents. ... The conviction took root [among managers] that this was ... systematic and deliberate resistance. ... One of the managers invented a term for what was going on – 'careful carelessness' – and this soon spread throughout the workplace.

Service workers can also undertake clandestine sabotage, sometimes in relation to disrespectful customers. In Bayard de Volo's (2003) study of a casino, the story is recounted of the casino workers reacting to a noisy, non-tipping group of customers by spiking their drinks with extra shots of alcohol, hastening the staggering exit of this troublesome (and soon-to-be-hungover) group.

Studies are beginning to show the importance of workers in platform work undertaking similar practices to shift the effort-bargain in their favour (Joyce and Stuart, 2021: 169):

> Research shows that platform workers, for instance grocery delivery drivers on Instacart in the US, have learned that rejecting low-paying jobs will train the algorithm to channel higher-paying jobs. One worker commented: 'I feel like I trained the computer what I'll do. Eventually that computer knows I'm not going to take all kinds of $10 orders. So they stop sending them to me and they send me more decent stuff' (Griesbach et al. 2019, p. 6). What is more, these workers had collectivised these tactics for training the algorithm via online social media groups. ... Effectively, these workers have reinvented the age-old practice of output restriction.

There may be other contemporary versions of age-old practices of resistance. For instance, online scrolling during work time by knowledge workers (Thompson, 2016) can be considered as analogous to Linda's slow walk on the factory floor.

Pursuit and defence of autonomy

Here, practices are very much about workers extending and defending the frontier of control. As outlined in Chapter 4, autonomy is central to the organization of knowledge work, although Adler's (2015) analysis suggests that there will be systematic conflicts around this. Hodson's overview of ethnographies of professional work finds relatively low levels of engagement by professionals in practices of resistance to defend their autonomy. Practices he considers include subverting managers and supervisors, withholding enthusiasm, turnover and 'playing dumb' (pretending not to understand hierarchical instructions). Hodson (2001: 157) states that 'professional employees exhibit relatively little overall resistance'.

Two analytical points may help to explain this apparent paradox of knowledge workers pursuing work autonomy but not engaging in acts of resistance to defend it. First, it may be that hierarchical attacks on autonomy, although present, are not as common as in other forms of work. This means that workers' resistance against such attacks will also be relatively less common. Second, it may be better to think of knowledge workers' active pursuit of autonomy as a central practice that is both supportive and resistive at the same time. Tam et al's (2005: 185) study of knowledge workers in large corporations shows that these workers operated in autonomous, collegial enclaves: 'Work teams of developers and dealers were imbued with the collegial ethos. These teams were egalitarian, autonomous and self-disciplining in the way they functioned ... these teams were like independent enclaves in the corporation.' The lived pursuit of autonomy comes out in statements from knowledge workers such as (Tam et al, 2005: 184): 'I don't believe in [project] management. The project manager has no tools to evaluate the task. In our case you cannot break the tasks into components, so you can't know how long it will take. Schedules cannot be valid in projects like this.' Although this autonomous organization of production may be supportive of the employer, it is clear that this was an autonomy linked heavily to a commitment to the occupation rather than the employer. Notably, the researchers found that discretionary effort was statistically significantly and strongly linked to *occupational* commitment, but not to *organizational* commitment.

In service work, the pursuit and defence of autonomy by workers is often played out through enacting labour to support service recipients in some way that is blocked or hindered by management policies. This comes out strongly in studies of care workers by Brown and Korczynski (2010) and Baines (2016) (also Karlsson, 2012). Baines' study of care work in Canada and the US shows that workers tended to position the employer as failing to provide structures for meaningful care to clients, and this is the context in which some workers sought out autonomous spaces away from the presence of managers. Two workers commented (Baines, 2016: 134) that 'lots of the staff don't like working morning shift because all the bosses are around', whereas in the evening and the night shift, 'you're on your own and you can do what you want without anyone looking over your shoulder all the time'. Doing 'what you want' tended to involve marginalizing management's (bureaucratic) demand for 'documentation' of care, and replacing this with the enactment of meaningful care to clients (Baines, 2016: 134):

> Workers sometimes left documentation incomplete. This is seen as a major problem by many managers. As one manager complained, documenting is 'the most important thing staff does on a shift,' but 'they let anything get in their way.' The frontline staff felt that the most important aspect of their job was that they 'cared about the service users' and that documentation took too much time away from doing this.

Sometimes, this was also manifest in the provision of unpaid work and gifts to clients (Baines, 2016: 131) – 'working through coffee breaks and lunch hour, staying late, taking work home, coming in on weekends, and taking clients home for birthday parties or weekend barbeques'. Brown and Korczynski (2010) studied the introduction of monitoring technology in (mobile) home care work in the UK. Here, the workers understood the introduction of monitoring as control that eroded their autonomy and the sense that they were not being trusted to do a good job of providing care, as noted by two workers (p 420):

> I don't agree with the system as I feel as if big brother is watching me and I am not trusted.
>
> A lot of people think that they are spying on you they don't trust you, watching what you do, it's that sort of scenario … you still feel that they are watching you and seeing how long you are taking with that client.

The more workers saw the new monitoring system as a controlling force that actually hindered the delivery of meaningful care, the less organizational commitment they had and the more (autonomous) discretionary effort they delivered to still enact some meaningful care for clients. The following statement is from a worker on her refusal to compromise on the delivery of meaningful care – note how she ends by articulating a strong principle of autonomy (Brown and Korczynski, 2010: 425):

> To start with, I felt that I was constantly clock watching the whole time, there was a bit of pressure put on us. I felt myself because you obviously have gaps between each client for travelling time. I've only got 5 minutes to get to somewhere, but I thought hang on I'm not going to get an accident a speeding ticket getting from one client to the next. After a while I managed to relax. Part of our job is to support the client and talk. I know my clients and I know what they need.

Egan's (2006) study of 'exotic dancers' gives a good example of service workers fighting for their autonomy after management altered the frontier of control. Originally, the dancers were able to choose the music to which they performed. Then the owner announced that to keep the club 'classy', only Top 40 songs could be played. These were songs that many of the dancers did not want to perform to. Collectively, they discussed (p 209) that 'we should all play what we want'. They tried to tip the disc jockey to avoid the new policy, and ended up succeeding in reversing the policy by enlisting regular customers to complain to the owner about it. They had reasserted an important part of their autonomy at the frontier of control.

As noted in Chapter 4, there are considerable areas of worker autonomy within the organization of platform work, which are strongly valued by workers, and that the processes of gamification (for example surge or dynamic pricing) can be thought of as (structured) or subordinated agency. Research into resistive practices by platform workers is beginning to show that workers understand that the platform is structuring their actions, and they respond by taking a form of autonomous action informed by horizontally sharing information with each other (Kearsey, 2023).

Sociological imagination – your turn

Meanings

One of the important process-related forms of meanings in knowledge work that we have discussed is 'flow'. Have you experienced 'flow' in your university studies – perhaps when devoting a focused period to a long piece of coursework? Would you like to have a job where opportunities for flow are present? What types of job are most likely to offer opportunities for the experience of flow?

Practices

Consider your own service work experience, or talk to a friend or family member about their service work experience. Have you deliberatively withheld effort in response to the behaviour of a customer or service recipient? By contrast, do you sometimes do extra (that is, perform discretionary effort) for some customers? Is there an informal pattern of such behaviour shared among your workmates? If so, where would you position such behaviour on Figure 5.1?

6

The Agency and Voice of Workers (2)

This is the second of the two chapters examining the agency and voice of workers. The overall structure of the two chapters is guided by Figure 5.1. The previous chapter examined meanings and informal practices. Continuing to move to the right along the horizontal axis of Figure 5.1, this chapter focuses on formal voice structures and mechanisms. It begins with an analysis of employer-initiated voice mechanisms. These, broadly, are assumed (at least by employers) to lead to voice from workers that is supportive of employer interests. In terms of Figure 5.1, these structures and mechanisms are mapped in the upper part of the vertical axis. The chapter then focuses on worker-initiated voice structures and mechanisms. Worker-led voice is more likely to be resistive in nature. Worker voice is workers' 'expression of ideas and opinions regarding their own or organizational interests through formal or informal mechanisms' (Khan et al, 2023: 1). This chapter focuses mainly, but not exclusively, on *formal* voice mechanisms, that is, those that operate through a recognized and named channel.

One of the most fundamental ways in which employer-initiated and worker-initiated voice mechanisms differ is the degree of control that workers have in these mechanisms. Voice mechanisms at their weakest involve just a way for management to share information – one way, *from* management *to* workers. Rather than being considered voice, this should be more accurately analysed as *listening*. This may occur within team meetings, for example. Next are mechanisms of *consultation*. Here, workers have the opportunity to put forward their views, but it is still entirely in management's power whether to act on those views or not. There is no redrawing of the frontier of control (see Chapter 5). Most employer-initiated voice mechanisms are mechanisms of consultation, from staff meetings to staff councils via staff surveys. Workers have a higher degree of control in voice mechanisms that involve *joint decision-making*. Here, management and worker representatives come together and jointly agree an approach on issues. This often involves a key role for independent worker voice. For instance, collective bargaining between employers and labour unions is the most important example of joint decision-making. Here, there is an important shift in the frontier of control in some areas – such as wages and conditions of employment – from being subject purely to management prerogative to being subject to a joint agreement between employers and workers. The highest degree of control for workers is when there is *self-management*: when decisions are placed in workers' hands, alone. The most important form of self-managing voice is the worker cooperative.

A final introductory point to make is that there is a disciplinary divide in the study of worker voice, with organizational behaviour (OB) scholars tending to focus on employer-initiated voice mechanisms, and industrial relations and sociology of work scholars tending to focus on worker-initiated voice. There is no good reason for this divide. Indeed, the divide is harmful for our understanding of overall voice, not least because the OB scholarship on voice is flawed through its lack of consideration of the fundamental issue of power relations. The sociology of work, in which a number of theoretical traditions analyse the employment relationship as a structure of power relations, is better suited to show employer-initiated voice mechanisms are much more likely to generate less resistive messages than the messages articulated through worker-initiated voice mechanisms (Donaghey et al, 2011). This difference is fundamentally important, but is not easily seen when the study of voice is separated across academic disciplines.

Indeed, because of this difference in message, in interests that are articulated, it may be useful to think that the analysis of voice is also the analysis of *silence*. It is about both what is said and what is *not* said – what often, effectively, *cannot* be said. A key driving argument in the first part of the chapter is that management effectively structure forms of worker silence in their structuring of voice mechanisms (Donaghey et al, 2011).

Employer-initiated voice mechanisms – and ensuing silences

Employer-initiated forms of worker voice mechanisms have come in waves, and under different labels – participation, empowerment, involvement, engagement and so on. Typical examples of such mechanisms, moving from the task level to the higher organizational level, are: team briefings, participatory team structures, quality circles, upward problem-solving groups, suggestion schemes, staff surveys, staff meetings and staff councils. Usually, employers put forward claims of a dual, win–win motivation for the introduction of such voice structures (Dundon et al, 2004) – the logic is that both the organization and the workers will benefit from such structures. The organization benefits by harnessing the insights, knowledge and experience of their workers to generate better decisions. Here, Wilkinson et al (2021: 693) note that in 'the so-called knowledge economy, which became prominent since the 1980s, management concepts such as empowerment, teamwork, lean production and total quality emphasize knowledge-sharing and creation as the central driver of corporate performance'. This motivation is the central one of interest to much OB scholarship on voice. Such scholarship even defines voice in terms of how it improves organizational effectiveness, for instance through preventing or correcting problems (Wilkinson et al, 2020; see too the important critique of such an approach by Barry and Wilkinson, 2022). In addition, employers point to gains for workers themselves. Workers have the opportunity to have a say on issues in their working life and to affect decisions on those issues. Voice structures create a greater space at work in which workers can flourish.

Dundon et al (2004) undertook insightful research in the UK to dig beneath the rhetoric of employer claims regarding the introduction of voice structures. They interviewed managers across organizations to see how they saw the voice structures in practice. They found (p 1149) that 'managers defined voice very much in terms of the perceived contribution to efficiency'. The following example is from a service firm (a betting business) where service workers' knowledge of customer practices helped improve organizational performance (Dundon et al, 2004: 1166):

> The Customer Service Manager at Bet.com comments:
> Our people have had some major new ideas that evolve from the customer contact they have which has impressed [the owners] no end. Because of some sloppy procedures at [head office] it was possible for customers to get bets on after the event. ... We've introduced a procedure that prevents that, and that came as a result of our team meetings and some inventive thinking by the agents.

Managers tended *not* to think of the voice mechanisms in terms of beneficial outcomes for the workforce.

An important question arising for this chapter is how workers react to these increasingly common forms of employer-initiated voice structures. Hodson's (2001) analysis is informative. He is aware that such structures may be part of an overall employer drive for greater effort and greater efficiency. However, his overview of ethnographies finds that workers tend to have a more positive experience of their working life where there are employer-initiated voice structures than where there are none. Furthermore, workers offer greater levels of organizational 'citizenship' where there are such voice structures than where there are none. However, the presence of employer-initiated voice structures has little effect on the likelihood of workers to undertake informal resistive practices. Hodson, being a sociologist based in the US, is sensitive to how the strong anti-union approach of US employers has actually underpinned some of the employer-initiated voice mechanisms. The logic in such anti-unionism is that workers are less likely to turn to independent voice (through unions) if they are provided with some form of formal voice structures within their organizations. He finds scant evidence of this working out in practice (Hodson, 2001: 189): 'There is little indication that team-based production systems have been successful in shifting workers' loyalties away from their coworkers and towards management.'

While it is important to know that workers react broadly positively to these voice structures, the crucial question left hanging is how loud and how meaningful worker voice is in these structures. It is useful to return to a point made in the introduction to this chapter, that, in the vast majority of these structures, voice is in terms of consultation: it is up to management, ultimately, to decide whether or not to act on the substantive points communicated by workers through the voice structures. This comes out as an underlying assumption in a statement by a manager interviewed by Dundon et al (2004: 1159), that 'voice is about corporate communications and the strategy is designed in such a way that all employees can represent their views to management, rather than it just being the other way around'. Note that voice is 'represented' to management. There is no sense that there is any obligation or assumption that management will act on what is represented to it.

It is important to be clear on what types of worker are presented with these structures. Chapter 4 showed that knowledge-work organization tends to have meaningful voice in decision-making on the organization of production (such as project teams, although see Hodgson and Briand, 2013). The voice structures being discussed here, rather, are primarily 'add-ons' to the organization of other forms of work, such as service work and manual work (voice for platform workers is discussed separately). Overall, these employer-initiated voice structures in these settings tend to offer a (welcomed) opportunity for workers to offer voice-as-consultation on a narrow range of issues mainly, but not exclusively, related to (improving) the efficiency of production. The fact that workers regard the opportunity to raise suggestions as a better state of affairs than there being no such opportunities should not blind us to the need to analyse these structures carefully.

Donaghey et al (2011) argue that limitations of these employer-initiated voice structures – for instance that they are primarily consultative, on a narrow range of issues and just 'add-ons' to the main organization of work – are so profound that it is appropriate to consider them also as structures that generate worker *silence*. Donaghey et al's (2011) argument centres on what is *not* on the agenda in these voice structures. They call on a wider tradition of social and political analysis that considers (p 61) 'how dominant groups can effectively organise out of the … arena issues of potential concern to other interest groups'. In this case, the dominant group is the employer, and the workforce is the group with concerns that do not make it on to the agenda in these voice structures.

What sort of concerns or interests could workers have that employers may want to keep off the agenda? Job security and higher pay would be base starting points. The review of structures of power in Chapters 3 and 4 and worker agency in Chapter 5 also suggest other important issues. One is work intensity. Chapter 4 has shown that the intensity of work has been increasing in recent decades, and Chapter 5 has shown that, at the same time, a key aim of many informal resistance practices by workers is the limiting of effort and work intensity. The coexistence of these two elements would suggest that, if voice is meaningful for workers, it should allow workers to articulate their voice on the intensity of work. Another important issue for workers is often meaningful work. Chapter 5 showed that, even in de-skilled Taylorist settings, workers, while partly accommodating to the structures facing them by espousing the importance of the extrinsic rewards of work, often seek to chisel out forms of meaning *within* work. Chapter 5 also showed that workers outside Taylorist settings often enact profound agency in pursuing meaning in the processes and ends of work. As such, it would appear reasonable to argue that, if employer-initiated structures provide meaningful voice for workers, it should be expected that meaningful work often joins work intensity, pay and job security on the agenda in these structures.

However, there is little evidence to suggest that these issues do come to the agenda (Waitling and Snook, 2003; Dundon and Rollinson, 2004). Rather, Dundon and Rollinson's (2004) study of non-union employee representation shows that workers could only contribute on matters deemed appropriate by management. The result is that, often, employer-imposed restrictions on what issues workers can raise lead to the diminution of the structures in the medium term. Put simply, when workers recognize such structures as 'all talk' and 'no voice', many of them turn away from a deep engagement with these structures (Waitling and Snook, 2003). Workers at a quality ideas (that is, voice structure) meeting at a factory I studied (Korczynski, 2014: 152) used the analogy of the three monkeys who 'see no evil, hear no evil, speak no evil' to articulate the dynamic of management silencing workers through the limiting of the agenda:

> At the quality idea meeting everybody's going, 'Oh bloody hell, why bother.' Tracey, who's the group rep, was just sitting up on the table and trying to explain the procedure [for the meeting] … Pete, William and Tony sit in a corner away from us, showing absolutely no interest, closing their eyes, putting their hands on their heads. At one point they do a skit of 'see no evil, hear no evil, speak no evil', with their hands in appropriate places. This gets a few laughs.

The growth of some limited employer-initiated voice structures (outside knowledge work settings) is the main picture, but it is not the only picture. The structuring by employers of platform-mediated work such that workers are not treated as workers but as independent contractors puts severe limits on the possibility of developing even the modest forms of voice structure just discussed (Wilkinson et al, 2021). A key argument of Kougiannou and Mendonca's (2021) study of workers for an online food delivery platform in a UK city is that positioning workers as independent contractors alongside algorithmic management techniques effectively constitutes a managerial silencing of worker voice. Gegenhuber et al (2020) studied five crowdsourcing platforms and found that, although they allow some limited articulation of voice about everyday work, the platform technology limits any significant influence over decision-making. As becomes clear in the following section, there is, however, evidence that workers in platform-mediated work still seek to articulate voice.

Independent voice mechanisms for workers

If employer-initiated voice mechanisms block off, or, at best, severely limit, the resistive voice of workers, it leads us to consider in this section the independent collective voice of workers that allows and supports the articulation of the resistive voice (bottom-right quadrant of Figure 5.1). The word 'independent' here means that it is not reliant on employer initiation. Workers, or people seeking to represent workers' interests, are the authors of these voice mechanisms.

It has been customary for industrial relations scholarship to primarily consider the independent collective voice of workers in terms of labour unions, or trade unions as they are known in the UK. Atzeni (2021) critiques such an approach, labelling the mono-focus on labour unions as a 'fetishism' of the union form. Atzeni argues that the almost exclusive focus on unions may have previously made some sense, in the context of a period of the Fordist compromise (see Chapter 3) when large trade unions represented workers in mass Taylorized industrial settings and bargained for high wages and job security in return for acquiescence to de-skilled work. However, key elements of the Fordist period are past. Globalization has considerably strengthened the power of employers over labour, and membership of unions has declined considerably as Taylorized mass workplaces have declined in advanced economies. In the US, Cornfield (2023) articulates a move in the sociology of work from a union-centred approach to one that is centred on a wider sense of worker agency. Moreover, the mono-focus on unions as *the* collective voice structure for workers, Atzeni (2021) and Bieler and Nowak (2021) argue, was based on a very Eurocentric form of scholarship. Bieler and Nowak argue that, if we have a postcolonial understanding – if we have an approach that centres on regions and countries previously marginalized in the world economy and industrial relations scholarship – it is more appropriate to see that, while workers may still strive to articulate and act on a resistive collective voice, it is often the exception, rather than the rule, that workers' collective voice is institutionalized in the union form.

This section takes a wide view of workers' resistive collective voice, considering social media campaigns, loose collectivities, civil society organizations, labour unions, statutory mechanisms for worker voice, worker cooperatives and workers' voice in global supply chains. By putting aside a focus on traditional unions, and 'adopt[ing] a more processual view of workers' collective organization away from pre-conceived forms' (Atzeni, 2021: 1352), we can see much more activity and energy in how workers' collective voices are being developed, organized and articulated.

Social media campaigns

In the wider polity, the Arab Spring of 2011 showed the considerable potential for dissenting collective voice to be developed, articulated and organized via social media (Howard et al, 2011). Just as social media helped to spread resistive voices across international borders in the Arab Spring, so we need to consider how social media can be used to raise and spread workers' voice across workplace boundaries. Consider the #MeToo movement – one of the most significant social media campaigns of the 21st century. Although it developed a wider focus, at its origins and in its central focus, it was about women workers exposing, and demanding an end to, work-related sexual harassment and assault (Jaffe, 2018). This was a social media-enabled movement with women workers' resistive collective voice at its heart.

The phrase 'Me Too' was originally used by African-American women's rights activist Tarana Burke in 2006. It became the name of a social (media) movement in 2017. *The New York Times* had just published a story about the repeated sexual harassment and assault of women employed (often in acting roles in the films he produced) by the film producer Harvey Weinstein. In response, actor Alyssa Milano, through the #MeToo hashtag, encouraged other women to join her in exposing sexual harassment and assault. The hashtag was used 12 million times in the first 24 hours.

Although much of the media discussion focused on the cases of celebrities, many of the voices in the #MeToo movement were those of ordinary working women. As Jaffe (2018) argues, what united these stories was the 'power of the boss'; the power to exploit the structures of power outlined in Chapter 3 and 4. Of course, it was nearly always a male boss sexually harassing and assaulting women in subordinate employment relationship positions. As Jaffe argues, #MeToo was simultaneously the collective voice of women workers and a voice against patriarchy. Regarding the former, Jaffe (2018: 86) outlines a key moment in the #MeToo movement:

> 700,000 women farmworkers of the Alianza Nacional de Campesinas, published [a letter] in *Time* magazine, that expressed solidarity with the Hollywood women who had come forward. 'Even though we work in very different environments, we share a common experience of being preyed upon by individuals who have the power to hire, fire, blacklist and otherwise threaten our economic, physical and emotional security.'

Tarana Burke, who had coined the use of 'Me Too', also pointed to the importance of structural power: 'I don't want to keep talking about individuals. You are all going to keep making boogiemen when we should be talking about systems. A person like Harvey Weinstein doesn't just exist in a vacuum' (quoted in Ozkazanc-Pan, 2019: 1212). Most of the social media contributions were made by individual women, but, by coming together in such numbers, women workers were effectively articulating their *collective* resistive voice. Ozkazanc-Pan emphasizes the importance of this collective agency enacted by women. Female actors (whose project-based industry made them, structurally, particularly vulnerable to the power of the male employer-as-hirer) responded to the solidarity shown to them by reciprocating (Jaffe, 2018: 87):

> The Time's Up fund, administered by the National Women's Law Center, began with over $13 million in donations from film stars and aims to provide legal support for those facing harassment. Their launch letter read:
> To every woman employed in agriculture who has had to fend off unwanted sexual advances from her boss, every housekeeper who has tried to escape an assaultive guest, every janitor trapped nightly in a building with a predatory supervisor, every waitress grabbed by a customer and expected to take it with a smile, every garment and factory worker forced to trade sexual acts for more shifts, every domestic worker or home health aide forcibly touched by a client, every immigrant woman silenced by the threat of her undocumented status being reported in retaliation for speaking up and to women in every industry who are subjected to indignities and offensive behavior that they are expected to tolerate in order to make a living: We stand with you. We support you.

The #MeToo case is a very powerful example of women workers' resistive collective voice in a social media-based campaign, but we also need to step back and consider, analytically, 'what does #MeToo imply for collective goal formation?' (Riordan and Kowalski, 2021: 599). Are workers' collective resistive voices per se likely to be facilitated by social media on an ongoing basis, or is #MeToo more likely to be a one-off?

There are two emerging approaches to this question by sociologists of work. The first is a contextualist approach, which sees some limited potential in the articulation of collective voice through social media campaigns, but which implicitly cautions against the likelihood of the development of any wider significant pattern. Khan et al (2023) develop such an approach, arguing that, to see the potential synergy of social media and collective voice, it is necessary to disaggregate both of these elements. Leaning on Treem and Leonardi (2012), they disaggregate social media by considering the different forms of potential that are offered by different types of social media. In a work-related context, the key potential qualities offered by social media are visibility, association, persistence, editability and anonymity. Khan et al (2023) go on to argue that these potential qualities will have different implications for collective voice depending on the type of voice that is being developed, for example whether it is a more supportive form of voice about improving production practices or whether it is a dissenting voice. For the dissenting voice (the focus in this section), Khan et al argue that, while social media's quality of association can help build and amplify collective voice, it is also the case that the qualities of social media can lead to a muting of minority voice.

By contrast, a second approach is put forward by Heckscher and McCarthy (2014), who make an energetic claim that collective resistive voice through social media is a central part of the future. The logic of the argument is that, as the trade-union form and its picket-line brother industrial solidarity were part of Fordist times, in contemporary post-Fordist times, there is emerging a new form of solidarity, collaborative solidarity, which is made up of multiple and transient forms of 'weak ties' between people (think of 'friends' on Facebook). Social media works symbiotically with transient collaborative solidarity by helping to generate multiple weak ties. In addition, social media becomes a key platform for the expression of collective voice that emerges through this new form of solidarity. Gone are the days of the stable institutional form of collective voice, the union. Enter the days of the transient flaring up and then dying down of flash mobs and social media campaigns (note the rise of Coworker.org, which supports workers in using petitions to initiate change in company policies). The debate between these two positions of Khan et al (2023) and Heckscher and McCarthy (2014) may be a crucial one for the future of collective resistive voice.

Loose collectivities

Loose collectivities appear to be an increasingly important contemporary mode of collective voice (Kochan et al, 2023). The focus here is upon workers coming together in quasi-formal, loose collectivities to raise their voice. There is an overlap between this form of resistive voice and some of the informal collective resistive practices that were discussed in Chapter 5. There is also some overlap between loose collectivities and social media campaigns in that loose collectivities also often involve the use of social media, but mainly as an organizing tool rather than being the main mode of articulating voice. Often, such loose collectivities are created around the articulation of voice on a single issue, after which they dissipate. We can see some of the energy in this form of collective voice by looking at examples across service work, knowledge work and platform work.

In the UK, during the height of the pandemic lockdown where critical COVID-19 cases in hospitals were at extremely high levels, nurses and other front-line health workers organized collectively, within hospitals, to claim a safe space for their own well-being. These spaces were called 'wobble rooms', with 'wobble' being the everyday term meaning an experience of feeling overwhelmed and being temporarily unable to cope (Pilling, 2020). Pilling describes the spread of wobble rooms, in and beyond the UK (Gurney et al, 2020), as a 'mass movement' in healthcare, which, in effect, was an interplay between workers' raising their voice, local nurse team leaders listening and the spread of the voice through social media, particularly Twitter. In terms of the concepts discussed in Chapter 5, wobble rooms can be analysed as simultaneously being a space for the creation of communities of coping, a collective symbol of the limits to healthcare workers' heightened discretionary effort during the pandemic and an assertion that workers' welfare and interests were still important.

In knowledge work, there have been a number of recent, high-profile and potentially significant cases where loose collectivities of workers have articulated a resistive voice. These have tended to flare up over a single issue, where a specific incident involving a corporation and a worker has acted as the immediate 'flashpoint' (Liu, 2023a), or catalyst, for the development of the resistive collective voice. Frequently, the issue concerns working conditions. This was the case in the walkout by 20,000 Google workers in 2018 (Bhuiyan, 2019). The two linked issues underlying this case were the organizational responses to sexual harassment (a key issue in the immediate wake of #MeToo) and the organizational restriction on workers' rights through the policy of having an enforced arbitration process for grievances that precluded the worker from taking their employer to court. The immediate flashpoint was Google's board of directors' approval of a $90 million payout to a male former Google executive despite the finding that a female worker's claims against him for serious sexual misconduct were credible. Perceiving that the employer-initiated voice mechanisms were not sufficient, workers organized themselves through an internal Listserv communication channel. Sensing widespread outrage, they initiated the walkout protest and demanded a reversal of the board's payout and an end to enforced arbitration. The latter demand was subsequently met by Google. A very similar process unfolded through the self-organizing of knowledge workers in the major Chinese tech firm Alibaba (Liu, 2023a: 313):

> In August 2021, as a protest against a workplace culture that discriminates against women, over 6000 tech workers signed an online petition demanding that their employer, Alibaba, investigate into what [workers] believed was a sexual crime in the workplace [by a senior male executive], as well as implement several institutional and policy changes intended to promote a better work environment.

Alibaba announced immediate action against implicated senior managers and set up a working party, led by women senior managers, to address the issue of suitable policy changes. Although key activists were sceptical about the likelihood of clear, concrete changes (Liu, 2023a: 322), one of them noted that 'at least ... it shows that the senior management is paying attention'.

Also in the tech sector in China was the 996 protest movement of 2019. This was aimed at limiting work effort and intensity, and it operated across the whole sector rather than being limited to a single firm (as in the Google and Alibaba examples). The name 996 refers to the standard expected work pattern in the tech sector in China: from 9 am to 9 pm, 6 days per week. The protest was focused against the intensity of work effort demanded in this work scheduling. This is clear in Liu's (2023b: 8) outline of the origins of the protest:

> A new user '996icu' created a project on a ... forum commonly visited by programmers around the world. As the project website stated in simplified Chinese, 996icu means 'the 996 schedule of work risks workers to the ICU (Intensive Care Unit)'. ... Within a month, this project went viral ... with thousands of workers flooding to the website to join the discussion, mostly making complaints about their job conditions.

A key flashpoint was the explicit support for 996 scheduling by Jack Ma, a major tech guru in China. He described the system as a 'huge blessing'. The protest was picked up in further social media and – very unusually for Chinese state media – it was portrayed sympathetically by state media. Specific demands were put forward to local governments for action regarding 996 scheduling, and protestors sent Jack Ma copies of the labour law to shame him for his support for the 996 system. Eventually, in 2021, the Supreme People's Court ruled explicitly that 996 was not legal within Chinese labour law.

Loose collectivities have played a central part in the development of resistive collective voice among platform workers. Cini et al (2022: 341) have noted that, 'since 2016, mobilizations of gig workers across European countries have become increasingly common within location-based services, such as food delivery'. Umney et al (2024) have developed a global dataset of media reports of platform-worker actions, ranging from withdrawals of labour (strike, or the platform equivalent of collective logging off) to protests via legal claims against platform companies. Crucially for this discussion, the authors have analysed the media reports in terms of how the platform workers are taking action – whether through established unions, new indie or grassroots unions, worker collectives, an informal group of workers or a law firm. They report that, globally, and indeed within all regions, the dominant pattern is that platform workers' collective resistive voice tends to be articulated through loose collectivities of workers – 80 per cent of disputes involve 'informal groups of workers', 20 per cent involve a 'workers' collective', 20 per cent involve a mainstream union and 13 per cent involve a grassroots, independent union (note that more than one type of collective voice mode may 'lead' a given action, so the numbers do not sum to 100 per cent). Where loose collectivities of workers are involved, the focus tends to be 'distributive' issues, such as pay. Typically, flashpoints for workers raising their collective voice involve a change announced by the firm either on the basis of payment (from an hourly pay rate to payment per gig) or the lowering of the pay rate (Cini et al, 2022). Notably, there is some emerging evidence of a shared emphasis on the importance of autonomy across both the organization of platform work and the mode of collective voice articulation by platform workers. Chapter 4 pointed to structured or subordinated agency as a core principle within the organization of platform work. This emphasis on self-determination and autonomy appears to be carried through into how platform workers raise their collective resistive voice. Cini et al (2022: 354) note that the Italian food delivery workers involved in the actions that they studied 'value highly the preservation of political and organizational autonomy in their mobilization practices'. Loose collectivities of workers are the mode of collective voice with the greatest space for such autonomy. Powell (2023) argues that, despite predictions that platform workers may start to turn to unions, it is likely that waves of uncoordinated collective resistive voice expressed through loose collectivities may be an enduring pattern.

Civil society organizations

The civil society organizations (CSOs) considered here cover community, identity-based, single-issue, campaigning and advocacy organizations (outside labour unions). Heery et al's (2012) careful study of CSOs shows that, collectively, they constitute 'a significant new actor' in UK employment relations.

Heery et al's study gives an indication of the breadth of organizations involved. CSOs that focused on discrimination and equality within employment included Age Concern, the Equal Pay & Opportunities Campaign, Stonewall, Arthritis Care, the Royal National Institute for Deaf People, Macmillan Cancer Support and Mind. CSOs that focused on caring and work-life issues included Carers UK, Counsel and Care, the Daycare Trust, One Parent Families Scotland and Working Families. CSOs concerned with protecting vulnerable workers included Citizens UK, Homeworkers World Wide, the National Group on Homeworking, the Migrant Rights Network and Refugee Action. Although many of the CSOs have a wider remit than work-related issues, Heery et al found that a substantial proportion of CSOs prioritize work-related activity. For instance, Stonewall, the LGBT rights organization, has not only consistently lobbied the government for stronger anti-discrimination laws and enforcement – contributing to the notable success of the introduction in 2003 of the Employment Equality (Sexual Orientation) Regulations that prohibit direct or indirect discrimination, victimization and harassment on the grounds of sexual orientation – it has also (Heery et al, 2012: 53):

> developed a substantial programme of work, including a Diversity Champions accreditation scheme for employers, an annual benchmarking survey, the Workplace Equality Index that is used to identify the top 100 gay-friendly employers in the UK, an annual Stonewall Workplace Equality Conference and a Leadership programme for gay and lesbian managers.

Significant impactful action has also been taken by Citizens UK (an arm of the US citizenship movement) (Heery et al, 2017). Citizens UK has a range of community, educational, religious and labour organizations as affiliated members. Citizens UK and its local chapters pursue a wide range of campaigns. The most significant is the Living Wage campaign. This calls for employers to pay all of their workers a Living Wage that is independently calculated, with the aim that it should provide 'for a decent, albeit modest standard of living, not conceived as minima' (Heery et al, 2017: 801). The Living Wage rate has been around 10–20 per cent above the state-arranged minimum wage. In its early years, the Living Wage campaign was rooted in migrant communities in East London, and it organized protests – which attracted considerable publicity – to shame corporations into raising the pay of workers such as cleaners and security guards to the Living Wage level (Wills, 2008; Wills and Lineker, 2014). Recently, it has moved more towards seeking to influence employers by making the argument that there is a 'corporate social responsibility' case against wages so low that they constitute in-work poverty. Over 3,000 employers have agreed to become accredited Living Wage employers, which has led to a direct rise in the wages of approximately 120,000 workers. Although this is not a trivial impact, Heery et al (2017) note the context that there are still six million workers being paid below the Living Wage rate. There is a strong case, however, that the Living Wage campaign's strongest effect has actually been an indirect one, by altering the terms of the debate on low pay. Notably, many large organizations, including the NHS in Wales and Scotland and some major supermarket chains, have agreed to pay the Living Wage, without becoming fully accredited Living Wage employers. More significantly, the UK government in 2016 took on much of the rhetoric of the Living Wage campaign when it effectively renamed the national minimum wage the National Living Wage. The government simultaneously increased the wage rate considerably for over-25s (although it is still well short of the Citizens UK Living Wage rate), and made the longer-term pledge that the rate should rise to two thirds of median earnings. This change in public policy is estimated to have raised the wages of around 1.6 million workers (Low Pay Commission, 2016).

Overall, although many CSOs tend to have activists rather than everyday workers as members, many of their actions can be seen as articulating the collective interests of different segments of the workforce (such as low-paid and LGBT workers). Heery et al (2012: 63) note that CSOs' voice on behalf of workers tends to have a distinct pattern: 'At lower levels, many CSOs have only an indirect presence at the workplace or enterprise, and focus their activity on the external labour market. At higher levels, there is a pattern of multiple engagement, principally targeting the UK state, but also embracing action at other scales.' This is in stark contrast to loose collectivities of workers that primarily operate at the workplace or enterprise level.

Kelly (1998) raises an important analytical issue regarding the rising importance of CSOs as a mode of articulating interests of workers (Heery, 2018). Kelly argues against a postmodernist understanding of the rise of CSOs and new social movements. A postmodernist approach sees the rise of CSOs and social movements here as emblematic of the increased polyvocality in the fractured social world, with an array of identity politics (for instance regarding sexual orientation), often pertaining more to the sphere of consumption than production, coming to dominate the terrain where class politics – based on a conflict between employers and workers, with *the* central voice role reserved for unions – used to hold sway. For instance, Piore and Safford (2006: 300) argue that social mobilization has fundamentally shifted 'from mobilization around economic identities associated with class, industry, occupation, and enterprise to mobilization around identities rooted outside the workplace: sex, race, ethnicity, age, disability, and sexual orientation'. Kelly (1998), writing from a Marxist perspective, argues that this portrayal of fundamental contrast between the two forms of politics is misplaced. Notably, new social movement and linked CSOs have concerns with their constituents in work settings as much as in consumption settings – a point subsequently supported, as noted, by the research of Heery et al (2012). Further, there is an important logic in the argument that the greater the power of employers and managers over workers generally, the more likely it is that specific characteristics of workers (such as sexual orientation) can be a point of disadvantage. This argument suggests considerable common ground between unions and class politics on the one hand, and new social movements and identity politics on the other. Kelly thus makes the case for a likely fusion between unions and new social movements. Here, Kelly's 1998 book *Rethinking Industrial Relations* makes much of the celebrated example of the support of gay and lesbian activists for striking miners in the 1984–85 coal-mining dispute (portrayed in the 2014 film *Pride*). Heery's (2018) perceptive article updates and supplements Kelly's argument regarding the potent fusion between unions and new social movements.

Jiang and Korczynski (2023) examine two cases of relations between CSOs and unions with regard the collective mobilization of migrant workers and point to a fundamental issue in the debate. In one case, of Polish factory workers, the CSO adopted a competing or contrasting framing between ethnicity and class and tended to work in tension with unions. By contrast, in the other case, regarding migrant domestic workers in London, the CSO adopted an intersectional approach, starting from the workers' lived experiences of migrant domestic workers and the interwoven ways in which class and ethnicity and migrant status tend to leave them marginalized, exploited and vulnerable. Here, the CSO, Justice 4 Domestic Workers, was able to work constructively with a union and develop the collective mobilization of the workers in an ongoing challenge to the power structures oppressing them. Connecting Jiang and Korczynski's observation with Kelly's fusion thesis, it appears that a form of intersectional politics is a fundamental process for the development of fusion as an outcome.

Heery makes the very important observation that Kelly's thesis of fusion is being played out in the contemporary articulation of workers' collective voice. He argues that the most important way that this has occurred is in the way that new social movements have affected unions. Heery (2018: 675) argues that unions have come to *absorb* new social movements and that this absorption 'has been one of the most powerful pressures shaping unionism over the past 50 years'. For example, regarding the union's internal representation of women (p 675):

> These changes include: setting up women's committees and conferences and establishing women's networks within unions; reserving seats for women on union decision-making bodies and delegations; appointing women's officers and other equality representatives who can prioritize the representation of

women's interests; and using women-only training courses and other measures to help women secure leadership and paid officer positions within unions. ... Internal representation of women and minorities within unions has often given rise to 'external representation': that is, the pursuit of their interests in political campaigning and lobbying, in litigation and in collective bargaining.

In Jiang and Korczynski's (2023) terms, unions, through the influence of CSOs and social movements, are moving towards articulating intersectional forms of collective voice (also Tapia et al, 2017). Notably, some unions have established general equality forums where groups representing women and minority interests can identify shared policy objectives (Briskin, 2008). This form of organizing to unite separate identity groups appears to be a clear mode of developing intersectional collective voice. Cornfield (2023) and Kochan et al (2023) emphasize the centrality of intersectional collective voice in their discussion of an upsurge in the labour activism in the US. All this leads to a consideration of ...

Labour unions

So far, this chapter has presented an analytical celebration of the vitality, imagination and strength shown in the development of workers' collective voice. In turning to consider labour unions, a different tone permeates the chapter: the wider context that workers' collective voice has been weakened through the rising power of employers over labour. This is the key context for understanding that union membership has been dropping across all countries for a number of decades. In some cases, the fall has been dramatic. In the UK, at the end of the 1970s, 54 per cent of the labour force were members of a union (Price and Bain, 1983). In 2021, the figure stood at 23 per cent (Department of Business, 2022).

Unions are organizations for fee-paying worker-members (the subscription is typically around £5 per week), which operate through democratic processes, for example voting on who is the leader and on whether to go on strike. Broadly, unions provide for members a mixture of collective representation (aiming to improve working conditions) and individual services (such as individual representation at complaints processes). Often, their collective representation occurs through a formal negotiation process with employers, known as collective bargaining. Blyton and Jenkins (2007: 220) make the important analytical point that the existence of unions fundamentally signals two things: that the interests of employers and workers are distinct, and that workers need to act *collectively* to, at least partly, offset the power of the employer.

Hyman (1997) argues that a useful way to analyse unions is to ask four analytical questions. Answering these questions is also a good way to understand the increasingly dominant 'organizing' strategy that unions are adopting as they attempt to revitalize themselves (Simms et al, 2017) and how that differs from the approach adopted by new, small, grassroots, or 'indie', unions that have emerged in recent years (Però, 2020). The first column of Table 6.1 is based on Hyman's questions. The other columns map the organizing approach adopted by long-standing unions, and the approach of indie unions.

Table 6.1: Two approaches to union strategy

	Main union 'organizing' approach	Indie unions' approach
Whom should unions organize?	Inclusionary approach	Marginalized, migrant workers
What interests of their members should unions prioritize in their actions?	Issues where there is conflict with management, but also attempt to move to bargaining relationship with employer	Moral demands for decent work conditions; no aim for formal bargaining relationship with employer
How should unions organize and represent their members?	Top-down push for greater membership participation	Member-led participatory democracy; forming coalitions in local communities
What is the ideology underlying their actions?	Implicit ideology of intersectional class conflict	Celebratory communities of struggle

Although there are some significant areas of overlap between the two approaches, there are also some points of difference. These differences can be understood by thinking of the emergence of indie unions as constituting a critique of the organizing approach at two key points.

First, although the organizing approach has been deliberately and explicitly an inclusionary one that seeks to include precarious, marginalized workers as much as the 'insider' constituency of workers with full-time, permanent employment contracts (Doellgast et al, 2018), in practice, sections of migrant workers have experienced mainstream unions as effectively continuing to exclude them. Però (2020: 905) quotes a leader of the indie union, the United Voices of the World: '[The union] was born ... due to a massive gap in the labour movement that simply wasn't addressing the needs of migrants. ... We are responding to a need.' Both Però (2020) and Cioce et al (2022) (regarding Italy) point to the greater sensitivity of the grassroots/indie unions to participative language translation among multi-ethnic migrant groups, and to the wider legal precarity that many migrants face, regarding the legal rights to work and to residence. Cioce et al (2022: 3) argue that what is at stake here in the relationship between precarious migrant workers and unions is a difference between, on the one hand, unions as 'participatory and multicultural projects' (as exemplified by emerging indie unions), and, on the other, unions as 'assimilationist facilitators in the society of arrival' (as exemplified by mainstream unions).

Second, the emergence of indie unions points to a fault-line in the main union organizing approach regarding the contradictions of a top-down push for member participation. In the wider context of the tension between representative and participatory democracy that pervades how unions organize themselves internally, Heery (2015) notes that, historically, moves towards greater participatory democracy in unions have been bottom-up and member-led. A leadership-led push to greater participatory democracy appears more difficult to achieve. Notably, studies emphasize the highly participatory forms of democracy within indie unions. Però (2020: 908) quotes Teresa, a cleaner and a founder of the indie union, Independent Workers' Union of Great Britain: 'Our union is run by workers, we take decisions with everyone ... we have meetings we consult everyone ... the worker has to have a voice and a vote ... workers gives us ideas on how to do things, how to help. ... We ensure members participate.'

In addition to bargaining with employers for better pay and conditions (with the back–up threat of striking to impose costs on the employer, if necessary), a key way in which unions have articulated a resistive collective voice, historically, has been through their political actions for enshrining improved conditions in employment law. In many countries, unions have played a key role in the founding of left–wing and social democratic political parties, and continue to play important roles in deciding policies, particularly regarding the sphere of employment, in those parties. For instance, in the UK, unions played a pivotal role in the founding of the Labour Party in 1900, and unions' support for a minimum wage was a key factor in the introduction of the first legal national minimum wage in the UK by the Labour government (as recently as 1998). The importance of employment law to long-standing mainstream unions also comes across in a tendency in how they have responded to the emergence of platform work. As noted, Umney et al's (2024) important overview of mobilization of platform workers shows that there are two distinct patterns to such collective voice. One, the more common, is led by loose collectivities and sometimes indie unions, and tends to have a focus on direct demands for higher pay and better conditions. The second, less common, tends to feature mainstream unions protesting for platform workers to be legally classed as workers/employees, so that they receive full access to employment law rights, such as the minimum wage and rights against unfair dismissal and discrimination. Here, unions are challenging the legal situation in many countries of accepting platforms' definition of platform workers as independent contractors, who, therefore, stand outside employment law.

The final important thing to consider in the analysis of unions is a sociological understanding of their current low membership numbers. Here, it is useful to return to the fundamental point of Blyton and Jenkins (2007), that unions represent two things – that workers understand that they have diverging interests from employers, and that workers understand that by acting collectively, they can effectively redress some of the power imbalance in the employment relationship. We can consider explanations of low levels of union membership in relation to each of these elements in turn. Regarding the first element, it could be that, now, only a small number of workers believe that their interests diverge in significant ways from those of their employer. Taking an overall view of the analysis of resistive norms, informal resistance and collective resistive voice in these two chapters, such a position appears difficult to sustain. Informal forms of (often collective) resistance appear still to be commonplace. Further, while union membership has fallen, there has been a rise in other modes for the articulation of workers' collective resistive voice (social media campaigns, loose collectivities, civil society organizations and some limited opportunity in employer-initiated voice mechanisms). This means that we are left with an explanation that centres on workers not seeing that collective action might be able to meaningfully redress some of the power imbalance in their employment relationship. Part of this relates to occupational trends, particularly the growth of knowledge-work occupations (as noted in Chapter 1; also Oesch and Piccitto, 2019). Given the strong labour market position of many knowledge workers (because of their high skills), many of them believe that they can act *individually* to meet their interests, for example by changing employers, by individually job crafting (Lazazzara et al, 2020) or by individually negotiating better pay. This was certainly the pattern found by Hyman et al's (2004) study of why software workers tend not to join unions. It is also relevant that workplace size in the high-wealth economies has reduced in recent decades. Recall the argument from Chapter 3 regarding the new international division of labour, with manufacturing increasingly located in low-wage parts of the global economy, and with high-wealth economies featuring more service and knowledge workplaces. Crucially, manufacturing workplaces are much larger than service and knowledge workplaces. Unionization tends to be lower in small workplaces. More fundamentally, this second element points to the logic that union membership is low because many workers do not believe that the union collective voice can be effective in redressing the power imbalance in the employment relationship (outlined in Chapter 3). They are, thus, less willing to pay membership fees to be part of a weak collective. Baccaro et al (2019: 7) suggest that 'if, under increased competitive pressure, negotiations become consultations, bargaining becomes concession bargaining and voice becomes mere expression, workers may be justified in wondering what trade unions are still for'. In the UK, highly restrictive laws imposed since the 1980s that significantly limit unions' ability to impose costs on employers, through strikes, solidarity strikes and picketing, make this observation even more telling.

Statutory workplace democracy mechanisms

> There is a ... paradox in the history of government in the West. The so-called absolutist monarchs of Europe overwhelmingly chartered republican [democratic] corporations – e.g., towns, universities, and guilds whose members elected their leaders. ... Yet, modern democracies themselves have overwhelmingly chartered authoritarian corporations – e.g. ... business corporations whose subjects have no vote. (Ciepley, 2023: 489)

It is the contrast between the explicitly proclaimed democracy of contemporary government systems and the lack of such democratic structures within people's everyday working lives that has informed movements for and debates about state-mandated forms of workplace democracy within firms. Many radical labour movements in Europe in the late 19th and early 20th centuries had, as a foundational aim, the establishment of workplace democracy (Gumbrell-McCormick and Hyman, 2019). Such workplace democracy was seen as both a good in itself and a foundation stone of a meaningfully democratic society. Across Europe, there has been a range of attempts to impose worker voice through law (Gumbrell-McCormick and Hyman, 2019: 92):

> One involved institutionalized collective representation at workplace level through councils or similar bodies, to provide collective voice in management

decisions. … A second envisaged employee representation on the decision-making boards of companies, with more ambitious versions providing parity between employee and shareholder representatives. A third set of solutions focused on 'direct participation' at the workplace, with the most radical versions envisaging workers' control of production, displacing the employer.

Overwhelmingly, such attempts, led by socialist (and sometimes social democratic) labour movements have been met by very strong resistance from employers, who call on arguments that the employer prerogative to direct labour derives from private property rights (Frega et al, 2019). This has meant that significant laws to mandate forms of workplace democracy have only been enacted in social junctures of crisis that present opportunities for radical changes to the prevailing institutions and norms, such as the context of revolutionary movements around the First World War, the immediate period after the Second World War and, partly, in the wave of democratizing protests in the late 1960s into the 1970s. Notably, there has been no significant surge of demand for workplace democracy since the 1970s in Europe. The Occupy protests that developed from North America, further to the global financial crisis of 2007 to 2009, articulated a broad democratizing ethos, but did not develop into a serious push for workplace democracy, partly because of the lack of connection to unions, civils society organizations and left-leaning political parties.

One of the strongest forms of statutory workplace democracy is in Germany, where there are elected worker representatives on the supervisory Board of Directors as well as works councils at the shop-floor level. Even here, however, commentators have noted significant limitations on the power of workers' collective voice, particularly in the context of recent decades of rising employer power. Notably, Streeck (2009), who, previously, had seen important benefits in the German workplace democracy structures – he had argued that they pushed German firms into adopting competitive strategies based on high-skill labour – argues that works councils are increasingly forced into company-level concession bargaining or else are bypassed by multinational employers. Jäger et al (2022) coldly note that existing codetermination laws convey little real authority to workers. Gumbrell-McCormick and Hyman (2019) make the strong case that, as capital has become global (think of MNCs and global commodity chains, discussed in Chapter 3), so national-firm forms of workplace democracy necessarily become stripped of significant power. In the UK, outside limited EU-level initiatives, there have been no statutory forms of workplace democracy. Union support for workplace democracy has historically been, at best, lukewarm, and employer opposition has been consistent and strong (Rees, 2023).

Worker-owned cooperatives

Worker-owned and worker-governed cooperatives are firms where 100 per cent of the equity is held by workers and where a system of democratic governance is enacted, often primarily through the principle of one person, one vote. The process of founding and running worker cooperatives can be seen as a form of resistive collective voice. Here, the resistance is at a different level and of a different form than most types of resistance covered so far in these two chapters. It is resistance not against a specific employer, or group of employers, but against how labour is organized and exploited under capitalism. Wiksell and Henriksson (2023: 1275) argue that worker-owned cooperatives are an example of 'constructive resistance', defined as 'the enactment – the construction – of alternative social orders in the here and now, that in the long run may replace undesired, dominant ways of organising society'.

The construction of alternative social relations of labour is present in the explicit principles underpinning worker cooperativism (Webb and Cheney, 2014). For instance, the principles adopted by the Mondragon group of cooperatives in the Basque region of Spain include not only 'democratic organisation' but also 'sovereignty of labour' and the 'instrumental and subordinate character of capital'. Workers' interests are thus positioned as of higher importance than that of capital. Equally fundamentally, the Mondragon principles also expound the aim of social transformation, understood as 'a process of expansion which will contribute to economic and social reconstruction and the creation of a Basque Society which is more free, just and solidary' (Ormaechea, 1993: 175). This is the aim not to coexist with capitalism, but to supersede it. Research into the nature of social relations within worker cooperatives tends to show a playing out of democracy, mutuality and a search for meaningful labour. The following quote from a member of a worker cooperative points to the sense of a profound difference in the social relations compared with when the firms were privately owned:

> I got here 30 years ago as last in line, and to find myself self-managing this factory here ... it's reaching an objective ... that is the maximum aspiration a worker that has been exploited can have, to say 'now nobody exploits me anymore, now it's my place [...] finally I feel at home'. (Giuseppe Terrasi, worker of the WRC Officine Zero metal works in Italy, quoted in Azzellini, 2018: 770)

This mirrors Zibechi's (2006: 352) discussion of Zanon, an Argentinian ceramics factory that the workers now own and govern:

> The difference between the current and previous management are striking ... 'We were not allowed to leave or go to the bathroom. ... It was like a jail' [stated one worker] ... [Now] once a month the factory calls a day-long meeting in which every member participates. It covers all topics – from the type of footgear necessary ... to the purchases they will make and external actions of solidarity in which they will participate. ... This way of functioning – democratic, participatory and horizontal – requires a lot of energy: 'It is exhausting, but it is productive because you find solutions to all of the problems, debating them with everyone.'

The Zanon worker cooperative is one of a wave of worker cooperatives in Latin America in which workers have tried to keep functioning previously privately owned firms that were about to close down (Azzellini, 2018). Azzellini estimates that there are 360 such worker-recuperated cooperatives in Argentina, involving 15,000 workers, and around 80 such cooperatives that employ 12,000 workers in Brazil. By contrast, most of the cooperatives in the UK are firms that were originally founded by the worker cooperators. In the UK, there are around 400 worker cooperatives, which are usually small- or medium-sized enterprises. Globally, there are several embryonic attempts by workers to develop worker-owned and -governed platform cooperatives (Cañada et al, 2023).

Research also shows that the tensions of the alternative social order that is the worker cooperative coexisting with a market that is dominated by private firms tend to lead to systematic tensions *within* cooperatives. Specifically, this becomes manifest in a tension between democratic – and, therefore, slow – decision-making and efficiency – demanded through market competition. Indeed, some scholars have put forward a 'degeneration thesis' that points to efficiency pressures inevitably leading to the de facto dominance of hierarchy over (increasingly empty) democratic structures within cooperatives (Cornforth, 1995). In recent decades, this has been countered by the practice of worker cooperators who, increasingly conscious of this endemic tension, become adept at reviewing and adapting their practices – for instance extending the tenure within job rotations where specialist knowledge in a role is important, and linking participatory and representative forms of democracy – in order to avoid degeneration (Webb and Cheney, 2014; Azzellini, 2018).

Voice in global supply chains

Chapter 3 began the analysis of global supply chains and pointed to their central role in the global economy. Chapter 4 argued that, through multinational corporations (MNCs) driving global supply chains, Taylorist work organization in manufacturing has been, to a significant degree, relocated from richer economies to emerging economies. This chapter now turns to consider workers' collective voice in global supply chains.

So far, the analysis of collective voice mechanisms has been conducted with two important, implicit assumptions: that there is a clear employing organization to which workers' voice is applied, and that this voice occurs within a given national–state boundary. However, neither of these conditions holds when it comes to the consideration of voice in global supply chains. Any given global supply chain may be driven and coordinated by a single identifiable MNC, but stages of production are dispersed across the globe in a network of suppliers. Recall the observation from Chapter 3 that Nike does not actually manufacture anything. The fact that these supply chains are located globally is very important for the potential operation of workers' collective voice. Because they occur outside of national–state boundaries, nations with emerging economies are put in a precarious position. If they enshrine strong labour rights and support the articulation of worker voice, they run the very real risk that MNCs may choose to relocate production to supplier firms based in a country with lower labour costs and weaker worker voice mechanisms. Indeed, there is an implication that national governments in emerging economies will tend to suppress workers' collective voice. This is part of the logic of the potential degradation of labour standards that is set in motion through the operation of global supply chains (noted in Chapter 3).

All this suggests that there are clear structural problems against workers autonomously establishing strong collective voice mechanisms at the sharp end of global value chain production. In this context, civil society organizations (mainly based in advanced economies) stepped forward to attempt to address the consequences of this structural collective voice vacuum. A key tactic of these civil society organizations has been to publicly shame MNCs at the head of global value chains regarding the labour conditions in which their (subcontracted) manufacturing activity occurs (Klein, 2001). Here, voice differs in two fundamental ways from the main modes of collective voice reviewed in this chapter. First, voice is made *on behalf of* rather than *by* the workers subject to poor conditions. Second, the power of collective voice here operates in the realm of consumption rather than in the realm of production (Reinecke and Donaghey, 2015). Campaigns are run to hurt the brand image of the MNCs and encourage consumers to boycott products linked to them. Klein (2001: 315) argues that the brand-centred marketing approach of many MNCs is highly vulnerable to such campaigns:

> If brands are indeed intimately entangled with our culture and our identities, when they do wrong, their crimes are not dismissed as merely the misdemeanours of another corporation trying to make a buck. Instead, many of the people who inhabit their branded worlds feel complicit in their wrong, both guilty and connected.

MNCs initially tried to distance themselves from the degrading work conditions highlighted in the brand 'jamming' campaigns run by civil society organizations, arguing that they were not responsible – that it was the responsibility of the subcontractors doing the manufacturing. However, such counter-arguments were quickly exposed as tenuous, and MNCs found themselves in as vulnerable a position as Klein suggests.

Cue the entry of 'corporate social responsibility' actions by MNCs who, realizing that they could not escape some responsibility for the harsh labour conditions in which their products were manufactured, turned to establish 'codes of conduct' regarding working conditions for the subcontracting firms in their global supply chains to abide by. Frequently, such codes of conduct were drawn up in *consultation* with civil society organizations, who were raising voice on behalf of workers exposed to poor conditions. Such codes of conduct can be thought of more as employer-led approaches to voice and working conditions than as independent voice mechanisms for workers. Reinecke and Donaghey (2023: 2) note that 'such private governance institutions show little concern with the democratic representation of those affected: workers and their representatives are not involved in social auditing'. Without meaningful independent worker collective voice either in the establishment of the codes of conduct or in the monitoring and enforcement of these codes, many commentators have criticized this MNC-led approach as, at best, lacking teeth and, at worst, as constituting a surface-level public-relations exercise regarding the problem (Klein, 2001). Locke (2013) argues that, while MNC-led approaches may lead to an initial improvement in labour standards in supply chains, this levels off when these standards meet the pressure of market competition within the supply chain model itself. Reinecke and Donaghey (2023: 14) position the deaths of over 1,100 Bangladeshi garment workers in the collapse of a manifestly unsafe building at Rana Plaza in 2013 (noted in Chapter 3) as occurring within the weak voice structures within the 'private governance' of labour standards: 'Without doubt, the sheer scale of the Rana Plaza disaster sent shock waves across the world. Yet over 1,100 people being killed in one site, on one day, was not an isolated event but an implication of Bangladesh being a paradigmatic case of the failure of democratic governance.'

It is becoming clearer to more and more commentators that there must be a central role for independent collective voice mechanisms for the organization and conditions of work to improve for workers at the sharp end of global supply chains. Klein (2001: 172) quotes a representative of the Workers' Assistance Centre in Rosario, the Philippines, saying that 'the more significant way to resolve these problems lies with the workers themselves, inside the factory'. Reinecke and Donaghey (2023) argue that such voice can be made up of unions directly representing the workers themselves, acting within the realm of production, as well as civil society organizations, who can pressure MNCs in the realm of consumption, acting on behalf of these relatively powerless workers. Pike (2020) studied a wider approach to governance of supply chains – the International Labour Organization's Better Works programme, which aims to involve global buyers, local governments, business and labour in social dialogue regarding compliance to labour standards and competitiveness. Pike highlights that a crucial element of this programme is its inclusion of labour at all levels of programme design, adoption, implementation, monitoring and evaluation. Pike finds that a meaningful voice of workers within the factories substantially helped the enforcement of standards. Echoing a wider theme of this chapter, Pike also argues that unions should not be thought of as the only form of meaningful collective voice for workers. Whether the meaningful collective voice of workers can come to be more widely articulated in the context of the logic of global supply chains, which works against such a voice, is, perhaps, the key question.

Sociological imagination – your turn

Think back to this section in Chapter 2. You were asked about the key points of tension and conflict that occurred in your job experience, or that of a friend. What mode of collective voice would be the best way for these points of tension and conflict to be raised and addressed? Consider both employer-led voice mechanisms and the wide array of independent, worker-led voice mechanisms discussed in this chapter. Consider *why* the voice mechanism you choose is the most appropriate one, and *why* other modes would be less appropriate.

7

Inequalities of Outcome: Income

This chapter and the one that follows focus on inequality related to work and employment. There are two key different forms of inequality in this regard. First, we can think about inequalities of *outcome*. The most important inequality of outcome in relation to employment is income inequality. That is the focus of this chapter. Most books giving an overview of the sociology of work have not considered overall income distribution or income inequality. Given that the distribution of income is a significant outcome of the social organization of work and employment, this is a curious omission. If Piketty (2013: 19) is correct when he argues that there is a 'need to put [income] distribution back at the heart of economic analysis', then there is clearly a corresponding need to put income distribution back at the heart of sociological analysis. This chapter focuses squarely on income inequality.

The second important type of inequality relates to inequalities of *opportunity*: systematic differences in the likelihood that different groups of people – for instance men and women – are able to occupy positions that give beneficial outcomes such as high income. Chapter 8 will focus on these inequalities of opportunity.

There are clearly important connections between these two types of inequality. For instance, if inequalities of outcome are very low, then the importance of inequalities of opportunity will lessen. Further, sometimes, these two types of inequality appear to blend into each other. Notably, in everyday speech, when people talk about class, they tend to use it in a way that links a particular type of outcome to a pattern of specific groups being more likely to occupy positions with that outcome. So, for example, if a person is described as being 'upper class', this tends to connote both that this person has a high-income position and that their educational and social background (as manifest in their spoken accent, for instance) has contributed to them occupying such a position. Here, the use of class in everyday speech relates to a persistence across generations of occupying a high-income position.

Despite the important connections between these two types of inequality, and despite the de facto blending of these types of inequality in everyday speech, our ability to analyse inequality is greatly aided by considering each type separately. That is why this chapter focuses on income inequality, as the key inequality of outcome, while Chapter 8 focuses on inequalities of opportunity.

First, this chapter lays out the building blocks needed to understand the key patterns of rising inequality of income. Then, it lays out those patterns, both in broad historical terms and in more detail regarding changes in recent decades. After that, we consider causes of the rise in income inequality. The last section of the chapter examines why rising income inequality matters, both in terms of health and social consequences and in terms of the issues that it raises for our understanding of class.

Building blocks for understanding income inequality

Before we can proceed to lay out the patterns of changing income inequality, we need to understand some basic elements in how income inequality is measured and to understand what elements are included in *income* inequality.

There is a range of measures of income inequality, and it is best to use a range of measures because, as Dorling (2019: 3) notes, 'inequality can be measured in many ways, and this can cause confusion'. There is little confusion, however, when the same pattern of rising inequality comes out strongly across analyses using different measures. Table 7.1 summarises the main measures of income inequality used in this chapter.

The overview in this section of changes in income inequality will reference the measures outlined in Table 7.1. The overview covers the UK, the US and (where possible) the European Union countries, by first giving a broad historical overview before focusing on the substantial changes since around 1980.

The main broad picture to be presented concerns changes in overall income inequality. Overall income comes from two sources. First, there is income from

Table 7.1: Measures of income inequality

Measure	Definition
Top 1% share	The share of the overall income earned in the country/region that is taken by the highest 1% of income earners. This measure has only come to be commonly used in the last two decades (Dorling, 2019).
Top 10% share	The share of the overall income earned in the country/region that is taken by the highest 10% of income earners.
Bottom 50% share	The share of the overall income earned in the country/region that is taken by the bottom 50% of income earners.
Gini coefficient	Named after the developer of the measure, Italian statistician, Corrado Gini, the Gini coefficient is a measure of income inequality across all income earners. It is an overall summary statistic of income inequality. The definition is a little too detailed to outline here (De Maio, 2007). The Gini coefficient ranges from 0 (representing perfect equality, where everyone earns the same income) to 1 (representing maximum inequality, where one person earns all of the nation's income). It has become commonly used in analyses of income inequality.

labour, comprising the wages that people earn in jobs. Second, there is the income that flows from ownership of capital. Capital here includes shares, bonds, savings, land and housing. Overall income inequality is affected by inequality in each of these sources of income. Here, it is worth stepping back to consider differences in sizes of inequality in these two sources. Inequality in income from capital ownership tends to be considerably higher than inequality in labour income. This holds true regardless of whether the society tends towards being more egalitarian or less egalitarian. As an example of a more egalitarian society, consider Scandinavia in the 1970s, at the height of the influence of socialist and social democratic parties in the Fordist era. In Scandinavian countries in the 1970s, all measures of inequality show that there was much greater inequality in capital ownership than in income from labour. For instance, the top 10 per cent share of capital ownership was 50 per cent, while the top 10 per cent share of labour income was much lower, at 20 per cent, and the overall Gini coefficient for capital ownership was 0.58, while the Gini coefficient for labour income was 0.19 (Piketty, 2013: 309–310). As an example of a highly unequal society, consider the US in 2010. Again, all measures of inequality show that there was much greater inequality in capital ownership than in income from labour. The top 10 per cent share of capital ownership was 70 per cent, while the top 10 per cent share of labour income was 35 per cent, and the overall Gini coefficient for capital ownership was 0.73, while the Gini coefficient for labour income was 0.36 (Piketty, 2013: 309–310).

The first sections of this chapter focus on *overall* income inequality. Overall income inequality is what emerges when people's income from labour and from capital ownership are combined. For a period of 50 to 60 years in the middle of the 20th century, there was a significant trend across advanced economies towards greater overall income equality. This led to Kuznets, an American economist, theorizing that although income inequality rises significantly in the first stages of industrial capitalism, as capitalist economies mature there are systematic tendencies (particularly the wide distribution of skill and knowledge) which will lead to a more equal distribution of income (see Piketty, 2013). However, as Piketty's widely praised important historical and geographical overview observes (2013: 19), 'since the 1970s, income inequality has increased significantly in the rich countries'. Overall income inequality has increased most significantly in the US and the UK.

Broad historical patterns

The graph in Figure 7.1 shows the changing share of income earned by the top 10 per cent of earners in the UK over a long historical period, from 1900 to 2020. The first pattern to note is that the top 10 per cent of income earners had a declining share of the overall income in the UK from 1900 until 1980. In 1900, the share of the income earned by the top 10 per cent was 56 per cent. By 1980, that stood at 29 per cent. The second notable pattern is that, after 1980, the share of income taken by the top 10 per cent of earners rose up to 36 per cent in 2020. This means that the top 10 per cent of earners' share in 2020 was the same as in the late 1930s, just before the start of the Second World War.

Figure 7.1: Top 10 per cent national income share, UK, 1900–2020

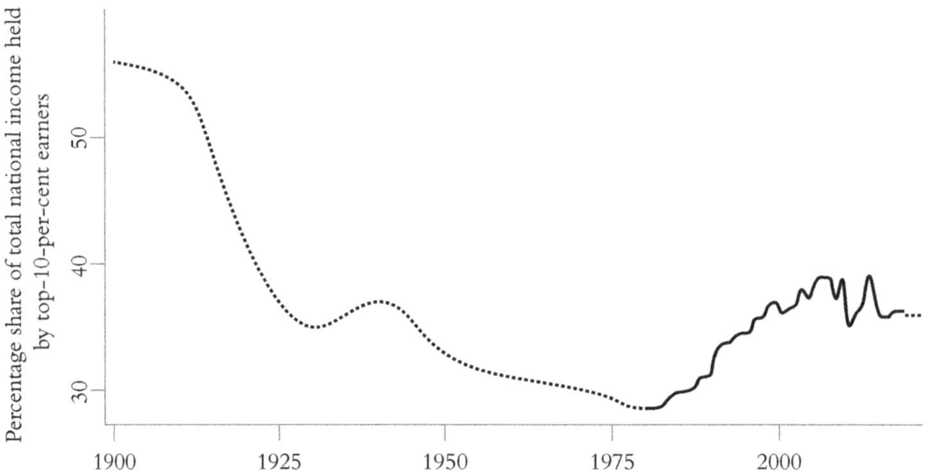

Note: The dotted line indicates an estimate based on extrapolations undertaken by the World Income Inequality database.
Source: World Inequality Database, shared under the Creative Commons licence 4.0

For the US, for the same time period, the share of income going to the top 10 per cent of income earners actually increased between 1900 and 1940 – from 40 to 49 per cent. Then there was decline until 1980, when the share going to the top 10 per cent was at the lowest point of the period – 34 per cent. From 1980, there was a sharp rise in the proportion of income going to the top 10 per cent, and in 2021, the share stood at 46 per cent. This is the same share as was taken by the top 10 per cent a century earlier, in 1919.

There is no similar data for the European Union countries as a whole, but it is possible to look at the same measure in Italy and Germany as two example countries. The pattern in both countries is similar to that in the UK. In Italy, in 1900, the share of income going to the top 10 per cent was as high as 58 per cent. This then fell to 28 per cent in 1980. Then there was a sharp rise, with the share in 2020 standing at 37 per cent. In Germany in 1900, the proportion of income going to the top 10 per cent of earners was 55 per cent. In 1980, the proportion was at its lowest for the period, standing at 29 per cent. In 2020, the figure had risen to 38 per cent.

Since 1980

The overview of the broad historical pattern showed a general decline in (one measure of) income inequality until 1980, and then a rise. This section of the chapter focuses on giving more detail, covering a range of measures, on the changes since 1980.

The UK

Table 7.2 gives information on four measures of income inequality in the UK in 1980 and 2018, and the proportional changes (taking 1980 as the base) between those two dates. The Gini coefficient, the statistic covering the nature of inequality across the

Table 7.2: Rise in income inequality across multiple measures, UK, 1980–2018

Measure of inequality	1980	2018	Proportional change
Top 1% share	7%	13%	+86%
Top 10% share	29%	36%	+24%
Bottom 50% share	23%	20%	−13%
Bottom 10% share	0.4%	0.3%	−25%
Gini coefficient	0.41	0.47	Not applicable

Source: Original analysis from data at the World Inequality Database website

Figure 7.2: Income distribution by decile, UK, 2018

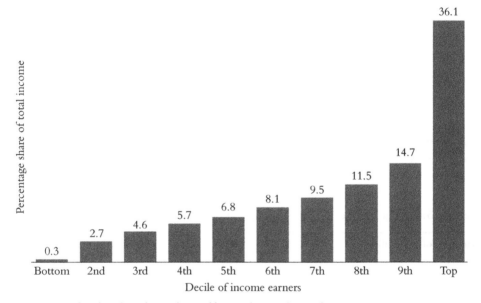

Source: Original analysis from data at the World Inequality Database website

whole of income earners, has risen from 0.41 in 1980 to 0.47 in 2018. Indeed, all of the measures in Table 7.2 show a rise in income inequality. The sharpest rise occurred in the share taken by the top 1 per cent of income earners. This nearly doubled – from 7 to 13 per cent. Notably, while the share accruing to higher-income earners rose, the share going to lower-income earners fell by 25 per cent.

It is worth considering the overall nature of income distribution in the UK after the sharp rise in income inequality from 1980 to 2018. Figure 7.2 gives a cross-sectional picture of income distribution in the UK in 2018. The vertical axis shows the share of the overall income that is earned by each of the ten deciles of income earners. The bottom 10 per cent of income earners is labelled as the 'bottom' decile on the horizontal axis, and the next 10 per cent of income earners is the '2nd' decile and so on. Figure 7.2 shows that income inequality is most pronounced at the top and bottom of the distribution. The top 10 per cent of earners accrued 36 per cent of the total income earned. The bottom two deciles of income earners – a fifth of income earners – together received only 3 per cent of the total income.

The US

Despite the US being a country with considerably higher income inequality than the UK in 1980, income inequality there between 1980 and 2020 rose even more sharply than in the UK. Table 7.3 gives information on four measures of income inequality in the US in 1980 and 2020, and the proportional changes (taking 1980 as the base) between those two dates. The sharp rise in overall income inequality comes out in the Gini coefficient, which rose from 0.45 to 0.57. The most dramatic changes were at the top and the bottom of the income distribution. The top 1 per cent of income earners experienced an 80 per cent rise in their share of overall income (up from 10 per cent to 18 per cent), while the bottom 10 per cent of income earners saw their share of overall income fall by 73 per cent (from 1.1 per cent to 0.3 per cent).

The European Union

Overall, for the EU countries in the period 1980–2020, Table 7.4 shows that there was also a rise in income inequality across all measures. However, the rise in income inequality was less pronounced than in the UK and the US. Notably, the Gini coefficient rose relatively modestly – from 0.44 to 0.48. In common with the UK and

Table 7.3: Rise in income inequality across multiple measures, US, 1980–2020

Measure of inequality	1980	2020	Proportional change
Top 1% share	10%	18%	+80%
Top 10% share	34%	44%	+30%
Bottom 50% share	20%	14%	−30%
Bottom 10% share	1.1%	0.3%	−73%
Gini coefficient	0.45	0.57	Not applicable

Source: Original analysis from data at the World Inequality Database website

Table 7.4: Rise in income inequality across multiple measures, EU, 1980–2020

Measure of inequality	1980	2020	Proportional change
Top 1% share	8%	12%	+50%
Top 10% share	31%	36%	+16%
Bottom 50% share	21%	19%	−10%
Bottom 10% share	0.3%	0.2%	−33%
Gini coefficient	0.44	0.48	Not applicable

Source: Original analysis from data at the World Inequality Database website

the US, however, the sharpest change was at the very top of the income distribution. The share of income accruing to the top 1 per cent of income earners rose from 8 per cent to 12 per cent – a proportional rise of 50 per cent.

Causes of rising income inequality

The previous section has provided an overview of research which shows that, since around 1980, there has been a dramatic rise in overall income inequality in advanced economies. This trend is at its strongest in the US and the UK. The shift has been so profound that it has effectively reversed the declining inequality that occurred during the middle decades of the 20th century. Atkinson and Jenkins (2020: 265) note that 'income inequality in the UK today is at least as high as it was just before World War 2'. Piketty (2013: 320) observes that, in the US in the 2010s, 'income from labor is about as unequally distributed as has ever been observed anywhere'. This research has now clearly dispelled the previous prevailing argument of Kuznets that there was a longer-term trend within the development of capitalism towards lower income inequality.

The focus of this section is upon considering the causes of this dramatic rise in overall income inequality. Given that Piketty's research has been pioneering in systematically laying out the scale of the change in income inequality, it is appropriate to start by considering his analysis of what has led to the rise in overall income inequality. Piketty's (2013) basic thesis is that there have been two separate things going on. First, he points to 'the rise of supermanagers'. He refers (p 379) to the emergence of 'top executives of large firms who have managed to obtain extremely high, historically unprecedented compensation packages for their labor'. Rather than 'supermanagers', it would be more appropriate to call them 'super-remunerated managers'. Fundamentally, Piketty derives this point from two observations. His first is that the most important element driving the dramatic rise in overall income inequality has been the increasing share of income claimed by the top 1 per cent of income earners.

Consider the data in Tables 7.2, 7.3 and 7.4. These show big rises in the share of national income taken by the top 10 per cent of income earners between 1980 and 2020 in the UK, US and EU countries. However, if we look in more detail, we see that a massive part of this rise has actually gone to the top 1 per cent of earners. For instance, Table 7.2 shows that the share of income in the UK claimed by the top 10 per cent of earners rose by 7 per cent (from a 29 per cent share to a 36 per cent share), and that nearly all of this rise went to the top 1 per cent of earners, whose share went up 6 per cent (from 7 to 13 per cent). Similarly, Table 7.3 shows for the US that, although the share going to the top 10 per cent rose by 10 per cent (from 34 to 44 per cent), a huge share of this went to just the top 1 per cent, whose share rose by 8 per cent (from 10 to 18 per cent). The top 1 per cent are the core of the dramatic rise in overall income inequality. Dorling (2019) concurs that these disproportionate gains made by the top 1 per cent are the key element in rising inequality in the UK. He makes this plain in the title of his book: *Inequality and the 1%*.

The second observation that underpins Piketty pointing to the importance of the rise of super-remunerated managers is that most of the rising share taken by the top 1 per cent has come from increasing wages, or income from labour. Focusing on the US, as the trend-leading case, Piketty (2013: 374) writes that the increase in the share of overall income taken by the top 1 per cent 'was largely the result of an unprecedented increase in *wage* inequality'. This dramatic rise in wage inequality was due to 'the emergence of extremely high remunerations at the summit of the wage hierarchy, particularly among top managers of large firms' (p 374). For Piketty, there has been 'a veritable separation of the top managers of large firms from the rest of the population' (p 32). This can be shown by considering the ratio of wages of a Chief Executive Officer compared with the average worker in their firm, and particularly the changes in this ratio. For the US, Mishel and Davis (2015) report statistics for the 350 private-sector firms with the largest revenues, regarding the average compensation (income plus stock-option bonuses) ratio between a CEO and the average worker in the industries covered. In 1978, the ratio was 30:1. In 2014, the ratio had risen dramatically to 303:1. For the UK, Kay and Hildyard (2020: 4) note that 'research suggests that the average FTSE 100 CEO is now paid around 126 times the average UK worker, compared to "only" 58 times in 1999'.

If the rise of super-remunerated managers is a core part of the story of the sharp rise in inequality of overall income, this still begs the question of why this rise has occurred. Piketty (2013: 32) rhetorically notes that 'one possible explanation of this is that the skills and productivity of these top managers rose suddenly in relation to those of other workers'. This, however, appears implausible. Piketty's main alternative explanation is that there was a profound change in the social norms that allowed corporations' remuneration committees to propose such high compensation packages for their senior executives. He suggests that the change in social norms was at its sharpest in the US and the UK, where the rise in super-remunerated managers was most dramatic. Even Piketty concedes, however (p 420), that this explanation 'only shifts the difficulty to another level. The problem is now to explain where these social norms come from'.

A basic sociological interjection here is that such social norms must be seen as related to and embedded in the social structures of the economy. This takes us back to the debates considered in Chapter 3 regarding the nature of contemporary capitalism, and asks us to dig even deeper into those debates. This is certainly a task for this section. However, before (re)turning to those debates, it is appropriate to conclude a full consideration of Piketty's analysis of rising inequality.

I noted that Piketty's analysis is that there have been *two* separate things going on that have informed the dramatic rise in overall income inequality. The first is the rise of the super-remunerated managers. The second is that, since 1980, there has been a greater share of the overall income going to capital-ownership rather than to labour (in wages). Recall the point that overall income comes from two sources: income from labour – comprising the wages that people earn in jobs – and income that flows from ownership of capital – shares, bonds and so on. Piketty's point is that a second major reason for the rise in overall income inequality is that *proportionally* more income is going to ownership of capital than to remuneration for the performance of labour. In socio-economic literature, this is discussed as a rise in the capital share of overall income (Fligstein and Goldstein, 2022). Piketty's meticulous data (2013: 278) show that, after falling for much of the 20th century, 'capital's share of income increased in most rich countries between 1970 and 2010'. Further, this was a large increase (p 278): 'capital income absorbs between 15 percent and 25 percent of national income in rich countries in 1970, and between 25 percent and 30 percent in 2000–2010'. If it is clear that there has been a greater share of income going to capital, this is important because, it was noted earlier, there is *much* greater inequality regarding capital ownership than regarding labour income. The bottom 50 per cent own barely 5 per cent of capital. So, if more income is accruing to the area where high inequality is structurally present, this will necessarily be part of the explanation of growing overall inequality.

If rising capital share of income is the second key part of the story of the sharp rise in overall inequality, we still have to ask the further logical question: what has been the cause of the rising capital share? Piketty's (2013) argument is a rather technical, economic one concerning a fundamental tendency for high returns to capital (relative to returns to labour) during longer periods of low growth, such as existed in the recent decades of rising inequality. Many commentators (Fligstein, 2014; Langman and Smith, 2018) have noted that again Piketty's unpicking of the key sources of growing inequality is stronger than his analysis of fundamental causes. Piketty warns (2013: 27) that 'one should be wary of any economic determinism in regard to inequalities of wealth and income', but then appears immediately to forget this danger in putting forward his argument.

It is appropriate here to make connections with scholarship on financialized capitalism and shareholder-value capitalism examined in Chapter 3. This is a literature that fundamentally has a focus on the changing nature of power embedded within the structures of capitalism. Occasionally, this is a view that Piketty sides with, but which he tends not to keep to: 'the history of inequality is shaped by the way economic, political and social actors view what is just and what is not just, as well as by the relative power of those actors, and the collective choices that result' (2013: 27–28). There have been a number of studies that seek to draw direct connections between the emergence of structures of financialized/shareholder-value capitalism and the development of rising overall income inequality (such as Huber et al, 2022). For instance, Flaherty's (2015: 417) study of 14 advanced economies finds that 'financialization has significantly enhanced top income share'. It is worth noting immediately that both developments – moves towards financialized capitalism and the advent of rising inequality – started simultaneously at the end of the 1970s and the beginning of the 1980s. Further, the research linking financialized capitalism to rising inequality has focused on both of the key patterns in rising inequality carefully pinpointed by Piketty: the disproportionately rising wages of the top 1 per cent of wage earners (the super-remunerated managers) and the rising capital share of overall income. Overall, the research points to a common fundamental cause of both of these key patterns. Fligstein and Goldstein (2022: 203) explain that, 'at the same time as shareholder value capitalism increased wage inequality among employees, the overall share of income going to employees also declined'.

Scholarship on financialized/shareholder-value capitalism points to the reorienting of corporations to maximizing short-term returns to shareholder investors. Fligstein and Goldstein (2022: 194) note that, although senior managers were initially resistant to this considerable change in the nature of the firm, 'managers came to adopt the shareholder-value orientation largely as a result of equity-based executive compensation'. In other words, senior managers' pay came to be directly linked to their ability to drive high short-term investor returns. Following the logic of that statement makes a link to both key elements highlighted by Piketty in the rise in overall income inequality. First, it points to the key mechanism through which the rise of super-remunerated managers occurred. Second, it shows that firms became structures that focused on raising the share of income going to capital ownership. One of the consequences of firms focusing on increasing short-term capital returns is to strengthen a drive to weaken unions – because unions lead to a greater capture of income for the performance of labour. De-unionization also raises wage inequality (Kollmeyer, 2018). This can be seen as a second-order effect of financialized capitalism on inequality. Fligstein and Goldstein (2022) argue that there are many such second-order effects.

Overall, the structures of financialized/shareholder-value capitalism may directly lead to greater inequality, but just as important is that they set in play a logic of consequences that frequently leads to rising inequality. For instance, Tridico's (2018) study of 25 advanced economies between 1990 and 2013 found a direct effect of financialization and a number of second-order effects. Tridico writes (p 1009) that the results 'clearly suggest that the increase in inequality over the past two decades is caused by an increase in financialization, a deepening of labour flexibility, the weakening of trade unions and the retrenchment of the welfare state'.

Finally, it is appropriate to make a connection between platform work (a thread in this book) and the argument that the rise of financialized/shareholder-value capitalism is a key factor driving rising income inequality. Fundamental to platform firms' business model is the stripping away of workers' rights to create greater shareholder returns. This approach fits perfectly into the logic of shareholder-value capitalism. Platform firms have completely thrown away the idea that there are multiple stakeholders in a firm whose interests need to be articulated and 'balanced' in some way. The logic of the platform firm business model points to a rise in the share of income going to capital compared with the share going to labour. Joyce and Stuart (2021: 174) note that:

> in the European Union, companies engaging a workforce on self-employed terms save the equivalent of around 25 per cent of their wages bill, by avoiding social security payments and other labour taxes, including paid vacations and entitlements for maternity leave. Moreover, in most jurisdictions, minimum wage regulations do not apply to self-employed workers.

Why rising income inequality matters

The dramatic rise in income inequality since around 1980 matters in a number of important ways. This section first considers health and social consequences of rising income inequality, and associated causal mechanisms for these consequences, before considering the implications for the sociology of class analysis.

Negative health and social consequences of income inequality at the societal level

At the same time as research was beginning to show the rise in income inequality, a quite independent stream of research was developing that began to investigate negative health and social consequences of income inequality. Much of this research was undertaken by health epidemiologists. Epidemiology is a good cousin to sociology in that it is concerned with analysing patterns of heath and disease in groups and across whole populations – rather than the health of any given individual. This considerable body of research was brilliantly distilled by Wilkinson and Pickett in their book *The Spirit Level* (2010) (also Pickett and Wilkinson, 2015). They show that the research overwhelmingly finds, when comparing whole populations – for instance populations of different countries – that, the greater the income inequality is, the worse the health outcomes are, across a range of measures. It is important to be clear that this link is *not* between overall country income and health outcomes in that country. For advanced economies, after a certain level of national income is achieved, 'there is no relationship between average income levels and health outcomes' (Picket and Wilkinson, 2015: 323). The relationship is between income *inequality* and negative health outcomes – at the societal level.

The body of research shows that, the higher the income inequality in a society:

- the lower the average life expectancy;
- the higher the rate of infant mortality;
- the greater the incidence of mental illness;
- the greater the incidence of drug and alcohol addiction;
- the greater the incidence of obesity.

A useful way to make these relationships clear is to consider the relationship between inequality and life expectancy. Wilkinson and Pickett (2010) ask us to consider two babies. Baby A is born in the US, one of the richest countries in the world. Baby B is born in one of the poorer advanced economies, Greece, where average income is around half that of the US. Whereas in the US the average person spends $6,000 on healthcare, in Greece the figure is less than $3,000. Wilkinson and Pickett ask (p 80), 'surely, Baby B's chances of a long and healthy life are worse than Baby A's?' However, because the US has much higher income inequality than Greece, the answer is that (p 80), 'in fact, Baby A, born in the US, has a life expectancy of 1.2 years *less* than Baby B, born in Greece'.

At the same time as this research was developing within epidemiology, a parallel research stream was developing in criminology that considered relationships at the societal level between income inequality levels and negative crime-related outcomes. The same pattern of findings emerges. At the societal level, higher income inequality is associated with: higher homicide rates, higher imprisonment rates (Wilkinson and Pickett, 2010) and higher levels of violence (Pickett and Wilkinson, 2015). As these links in health and criminology research became established, researchers began to look at associations, at the societal level, between income inequality and a range of negative social outcomes. There are now bodies of evidence linking, at the societal level, income inequality to lower levels of trust, lower levels of children's educational performance and higher rates of teenage pregnancy. Another important finding (and one that we return to in the following chapter on inequality of opportunity and social mobility) is that income inequality at the societal level is strongly linked to lower social mobility. This means that, in the societies with higher levels of income inequality, like the UK and the US, the rates of social mobility – the rates of people moving between classes – are much lower than in countries with lower levels of income inequality.

Many criticisms were raised following the publication of *The Spirit Level*, but Wilkinson and Pickett wrote a robust response to the key points of the criticism (2010: 273–300). They emphasized that they were summarizing bodies of accumulated research from a range of academic disciplines. Further, Pickett and Wilkinson (2015) carefully argue that not only is higher income inequality, at the societal level, linked to the range of negative outcomes just noted, but it is a causal link. The argument is that income inequality *causes* these negative outcomes. Pickett and Wilkinson lay out the key criteria for arguments of causation within the discipline of epidemiology – consistency, temporal order, the absence of alternative explanations and plausibility – and argue that these criteria are met.

Perhaps the least convincing element in Wilkinson and Pickett's case concerning causation relates to the causal mechanism that they point to as linking, at the societal level, higher income inequality and worse health and social outcomes. An argument regarding causation should have at its heart a convincing outline of the processes that lead from cause (higher income inequality) to effect (worse health and social outcomes). In their key works (Wilkinson and Pickett, 2010; Picket and Wilkinson, 2015), they elusively point to a group of linked causal processes. They argue that 'inequality affects the whole social fabric' (Wilkinson and Pickett, 2013: 176). Income inequality worsens social relations in the sense that (Pickett and Wilkinson, 2015: 323) 'income inequality is linked to lower social cohesion and generalised trust, suggesting that it acts as a social stressor'. Further, they tend to emphasize that this inequality as a social stressor becomes particularly manifest in social interactions between poorer and richer, where they see a tendency for people with lower incomes to internalize a sense of shame, a sense of their lesser worth. Peacock et al (2014: 391) note that 'invidious shaming comparisons ... are emphasised in *The Spirit Level*'. A very strong example of this process comes from research by Charlesworth (2000). The example (quoted by Wilkinson and Pickett, 2013: 165) concerns a working-class man's experience in a social security/unemployment benefit office in Rotherham:

> I went in to the social [Social Security Office] the other day ... there were chairs and a space next to this stuck-up cow, you know, slim, attractive, middle class, and I didn't want to sit with her, you feel you shouldn't ... I became all conscious of my weight, I felt overweight, I start sweating, I start bungling, shuffling, I just thought 'no, I'm not going to sit there, I don't want to put her out', I don't want to feel that she's put out, you don't want to bother them ... you know you insult them ... the way they look at you like they're disgusted ... they look at you like you're invading their area ... you know straight away ... you feel 'I shouldn't be there'.

Sennett and Cobb's (1973) study of working-class men in Boston in the 1970s came up with the term 'the hidden injuries of class' to encompass such experiences (see also Sayer, 2005). More recently, Owen Jones argues that we can see the mainstream shaming of working-class people in the UK in the widespread use of the derogatory label 'chavs' (2020: 23):

Comedians dress up as chavs for our amusement in popular sitcoms such as *Little Britain*. Our newspapers eagerly hunt down horror stories about 'life among the chavs' and pass them off as representative of working class communities. Internet sites such as 'ChavScum' brim with venom directed at the chav caricature.

Jones (2020: 27) argues that it is the high inequality in the UK that gives rise to this phenomenon: 'Chav-hate is ... in part ... the product of a deeply unequal society'.

The argument of Wilkinson and Pickett that a key causal mechanism in the connection between higher inequality and worse health and social outcomes lies in interactions involving shaming between richer and poorer has, however, been subject to criticism. Notably, Peacock et al (2014) argue that Wilkinson and Pickett's approach is sociologically thin primarily because it neglects the agency of people in creating frames of meaning in which they can protect themselves from shame. They reference Lamont's (2000) study of French and US male workers which shows that both sets of workers created meanings that in part protected them from invidious social comparison with the richer in their societies, although the French workers were more successful here in that they drew on a *collective* sense of class position. There is an overlap here with the findings of research (noted in Chapter 5) in 'dirty work' occupations, which show how workers collectively create patterns of meaning that protect them from negative social stigma.

Furthermore, if shaming social interactions between poorer and richer are an important part of the causal mechanism from higher inequality to worse health and social outcomes, we should expect that research within the sociology of work would have found such shaming to be a common pattern where workers in low-wage service jobs provide services to high-income customers and clients. However, this is *not* a common finding in studies of such service jobs. For instance, Sherman's (2007) study of workers and wealthy customers in luxury hotels in the US finds that neither do customers disdain workers nor do workers tend to resent the customers. Even if patterned deference is embedded within key aspects of the labour process (Hanser, 2008; Chen, 2023) – for instance in the unreciprocated terms of address ('Sir', 'Madam') from service worker to customer – this does not mean that service workers tend to experience social shame in service interactions.

Overall, there is further research needed on the causal mechanism between higher income inequality and worse health and social outcomes, at the societal level (Patel et al, 2018). Indeed, even Pickett and Wilkinson admit that further research is needed to develop understanding of the causal processes (2015: 324). It may be that the focus on shaming interactions can only give limited insight, and that a more fruitful avenue of research could focus on the more direct causal route of the social meanings people create regarding relative incomes.

Implications of rising income inequality for the sociology of class

Here, we examine what the implications of rising income inequality are for sociological thinking, particularly whether such rising income inequality should lead to greater attention to the concept of *class*. Historically, class has been one of the most contested concepts within sociology (Crompton, 2008). For the purposes of giving a quick, broad overview, it is possible to point to three main approaches to class within sociology.

The Marxist approach centres on Marx's core idea that class relates to people's relationship to the means of production. In capitalism, the means of production is capital, and so there are fundamentally two classes: one that owns the means of production – the capitalist class (the bourgeoisie) – and one that does not own capital but only labour power to sell to the capitalist class – the working class (the proletariat). In light of the lack of emergence of two such sharply delineated classes, subsequent Marxist-informed analyses of class have also attended to the importance of authority and control within the labour process (Wright, 2015).

The second main approach to class is the Weberian one. Like Marx, Weber also saw the selling of labour as central to the definition of class, but he differed from Marx by specifying a range of market situations in which the sale of this differentiated labour was associated with different levels of rewards, giving rise to different classes. There is an important element of this Weberian approach in the sociological approaches of laying out a gradient of classes. This approach, in turn, informed official state classification schemes. In the UK, this was through the National Statistics Socio-Economic Classifications (Crompton, 2008). A typical classification is (Crompton, 2008: 65):

1. Higher managerial and professional occupations
2. Lower managerial and professional occupations
3. Intermediate occupations
4. Small employers and self-employed workers
5. Lower supervisory and technical occupations
6. Semi-routine occupations
7. Routine occupations
8. Never worked and long-term unemployed.

The third important approach to class analysis is the one informed by French sociologist Pierre Bourdieu. Bourdieu emphasizes the importance of hierarchical distinction that groups make between each other through patterns of culture, taste and lifestyle (1984). Sociologists have seen this as a key way to examine how classes coalesce and how the potential for social mobility for people between classes is, in practice, highly limited. Umney (2018: 19) says: 'Bourdieu provides a very good way of explaining why social inequalities do not change, and why there is little social mobility.' Umney (2018: 21) also makes a sharp statement to show the difference between a Marxist and a Bourdieusian approach to understanding class:

> Someone who depends on selling their time and skills in exchange for a wage may have conflicting interests with someone who depends on making a profit by manufacturing and selling goods at a competitive price. This is the case even if they both have the same views on the relative value of the opera versus *The X Factor*, have the same accents and went to the same school.

Wright (2015), discussing the debates over the nature of class, made the acute observation that the usefulness of a specific concept of class relates to the research question being addressed. The key research questions, further to the rise of income inequality, are whether class is useful in making sense of the rising inequality of income, and if so, which concept of class? The three most notable features in the rise in income inequality are:

- The rise has been substantial over a sustained period since around 1980, such that current levels of income inequality are historically high.
- One of the key sources of rising income inequality has been the greater share of income going to capital rather than to labour.
- The second key source of rising income inequality has been the dramatic pulling away by the top 1 per cent of those earning income from labour (the rise of the super-remunerated managers).

Further to the first point, it is noteworthy that income inequalities in many advanced economies are at levels equivalent to historical high points. Given that it has been common to refer to societies at these historical high points as *class* societies, a prima facie case can be made that it may now be appropriate to understand current societies as strongly informed by class-based inequalities. Acknowledging that class has become a much less common term in everyday speech and thinking, Crompton (2008) argues that class can still be a potentially useful analytical concept for sociologists.

So, which concept of class would be the most appropriate to use? The strength of the Bourdieusian approach to class relates primarily to the issue of (im)mobility between classes. The issue of immobility is not part of the focus here on patterns of income inequality, so it is reasonable to say that we need not turn to a Bourdieusain approach in characterizing current societies with a high degree of income inequality as class societies.

Although the Weberian approach to class does consider patterns of income inequality, there are also some problems in trying to apply this approach to the current rise in income inequality. First, the Weberian approach can do little to account for changes in the share of overall income going to capital rather than to labour. Second, the Weberian approach emphasizes the range of differentiated market situations for selling labour and consequently the range of differentiated class categories, which is out of kilter with the rise in income inequality not being about a broad stretching of income brackets but being primarily about the pulling away of the super-remunerated managers.

Finally, what of the relevance of a Marxist approach to class? The Marxist emphasis on differentiating a capitalist class and a class dependent on money from selling labour power does resonate with the rising share of overall income that is going to capital rather than labour. Further, a Marxist approach could point to the pulling away of the top 1 per cent of those earning income from labour as part of the development of two fundamentally distinct classes, with the super-remunerated managers becoming part of the capitalist class. Indeed, this is precisely the point made by Duménil and Lévy (2018) whose broad argument is that contemporary economies are forms of 'managerial capitalism'. It may be that the terms partly popularized by the 2011 Occupy! protests – differentiating the 1 per cent and the 99 per cent – are becoming the new way to talk about class (curiously, of course, without talking directly about class) in a way that resonates with patterns of overall income inequality.

Sociological imagination – your turn

This chapter has summarized research showing that overall income inequality levels have risen dramatically since around 1980 such that they are at levels similar to the highest levels in the early part of the 20th century. Do you find convincing the argument put forward that this rise in income inequality is due to the rise of financialized capitalism? What could other causes of rising income inequality be?

The chapter also outlined debates concerning the causal mechanisms and processes, at the societal level, between higher income inequality and a range of negative health and social outcomes. What do *you* think is the most likely causal mechanism between higher income inequality and negative health and social outcomes?

8

Inequalities of Opportunity

The introduction to Chapter 7 pointed to two important types of inequality. This chapter focuses on the second important type: inequality of *opportunity* – systematic differences in the likelihood that different groups of people (for instance people born to working-class or upper-class parents) are able to occupy positions that provide beneficial outcomes, such as high income. The chapter examines, in turn, four types of inequality of opportunity: overall social (im)mobility, barriers related to gender, barriers related to ethnicity and global inequality between countries as a context for international migration. As in previous chapters, woven in are examples from customer service work, knowledge work and platform-mediated jobs, where appropriate.

Overall social immobility

This section focuses on overall social (im)mobility. Research increasingly shows that 'the workplace is as at least as important as education in determining mobility prospects' (Eyles et al, 2022: 4). Therefore, it is important that social immobility is considered in this overview book on the sociology of work. The section begins by laying out what is meant by social mobility, and how it is measured. Then it lays out the patterns of social (im)mobility in the UK, before putting the UK experience in an international context. This leads to a consideration of workplace-related factors that contribute to the contemporary pattern of limited social mobility.

Social mobility, here, refers to change in a person's socio-economic position, compared with their parents' socio-economic position. This is sometimes also called relative intergenerational mobility. The study of social mobility looks for patterns in whether societies have high social mobility – such that a person's parents' position tends to have little relationship with the person's socio-economic position (as an adult), or whether societies have low social mobility – where a person's parents' position tends to be the same as the person's socio-economic position (as an adult). In terms of measuring social mobility, it is clearly important that the second-generation person has become an adult with a set pattern of income. This means waiting until the person is middle-aged. Eyles et al (2022) suggest that this makes social mobility researchers similar to astronomers, who are only able to observe a star exploding long after it has actually occurred. The analogy is that major changes may be occurring now in patterns of social mobility, but researchers cannot observe this until a considerable time in the future.

Sociologists and economists have both been involved in the study of social mobility. When measuring a person's (and their parents') socio-economic position, sociologists have tended to locate a person's position within a social class. Sociologists then consider whether the person occupies the same social class as that occupied by the parents or a different one. Upward mobility occurs when the person's social class position (as an adult) is higher than their parents' position. Downward mobility occurs when the person's social class position (as an adult) is lower than their parents' position. Immobility occurs when the social class position of the person and their parents is the same. Economists tend to define a person's socio-economic position in terms of where they are located in relative income rankings, for instance within the top 10 per cent (decile) of income earners. Much of the research on social mobility up to the 1990s relied on relatively small research samples, but, in recent decades, considerable developments have taken place in social mobility research, although gaps do still pertain regarding research data on the mobility of women and people from minority ethnic groups (Eyles et al, 2022).

The main pattern in the research findings on contemporary UK social mobility is one of restricted social mobility, with particular 'stickiness' or immobility at the top and at the bottom of the socio-economic rankings. Although there is some open mobility among the middle socio-economic classes, the likelihood of social immobility – of a person staying in the same social class as their parents – increases substantially when the parents are in either the bottom social class or the top social class. This pattern of stickiness at the top and bottom pertains to whether the measure of socio-economic position is social class or income bracket. Eyles et al (2022: 38) state that 'the UK is associated with particularly stark intergenerational persistence of poverty and privilege – immobility among those on low and high incomes'. Bukodi and Goldthorpe (2019) note that the chances of a child whose father is from the highest social class also ending up in the highest social class rather than in a working-class position are up to 20 times greater than the chances for a child with a working-class father ending up in the highest social class rather than the working class. Focusing on the immobility at the top, Friedman and Laurison (2019: 12) offer a more straightforward comparison of the likelihood of ending up in the top social class, that 'people from upper-middle-class origins have about 6.5 times the chance of landing an elite job compared to people from working-class backgrounds'.

Table 8.1 outlines key findings from Major and Machin's (2018) analysis of a study of a cohort of males born in 1970 (recall that it takes a long time in the playing out of intergenerational mobility). It shows that 41 per cent of sons born to parents who occupied the top fifth income bracket also occupied that income bracket. By comparison, only 8 per cent of sons whose parents were in the bottom fifth were able to occupy jobs that put them in the top fifth of income earners. It also shows that 35

Table 8.1: Intergenerational mobility across income brackets

		Where parent was in lowest fifth	Where parent was in highest fifth
Son's income bracket (as an adult)	Highest fifth	8%	41%
	2nd highest fifth	14%	19%
	Middle fifth	18%	18%
	2nd lowest fifth	25%	12%
	Lowest fifth	35%	10%

Source: Major and Machin (2018: 4) analysis of 1970 cohort study

per cent of sons born to parents who occupied the bottom fifth income bracket also occupied that income bracket.

It is also important to be aware of how the UK's record on social mobility compares with other advanced economies. Apart from the US, the UK has the lowest social mobility among advanced economies (Major and Machin, 2018). The acute reader would have anticipated this statement given that Chapter 7 noted that income inequality, at the societal level, is associated with lower social mobility (Wilkinson and Pickett, 2010). By international standards, the UK has high levels of income inequality and low levels of social mobility. An important overview report on international levels of social mobility concluded that the UK was actually at the bottom of the income mobility league table (with the US close beside the UK) (Causa and Johansson, 2010). It concluded (p 9) that, in the UK:

> 50 per cent of the economic advantage that high-earning parents have over low-earning parents is passed on to the next generation. ... By contrast, intergenerational persistence is comparatively low in the Nordic countries, Australia and Canada, with less than 20 per cent of the earnings advantage passed from parent to offspring.

A nicely intuitive way of thinking about comparing the social mobility of countries is in terms of the likelihood of the American Dream occurring, in which an offspring comes to occupy the top fifth of income after being brought up by parents occupying the bottom fifth of income. Ironically, the US comes out at the bottom of the American Dream league table, with just 7.5 per cent of children born to parents in the poorest fifth of households rising into the richest fifth as adults. The UK was close to the US at the bottom of this league table (reported in Major and Machin, 2018).

In the early decades of social mobility research, emphasis was placed on analysing education as a key process that informs the passing on of intergenerational advantage and disadvantage. Although hope had been placed on the education system as a great leveller for each new generation, more critical scholarship has argued that education actually constitutes a machinery for the stratification of society (Eyles et al, 2022). Private tutoring and the richer buying houses close to high-performing state schools are important mechanisms for the rich passing on advantage to the next generation through the processes of education. And, of course, there is the not insubstantial role of private schooling. Eyles et al (2022: 23) report of the UK: 'In 1991, privately educated 33–34 years olds were earning on average 25 per cent more than their otherwise similar state educated counterparts. In 2004, the pay premium had increased to 41 percent.' Research has also found an important role for socialization, parenting activities and home ownership as key mechanisms in the passing on of advantage across generations.

More recently, social mobility research has also begun to understand that social processes in employment also have a key role to play in the low levels of intergenerational mobility at the top and bottom. Rather than seeing the workplace as a neutral site where the second-generation person simply lands, researchers have begun to engage with sociology of work to examine processes that play a significant part in how intergenerational (im)mobility unfurls. The most directly penetrating research has examined how social processes within employment contribute to the passing on of privilege from one generation to the next.

Notably, Rivera's (2015) pioneering study of processes of job hiring among elite knowledge-work positions in US investment banking, consulting and law found that the social (classed) construction and evaluation of merit in hiring by elite employers was a key reason that these firms were populated overwhelmingly by people who had parents in high socio-economic positions. First, recruiters favoured those from higher socio-economic backgrounds by eliminating nearly all applicants who had not attended an elite college or university. Second, recruiters put applicants through a series of 'informal' recruitment activities, such as cocktail parties and mixers, that are most comfortable and familiar to those applicants from a higher socio-economic background. Finally, when in the formal interview process, selectors tend to evaluate candidates less with reference to formal criteria and more with reference to how at ease they appear, whether they build rapport in the interview and whether they share common interests. Rivera uses sociological analysis to describe these processes as 'cultural matching'. Overall, while the recruiters believed that they were enacting socially neutral processes that focused on 'merit', Rivera reveals that social construction of merit was class-based because a shared world-view, class-specific tastes, comportment and interaction styles gave candidates from affluent backgrounds a clear advantage in who was hired. In the UK, in the context of elite City of London law, accountancy and banking firms, Ashley (2022) similarly finds that recruiters tend to misidentify classed performances of cultural display as 'talent'.

While these studies are important in analysing the processes at the point of entry to the employing organization, Friedman and Laurison (2019) primarily focus on what processes there are *within* employment that can also contribute to the dominance of elite knowledge-work jobs by people whose parents occupy high socio-economic positions. They find (p 21) that, in elite professional and knowledge work, the relatively few people from working-class origins who manage to convince the recruiters to hire them come to earn 16 per cent less than people who come from privileged backgrounds. This previously undetected 'class-based pay gap' is multiplied for women and for black, Bangladeshi and Pakistani workers. Friedman and Laurison argue that, in elite professional and knowledge-work occupations, a '*class* ceiling' operates that limits the career advancement and income of those from working–class backgrounds.

This class ceiling is made up of subtle, informal, almost invisible social processes. Friedman and Laurison (2019) unpick these processes through an in-depth study of workers in four 'elite' fields – accountancy, acting, broadcast television and architecture. They began their study by asking interviewees about criteria for advancement in these elite occupations, and received a common answer that emphasized the importance of an individual having 'confidence'. The authors argue that the term 'confidence' serves to cover a number of important social processes that cumulatively produce a class ceiling. First, those from privileged backgrounds had more resources to fall back on in having the confidence to make risky decisions regarding career advancement. Economic resources provided by parents from high socio–economic positions allowed people to make 'confident' moves. People from lower socio–economic backgrounds did not have the back-up parental resources to allow them to make confident, risky moves. Second, those from privileged backgrounds were more likely to enact confidence in terms of proactively asking for pay rises and promotion. Such confidence tended to be socially created in that these moves were often prompted by advice from senior advocates within the occupations. Crucially, 'sponsor relationships were rarely established on the basis of work performance. Instead, they are almost always forged, in the first instance at least, on cultural affinity, on sharing humour, interests and tastes' (Friedman and Laurison, 2019: 25). Such cultural affinity is very frequently based on sharing the same (privileged) class background. This means that workers in these fields from working–class backgrounds tend not to have the same confidence in asking for a pay rise or promotion. Third, those from a privileged background act in more 'confident' ways in workplace settings, such as meetings, and this contributes to their career advancement.

Friedman and Laurison (2019) argue that this appearance of confidence is actually about workers from privileged backgrounds being more at ease in, and better able to read, the cultural codes enacted within workplaces. In elite occupations and firms, these cultural codes are class codes: they represent the normalized patterns of expectations and behaviour of those from privileged backgrounds. Workers from working–class backgrounds do not lack confidence per se, but may appear to lack confidence in settings where the class codes are unfamiliar. Finally, a key process that hinders working–class entrants from advancing in these occupations is that they tend to 'self–eliminate': they step back either from the occupation or from attempts to advance far in the occupation. This may appear like a lack of confidence, but Friedman and Laurison interpret this rather as a logical response to the very real class–based barriers that stand in the way of these workers.

It is important to be aware of the class ceiling in elite firms and occupations that hinders people from working–class backgrounds. It is equally, if not more, important to consider what elements in employment settings contribute to the tendency of people from working–class backgrounds to occupy working–class employment positions. If there is a class ceiling in workplaces limiting the extent of upward social mobility, there may also be a wet concrete floor in workplaces, keeping people stuck at the bottom.

The considerable amount of social mobility research regarding stickiness at the bottom tends to concentrate on *educational* mechanisms and processes, often in terms of working-class children being left with restricted qualifications (for example Willis' classic 1977 study, *Learning to Labour*). However, strands of sociology of work scholarship can be interpreted as pointing to potentially important *workplace* processes in the stickiness at the bottom. What is particularly relevant is less how people from working-class backgrounds come to apply for and be recruited into low-income jobs, and more on *the nature of such jobs and how people come to stay in them*. Here, concrete structures rather than subtle, invisible social processes are important (suggesting that the metaphor of a wet concrete floor as a complement to the class ceiling metaphor may be an appropriate one). These structures relate to a lack of career ladders (Chapter 4), a lack of training (Chapters 3 and 4) and, at a more macro-structural level, the international division of labour (Chapter 3) and the sharp rise in income inequality itself (Chapter 7). As the parentheses indicate, these structures have been already examined in this book. Here, I will briefly outline how they connect to the issue of social immobility at the bottom.

Chapters 3 and 4 outlined the structures that have led to severely limited career ladders and training opportunities in low-skill jobs in the UK. For instance, careers are now embedded more in the external labour market than in the internal labour market of a firm that offers career ladders alongside long-term employment. At the most extreme case of platform-mediated jobs, the employer abrogates even limited commitment to supporting training for employability. Job mobility comes to be played out in terms of a hustle search for short-term opportunities in similar low-paying jobs. While these short-term opportunities may allow people to keep their heads above the water, they do not offer a ladder out of the water. For customer service jobs, I argue (Korczynski, 2002) that there is a tendency for these to become 'dead zones' for career opportunities. Under financialized capitalism, there is a logic for training to be restricted to narrow immediate task proficiency. Training for customer-facing interactions (the immediate task of customer service workers) tends to have limited salience for wider career development. People from working-class backgrounds who come to be in low-paying platform-mediated jobs and customer service jobs may want to develop their careers upwardly, but workplace structures tend not to support such aspirations. In this context, state involvement to sponsor and develop apprenticeships, which allow people both to earn while they learn (particularly important for people from low-income backgrounds) and have a ladder upwards through skill development, becomes crucial (Major and Machin, 2020).

Regarding more macro-level employment-related structures, the international division of labour sets a crucial material context for social immobility at the bottom in advanced economies. Chapter 3 outlined the broad tendency for many manual jobs in manufacturing to be globally outsourced, leaving advanced economies as increasingly focusing on service work and knowledge work. Given the difficulty for people from working-class backgrounds to access knowledge-work occupations, the previously noted 'dead zones' of customer service jobs become both the logical main entry point and the staying point for employment. For working-class men who experience service work as running counter to their sense of masculinity, customer service jobs may not even be an entry point (Nixon, 2009).

Finally, it can be argued that the structures of employment matter for social immobility at the bottom because a key outcome of the changing structures of employment has been the sharp rise in income inequality (discussed in Chapter 7). Earlier in this chapter, we noted the strong correlation between income inequality and social immobility: the higher the income inequality in a society, the lower the levels of social mobility. An important question concerns whether this is a correlation or a causal relationship (Eyles et al, 2022). Major and Machin (2020) argue that it is a causal relationship in that greater income inequality when children are young leads to greater restrictions on mobility. However, the issue may be less about seeking directions of causation between the two, and more about seeing how high income inequality and high social immobility are *joint* outcomes of structures of an emerging form of financialized capitalism. The big picture, overall, is that both the wet concrete floor and the class ceiling in workplaces are being recognized as significant factors in the playing out of social immobility.

Inequalities for women

Legislation for equality of opportunity, for equal pay and against sex discrimination has been in place for many decades in most advanced economies. Despite this, there is a persistent and considerable gender pay gap across many economies. The UK is positioned low down the international league table for income equality between men and women.

This section outlines the nature and extent of the pay gap before considering how the gender pay gap is intimately linked to inequalities of opportunity. Hence inequalities of outcome and opportunity for women are considered here together. Key patterns of horizontal segregation (women work mainly in women–dominated occupations) and vertical segregation (related to the glass ceiling) are outlined. We examine research that seeks to account for the gender pay gap. This research consistently shows a large 'unexplained' element in the gender pay gap. Further to this, we review qualitative sociology of work research and theorizing that points to important gendered processes that are likely to play a key role in the 'unexplained' part of the gender pay gap.

The gender pay gap refers to the difference between the average hourly pay of men and the average hourly pay of women. This difference is expressed as a percentage of the average hourly earnings of men. For 2022 in the UK, the gender pay gap was 14.9 per cent (Office for National Statistics [ONS], 2022). In other words, for every £100 income earned by male workers, on average, female workers earn £85.10. Women constitute 47 per cent of the UK labour force. The gender pay gap has been gradually declining over many decades. It was 27.5 per cent in 1997, and 19.8 per cent in 2010. If the comparison between male and female average earnings is limited to full-time workers only, then the gender pay gap statistic is lower. For 2022, the gender pay gap for full-time workers only was 8.3 per cent.

In international terms, the UK's gender pay gap is relatively high (Piketty, 2013). Figure 8.1 shows the UK's position for gender pay gap alongside many other advanced economies, as well as against an overall EU average. The graph is based on OECD figures, which report the UK gender pay gap at 14.5 per cent, rather than the 14.9 per cent noted earlier. Note that, while the UK's gender pay gap is far below that of Japan (22.1 per cent), and some way below the US (17 per cent), it is much higher than

Figure 8.1: Gender pay gap in selected countries, 2021

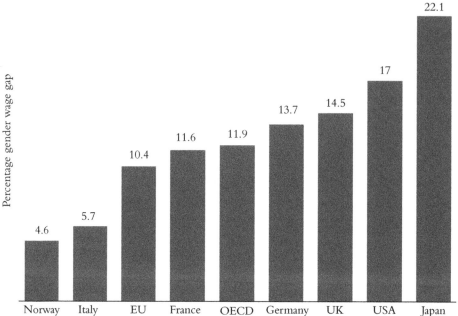

Source: OECD (2022), 'Gender wage gap', data.oecd.org/earnwage/gender-wage-gap.htm

both the average for the 38 OECD countries (of advanced economies with democratic systems) and the average for the EU as a whole. Continuing the strong record on overall income equality (reported in Chapter 7), Scandinavian countries have, by international standards, low levels of gender pay gap, with Norway standing at 4.6 per cent.

Some readers may be perplexed by the coexistence, in the UK, and in most advanced economies, of long-standing equal pay legislation and the continuation of a considerable gender pay gap. Explaining the coexistence of those two things is actually a good starting point for a sociological analysis of the gender pay gap. The main crux of the equal pay legislation is to make it illegal for an employer to offer different pay rates for doing the same job simply on the basis of a person's sex. There is no question that this legislation has successfully stopped the practice that it made illegal. So, the gender pay gap is not driven by employers explicitly offering different pay rates for the same job on the basis of sex. To understand how there can still be a gender pay gap in this context, we need to understand how men and women tend to occupy different jobs in the economy. Sociologists tend to use the term 'occupational segregation' when writing about the processes that lead to men and women occupying different jobs. There are two important forms of occupational segregation: horizontal and vertical.

Horizontal occupational segregation

Horizontal occupational segregation means that men and women tend to work in different occupations. Crucially, women tend to work in women–dominated

Table 8.2: Examples of female-dominated occupations in the UK

Occupation	Percentage of female workers	Number of women employed (1,000s)
Nursing	76%	927
Nursing assistant	76%	350
Caring assistant	77%	949
Care worker and home carer	80%	458
Secretary	77%	811
Sales assistant	63%	759
Cleaner	69%	433
Teaching assistant	90%	246
Waitering	68%	130

Source: Original analysis of data at GOV.UK (2022)

occupations – rather than workplaces; the difference is important – and men tend to work in men-dominated occupations. Although there has been some significant change in that pattern in certain professions, the overall level of occupational segregation by sex has remained stable internationally over recent decades (Wong and Charles, 2020). Table 8.2 gives some examples of female-dominated occupations.

As suggested by Table 8.2, women-dominated occupations (which is where women mainly work) tend to have low pay and poor conditions. Notably, when the UK national minimum wage first became law in 1999, of the one and a half million workers whose wages were raised, one million (two thirds) were women (Low Pay Commission, 1999). This, then, is the first stepping stone to understanding the gender pay gap: women tend to work in low-paying occupations and, more pertinently, in occupations that are lower paying than the occupations men tend to work in. As a report by the Equality and Human Rights Commission (EHRC, 2017b: 55) notes, for the gender pay gap, an 'important factor is the disproportionately high number of women in poorly paid occupations'. However, there are still some important sociological questions begged in the laying of this first stepping stone. First, why do women dominate in these specific occupations? Here, there is a tendency for sociologists to point to socialization of people from a young age into gendered norms regarding which jobs are appropriate for men and which are appropriate for women. Dunford and Perrons (2014: 474), for instance, argue that there are 'deeply embedded cultural practices and gendered social norms; norms which uphold and reinforce existing enactments and understandings of appropriate roles for women and men'. This is essentially an argument that emphasizes the supply of labour: certain occupations are dominated by women because this is where women (due to gendered socialization) want to work. Sociology of work research focusing on customer service occupations (many of which are dominated by women) also points to a key role for employers here. Employers are not just neutral bodies simply receiving job applications from those who have experienced gendered socialization. Belt's (2002) study of how call-centre customer service assistance came to be a female-dominated occupation (also Scholarios and Taylor, 2011) reveals that employers also have a significant role in the gendering of the job. Belt shows that the marketing by the financial service firms she studied used images of smart, smiling female call-centre agents in their advertising. They were encouraging their customers to have gendered expectations of what customer service constitutes. Further, Trentham and Larwood (1998) argue that service managers come to have a discriminatory 'rational bias' regarding women by making hiring and other decisions based on the real or perceived customer preferences about the appropriate gender of the service worker.

The second question begged by the observation that women tend to work in women-dominated, relatively low-paying occupations is why do these occupations (in which women dominate) have low pay and poor conditions and, specifically, are the poor pay and conditions *linked* to the high percentage of women in the occupations? Feminist-informed 'undervaluation theory' argues that society and employers undervalue certain work *precisely because women do it* (EHRC, 2017b). Perales (2013) for the UK, and England (1992, 2005, 2010) for the US provide research support for this with the finding that the level of feminization of an occupation is negatively correlated with the wage in that occupation. Again, studies of service-work occupations provide insight into important processes here. There is a tendency for employers to undervalue skills in service occupations (dominated by women). What is and what is not recognized as skilled work is socially constructed, and gender has a crucial role to play in this social construction. Skills in service work, such as empathetic listening and other forms of emotional labour, are regarded less as skills and more as 'natural' attributes of women's personalities (Korczynski, 2002: 163). This has concrete implications for pay through the process of job evaluation in organizations. Job evaluation is the process in which tasks within a job are given ratings that are summed up and lead to jobs being placed in bands linked to pay levels. A report from the EHRC (2014: 10) notes that frequently overlooked job characteristics in job evaluation exercises are often central elements in service occupations (undertaken mainly by women): 'Communication skills or meeting emotional demands are undervalued because they are thought to be the skills or attributes that women either naturally possess or acquire through life experience, and so may be omitted from a job evaluation.'

Legislation regarding equal pay for work of equal value (called 'equal worth' in the US) provides a route for such undervaluing to be challenged. The principle of equal pay for work of equal value is that equal pay should be given to jobs of equal value, under the same employer, irrespective of the composition of the occupants of those jobs. This allows women to make the legal case that, if their jobs are of equal value to higher-paying jobs mainly occupied by men, they should receive pay at that higher rate. Female checkout workers at Sainsbury's supermarket made the successful case that their job was of equal value to the higher-paying (and male-dominated) job of a warehouse worker (Dickens, 2000). Similar cases are being made by female workers in Asda and Next (Stewart, 2023). Although legislation does provide some scope for challenging the undervaluing of skills in women-dominated occupations, such legal challenges are lengthy and costly. What these legal cases reveal is that the undervaluing of skills in women-dominated occupations is ongoing.

Vertical segregation

Vertical segregation refers to the tendency for women to occupy lower-ranked and lower-paid positions within occupations than men. In everyday terms, this is often discussed in terms of the 'glass ceiling'. 'Glass ceiling' refers to a situation where there is an apparent opportunity for women to rise within an occupation but subtle, informal, invisible processes mean the opportunity to rise is more apparent than real. There is a tendency for the metaphor of the glass ceiling to be used mainly with reference to senior managerial and professional positions, for instance with regard to the fact that only 25 per cent of board members in major companies in the UK are women (EHRC, 2017b). One strong argument developed by feminist writers is that, in these senior positions, there is a tendency for hiring and promotion decisions to be made with reference to an ideal worker, who is, implicitly, male (Moen and Roehling, 2005). Sweet and Meiskins (2008: 77) put it thus:

> Ideal workers, in today's economy, are people who can put in long hours, uninterrupted throughout their careers. They are available when the company needs them, can work late when called upon, can spend weekends in the office and will not have any prolonged absences from the job. Their performance will not be hindered by sickness, aging parents, children or pregnancy. These expectations are largely insensitive to the normal life course of women and their roles off the job. In a word, ideal workers are men.

Indeed, the ideal worker as male is part of Acker's (1990) wider feminist theorizing of the 'gendered organisation' (discussed in Chapter 2). Overall, although the increasing numbers of female graduates suggest that women may be breaking down the horizontal segregation that has kept them out of professions, it tends still to be the case that significant, albeit declining, vertical segregation (the glass ceiling) occurs in these senior occupations (Bolton and Muzio, 2008; Watts, 2009). An important addendum to the analysis of vertical segregation is to note that we should not be trapped by the everyday linking of the 'glass ceiling' to senior occupation into failing to see that vertical segregation occurs across all types of occupation. It occurs, for instance, in nursing (Korczynski, 2002: 166) and call-centre work (Scholarios and Taylor, 2011), where, even though the occupations are female-dominated, male nurses and male call-centre workers have a better chance of promotion on average than female nurses and female call-centre workers.

The feminist argument regarding processes contributing to vertical segregation is countered by advocates of human capital theory, which is primarily based on economics scholarship. The argument here is that positions in income hierarchies are primarily based on individuals' human capital – their skills, knowledge and experience – which, in turn, influences productivity. So, if there appears to be vertical segregation relating to gender in an occupation, this is a secondary observation. The primary observation is that there is vertical ordering according to human capital, and the secondary observation relating to gender arises simply because women tend to have less human capital than men (Becker, 1991; Manning and Swaffield, 2008).

Although there is evidence that men's advantage in human capital has weakened over time – not least because of the substantial relative rise in women graduates – men do have the advantage, because of their lesser domestic work responsibilities, in being able to invest time and resources into their education and career (EHRC, 2017b).

This debate has led to research that examines the factors contributing to the gender pay gap (Olsen and Walby, 2004; Olsen et al 2010a, 2010b, 2018; EHRC, 2017b). This research directly considers the human capital theory by measuring education and work experience and looking at differences between males and females who have the same level of education and work experience (so, the same human capital). In addition, this research considers the impact of occupational segregation by gender on the gender pay gap.

Although there are some important differences between the findings in this important and pioneering research, there are also some significant shared findings. The research tends to show that occupational segregation, the greater tendency for women to work part-time and human capital differences between men and women (in terms of labour market histories) are key factors that drive the gender pay gap. Note that some of the variables that are shown to impact the gender pay gap (occupational segregation and so on) themselves are informed by prior gendered behaviours and discrimination. As the EHRC (2017b: 50) puts it, 'some of the explanatory variables might obscure various levels of discrimination that work indirectly'. In addition, what is just as important in the findings is that a very large part of the gender pay gap remains 'unexplained' by the variables in the studies. Olsen et al's (2018) study found that 35 per cent of the gender pay gap cannot be accounted for by occupational segregation, human capital differences and so on. For the EHRC (2017b) study, this statistic is even higher, at 42 per cent. Some of this may be due to the need for better measures in studies, but Olsen et al (2018: 23) state that, 'while we are unable to definitively identify why "unobserved" criteria continue to be such a large driver of the gender pay gap, it is likely to be a function of an unknown combination of discrimination and gendered behaviour'.

This observation comes as little surprise to a rich tradition of (mainly) qualitative research in the sociology of work that has unearthed subtle forms of gendered behaviour with discriminatory implications. For instance, Gregory's (2009) study of the informal 'locker room' culture among male elite knowledge workers – creative workers in the advertising industry – is instructive. Gregory shows how the locker room culture among male employers and knowledge workers helps men to retain their dominant position in the industry. In effect, the locker room culture acts in an exclusionary manner towards women as it reinforces behaviour such as the use of sports, macho humour, banter, sexualization of women, drinking and going to strip clubs. Gregory (2009: 338) quotes a male senior creative advertising executive giving a disarmingly frank overview of the picture:

> There's a locker room sense of humour in most creative departments, especially when it comes to women. The whole sense of a male environment is the same, whether you're talking about a male locker room, or a creative department. Being in a male environment we talk about a lot of male things, especially

when it comes to sex and making sexual innuendos. Men dictate the rules of their environment, and the rules of a football club and a creative department are exactly alike. You could exchange them for one another because the moods are so similar.

Williams et al's (2012) important study of knowledge workers (geo-scientists in the oil and gas industry) shows less stark, but equally important, gendered patterns that operate in a way that effectively lessens women's chances of rising in an occupation. Williams et al note that Acker's (1990) concept of the gendered organization was strongly oriented around the bureaucratic organizational form, and they aim to consider if the concept of the gendered organization is relevant for the analysis of the more network-oriented (or community of practice-oriented) form of knowledge work primarily organized around project teams. This is their conclusion (Williams et al, 2012: 569):

> Our research suggests that teams, career maps, and networking reflect gendered organizational logics. To excel at teamwork, individuals must be able to engage in self-promotion, which can be difficult for women in male-dominated environments – even though they are the ones who may need to do it the most. In contexts where supervisors have discretion over careers, gender bias can play a significant role in the allocation of rewards. And networking is gendered in ways that disadvantage women.

Given the predominance of women in low-paying jobs, it is appropriate also to reference insightful studies of gendered behaviour with clear implications for the gender pay gap within customer service work. Scholarios and Taylor's (2011) study of women in call-centre work finds that women's career trajectory was constrained not just by having lower educational qualifications than men (as per human capital theory), but also by having greater domestic work responsibilities, which limited their career search, and by the tendency for (important) informal supervisor support to be offered more to men than to women. Here, we see how gendered behaviours both outside the workplace (women have greater domestic work responsibilities) and inside the workplace (gendered patterns in supervisor support) come together to limit women's possibilities.

Inequalities for people from minority ethnic groups

The UK, like many advanced economies, has become more ethnically diverse in recent decades. In 2001, people from non-white ethnic groups accounted for 6 per cent of workers. In 2023, this figure was 14.7 per cent (Office for National Statistics [ONS], 2023). Despite the existence of anti-discrimination legislation, there is evidence of a persistent negative ethnicity wage gap for a number of important groups.

This section lays out the nature of the ethnicity wage gap and considers research into factors that inform the gap. As in the case of the gender wage gap, issues of inequality of outcome and opportunity are intimately linked.

The ethnicity wage gap is defined as the difference between the average hourly pay of minority ethnic people and white British people, expressed as a percentage difference, with white British people's earnings representing 100 per cent. While it is meaningful to give a headline overall statistic for the gender wage gap, this is not the case for the ethnicity wage gap. There are several reasons for this.

First, there is a big difference in the ethnicity wage gap between men and women. The ONS (2020) estimates that, in 2019, minority ethnic men earned 6.1 per cent less than white men, while the hourly pay of minority ethnic women was actually 2.1 per cent *more* than that of white women. The significant difference between men and women is one of the enduring puzzles of research into the ethnicity wage gap. Much of the research concentrates on understanding why and how the negative ethnicity wage gap *for some groups of men* occurs.

Second, there are also significant differences in the experience of different ethnic groups. Although the ONS (2020) aggregates all minority ethnic people into one overall category to allow them to give the statistics noted in the paragraph above, it is more common (and more meaningful) for comparisons to be made between the earnings of white British people and the earnings of specific minority ethnic groups. For instance, current research suggests that, for men, the two groups with the highest ethnicity wage gap are Pakistani and Bangladeshi workers, while some studies estimate that, on average, the hourly earnings of Indian men are actually close to or even slightly higher than the hourly earnings of white British men (EHRC, 2017a). Further, although the overall picture for ethnicity pay gap is more positive for women, it is the case that Pakistani and Bangladeshi immigrant women had lower earnings on average than white British women (EHRC, 2017a).

Third, there is also a considerable variance in the gap depending on whether place of birth is considered. The clear picture is that the ethnicity pay gap is *lower* for people born in the UK from a given ethnic minority compared with the gap for people from that same ethnic background who are born outside the UK: 'pay gaps are much larger for ethnic minority men born abroad than for those born in the UK' (EHRC, 2017a: 10). For instance, the EHRC estimates the wage gap for black Caribbean men born in Britain to be 6.9 per cent, while the figure is 17.4 per cent for male black Caribbean migrants. The EHRC notes that migrant workers from a minority ethnic group may have a weaker ability in English language, lack the social networks that are often important in the job search process and, crucially, their qualifications – earned in their country of birth – are often left unrecognized by employers in the UK (the following section has further discussion of this).

Finally, there are also some differences in the findings between studies, depending partly on different datasets being analysed and partly on different assumptions made in the methods underpinning the studies. Generally, however, the differences between studies are relatively small.

One consistent pattern in the findings for male workers is that, with some exceptions, the ethnicity wage gap has tended to be relatively constant in recent decades. There is no evidence that there are trends for the ethnicity pay gap to diminish in general. Mirza and Warwick (2022: 62) give the overview picture that, 'for most ethnic minority groups, male median earnings relative to those of the ethnic majority were comparable in 2019 to those in 1995'. Mirza and Warwick and others have conducted research into analysing factors that 'explain' the ethnicity pay gap – in a similar way to the research noted in the previous section on factors 'explaining' the gender pay gap. Mirza and Warwick (2022: 69) state that, 'though Indians earn more than White individuals on average, and Black Caribbean men earn less, both earn less than would be expected given their qualifications and job characteristics'. Indeed, their analysis (p 68) offers the startling observation that, 'almost uniformly, "basic controls" (which include region of residence and age, for instance) would indicate that … minority groups … should earn *higher* wages than White British individuals' (emphasis added).

For the most part, previous research into the ethnicity pay gap has focused on assessing the role of education, based on the assumption that there is something in the education system that leads to lower qualifications for certain ethnic groups, which in turn is seen as the key driver of the ethnicity pay gap. This has meant that public policy interventions to improve the ethnicity pay gap have tended to focus on the arena of education. Mirza and Warwick (2022: 70), however, note that, 'while the evidence … has shown that education does provide a partial path to closing existing gaps, it is also clearly not a panacea'. They argue that there are likely to be crucial processes occurring within the labour market and within employment relationships that underpin existing, and enduring, ethnicity wage gaps.

Research has found recruitment to be a key point for discrimination based on ethnicity to occur. A common approach here is the field experiment study in which researchers send in fictitious CVs to real job vacancies. The CVs are equivalent in terms of the ability of the applicant to perform the job but the race or ethnicity of the candidate is apparently revealed by their name. There is now a considerable body of such research. Quillian and Mitdbøen (2021) offer an overview of 140 field-experiment studies of hiring discrimination against ethnic minority groups in 30 countries. Their conclusion is clear (p 391): 'these studies show that racial and ethnic discrimination is a pervasive international phenomenon that has hardly declined over time'. Wood et al's (2009) UK-based study is a typical one. They sent applications to various job vacancies for nine types of occupation, including IT, accountancy, care and sales. They found that job applicants with apparently foreign names were less likely to be offered an interview than those with British-sounding names.

Another key process that contributes to the ethnicity wage gap is the tendency for workers from some minority ethnic backgrounds to be disproportionately located in low-paying occupations. As Mirza and Wood (2022) note, this became particularly apparent during the pandemic lockdowns where the high proportion of (low-paid) key-worker roles occupied by people from minority ethnic groups was exposed. For instance, black African men work in social care roles at seven times the rate of white British men, and black African women are four times as likely as white British women to do so.

Platform-mediated work is the latest form of low-paying work to be disproportionately undertaken by people from minority ethnic groups – specifically, by *migrants* from minority ethnic groups. Van Doorn et al (2023: 1101) see 'growing evidence that migrant workers … provide a large share of the labour power driving gig platforms in cities ranging from New York to Paris and from Bogotá to Cape Town'. Van Doorn and Vijay (2021) show that this occurs through structures of power in states and in the labour market that funnel the agency of migrant workers into these jobs. In the context of labour markets where discrimination occurs against job applicants with foreign names, and where employers do not recognize qualifications gained outside a narrow set of countries, Van Doorn and Vijay reveal how platforms operate in such a way as to become part of the technology of migration. They state (2021: 16) that 'migrants do not just use social media platforms to support and plan their migration trajectories, they also increasingly turn to gig platforms for work once they arrive in a foreign city'. However, platform-mediated work is double-edged. It simultaneously opens opportunities for immediate income-earning for migrant workers and offers relatively poor pay and conditions. Furthermore, while many migrant workers enter platform-mediated work with the idea that it is a temporary stepping stone to something better, there is a logic that they may become ensnared in these positions, where career structures are reduced to short-term, individual hustles (see Chapter 4). Van Doorn and Vijay (2021: 15) argue: 'Due to their mix of accessibility and "generative entrenchment" … they [platforms] also have a penchant to ensnare migrants who already face structural barriers to the labor markets and welfare provisions of host countries. In other words, it's easier to access a gig platform than to leave it.'

Support for the argument that processes of discrimination continue to occur after hiring comes from research which shows that many people from minority ethnic backgrounds perceive they are subject to discriminatory processes in the sphere of employment. Rolfe et al (2009) sought to analyse these perceptions. They stress that people from black and minority ethnic groups commented on the predominance of white British managers and how that set the tone for an organizational culture that was implicitly discriminatory. Clark and Nolan (2021: 1) find that 'specifically Black [male] groups – face an apparent glass ceiling barring access to well paid jobs'. Clarke and Smith's (2024) study of informal career processes in the most senior ranks of the London Metropolitan Police shows what this means in practice. Through in-depth interviews with senior officers, the authors point to the existence of an implicit 'club', composed of white senior officers, that provides an invisible guiding hand that identifies, pursues, advises and sponsors white officers who fit the existing leadership composition. One senior officer reflected on the 'club' (p 2):

> It's almost like an unholy club at times. And when I say club I don't mean it's a select club which is being defined and there's an intention behind it. But it's behaving like a club and the club then becomes strengthened and further engendered by the way people are recruited and the way people are then groomed to be a part of their club. Institutionally throughout the decades and the years, we just sort (sic) to recruit people from its own image … and that's why it's hard to break into the circles and any degree of difference that isn't similar to their own characteristics becomes uncomfortable for this institution of Chief Officers.

Officers from minority ethnic backgrounds are effectively marginalized from promotion to senior ranks here, all within a framework of an organization that formally adheres to equal opportunities policies.

Global inequalities of income and opportunity: migration

As Bhambra (2007) has argued, postcolonial sociology must consider not just inequalities *within* countries, but also inequalities *between* countries. In that spirit, this section places the important contemporary phenomenon of international migration in the context of global income inequality. In the structure of global income inequality, a key reason that people move country is the aim of improving their income and overall life chances. As Faist (2016: 323) puts it, 'cross-border migration is a visible reflection of global inequalities'. This section considers the structures of inequality between countries along with the simultaneous demand for migrant labour from employers in advanced economies and the barriers to the entry of migrant labour put in place by those countries. These are the key structures that migrant people seek to navigate in higher-income destination countries.

Although it has been closing in recent decades, there is still considerable income inequality between countries across the globe. The most common way of comparing income inequality between countries is to look at the Gross National Income (GNI) per capita: the total income earned by individuals and corporations in a country divided by the number of people in the country. The World Bank has created a four-level classification of countries based on the average GNI per capita. Table 8.3 outlines the population contained within each category of country, and the overall average GNI per capita within each category for 2022. Note that only 15.7 per cent of the world's population live in countries categorized as 'high income' (those with a GNI per capita above $13,845). The UK, with an average GNI per capita of $48,890, is classified as a high-income country. The average GNI per capita in the high-income countries towers above that in all of the other country categories. The average GNI per capita in the high-income countries is around five times that in upper-middle-income countries, around 20 times that in lower-middle-income countries and approximately 70 times that in low-income countries.

Table 8.3: Average income levels for country groups, 2022

Category of country	Population (millions)	Population as percentage of total population	Average GNI per capita ($)
Low income	704	8.9%	721
Lower middle income	3,190	40.3%	2,517
Upper middle income	2,784	35.1%	10,530
High income	1,245	15.7%	51,087

Notes: Low-income economies are those in which 2022 GNI per capita was $1,135 or less. Lower-middle-income economies are those in which 2022 GNI per capita was between $1,136 and $4,465. Upper-middle-income economies are those in which 2022 GNI per capita was between $4,466 and $13,845. High-income countries are those in which 2022 GNI per capita was more than $13,845.

Source: World Bank, World Development Indicators, wdi.worldbank.org/table/WV.1#

This means that, to a very large extent, the range of income a person is able to earn is based on which country a person happens to be born in. The accident of where a person is born bequeaths to some a world filled with opportunity, and condemns others to a life with little opportunity. Schachar (2009) calls this 'the birthright lottery'. Faist (2016: 327) notes that, 'nowadays, more than half of global income differences can be attributed to huge gaps in average income between countries'. Milanovic (2015: 458) confirms this picture: 'more than half of variability in income globally is explained by circumstances given at birth'. Milanovic argues that this constitutes a 'global inequality of opportunity'. This outline of the very high levels of average income inequality between countries is important in itself. Also, recall from the discussion in Chapter 3 of globalization and the international division of labour that there are important arguments that, although individual countries may be able to go up and down the ladder of inequality, structural factors make the overall core patterns of inequality between countries enduring.

This global inequality of average income between countries is also important because it constitutes the key structural context that drives most migration. Milanovic (2015: 458) summarizes the three ways to try to raise their income for the 84.3 per cent of people not lucky enough to be born in a high-income country: 'own efforts [in country of birth], hope that one's country does well, and migration are three ways in which people can improve their global income position'. Faist (2016: 325) points out that 'the path of cross-border migration, though often requiring a high level of courageous determination, tends to offer much more immediate and certain returns'. Further, research (Faist, 2016: 326) shows that:

> On average, cross-border movement yields more income [to individuals] than internal migration, and intercontinental migration usually yields the most. This is because the most attractive destination countries are OECD [high-income] countries located in Europe, North America, Australasia, and the Gulf states, whereas the main emigration countries are located in Africa, Latin America, the Middle East, and South and Southeast Asia.

Pointing to large inequalities of average income between countries as the key context for migration is not to reduce migration to a simple economic cost and benefit analysis. There is a considerable body of scholarship which shows that there can be a range of motivations for migration. A notable case is forced migration further to wars, political instability, political persecution or dramatic environmental changes. There is consensus that migration should be seen as a multi-causal phenomenon and one that is rarely taken lightly. Potential for higher income is often a key factor, but it may be more appropriate to see it as just one factor within a wider consideration of differences in overall life chances in a new country compared with the country of birth. Overall, migration and inequalities are intimately linked (Safi, 2020).

Migration is certainly an important contemporary phenomenon. Castles and Miller (2019) call the contemporary era the 'age of migration', with the global numbers of people on the move doubling in recent decades. To put this in context, however, people living in a different country from that in which they were born only constitute around 2 to 3 per cent of the world's population. Although current flows of migration have become complex (Castles and Miller, 2019), we have already seen a key pattern of flow being towards countries with higher average income. The following part of this section turns to concentrate on examining social structures, particularly in the UK, facing migrants both on their journey to and in the stage of reception in the host country. These social structures are significant factors that position migrants at a disadvantage in the host country compared with people born in that country, including an income disadvantage noted in the previous section on the ethnicity pay gap.

Schierup et al (2006) usefully outline how the structures facing migrants are linked to key forms of political economy. Overall, their analysis points to two distinct patterns. They argue that, from 1945 to the 1970s, in the Fordist period, demand for migrant labour occurred in a context of almost full employment. Migrants tended to be recruited into large workplaces where unions were able to negotiate good pay and conditions, and social democratic parties introduced welfare provisions to protect workers and their families, including migrants. Invitations to migrants tended to be offered to countries previously occupied by the host country (in the UK, these were the Commonwealth countries – those occupied and annexed to become part of the British Empire). The entry of each new wave of migrants from a specific country could be embedded in networks set up by the first wave of migrants from that country.

As noted in Chapter 3, the Fordist model of capitalism collapsed at the end of the 1970s, and so, Schierup et al (2006) argue, did the social structures facing migrants. After an interim period, they identify a clear pattern emerging from the 1990s, in which the demand for (unskilled) migrant labour occurs further to the recreation of sweatshops and other exploitative work in advanced economies. The context of reception for new migrants was now very different from that in the Fordist period. Schierup et al characterize that context as a laissez-faire state that offered little protection to workers and had weak unions and fragmented labour markets that opened the door for exploitative employment practices. The previous situation of ethnic communities being able to support new migrants was also partly undermined by the rise of the informal/illegal 'migrant transition industry' that arose as a way to get around the barriers to entry for migrants that are increasingly being put up in advanced economies. Here, a typical pattern is that migrant people not only pay a high initial fee to be transported to a higher-income country, but they also promise to make further payments once they have arrived. This creates conditions of great dependence between the migrants – who, being undocumented, have little recourse to support from state authorities or formal institutions – and those who transported them.

This was the structural context for the largest work-related disaster in the UK of the 21st century – the deaths of 23 people in 2004 in Morecambe Bay on the north-west coast of England. The dead were all undocumented migrant workers from China who had been put to work to pick cockles in the sands of Morecambe Bay. The workers became trapped on the sands at dusk as the tide came back in, and drowned. This case also connects to Schierup's arguments concerning the role of the 'laissez faire' state. In this context, the state body concerned with safe working conditions, the Health and Safety Executive, has been increasingly underfunded and marginalized in regulating safety conditions in the economy. Bernat and Whyte (2017: 82) acidly observe that, 'in the months and weeks leading up to disaster, cocklers on Morecambe Bay might have had a chance of seeing immigration officers, but would have had little chance of seeing workplace safety regulators'. Burnett and Whyte's (2010: 9) research into the dangerous working conditions in which undocumented migrants are placed argues that the Morecambe Bay deaths were just an extreme example of a wider pattern:

> This report begins to unravel a story that is normally only told in the context of catastrophic events such as the Morecambe Bay disaster. But what follows provides a more mundane way of interpreting the dangers that migrant workers face. For, as the data analysed here reveals, those risks are everyday, routine, and in many ways part of the normalised experience of undocumented workers in the UK.

In extreme cases, the structural dependency between the undocumented migrant workers and their transporters and/or employers can become a form of bonded labour, which is also increasingly being labelled as 'modern slavery' (Kara, 2017). In Qatar, the structural dependence of formally recognized and recruited workers upon their employer – who had to continue to sponsor them for them to be able to remain in Qatar – led to strong condemnation from the International Labour Organization with regard to labour linked to the 2022 football World Cup. In 2021, *The Guardian* estimated that 6,500 migrant workers had died in Qatar over the previous ten years (Pattison and McIntyre, 2021).

While forms of bonded labour for undocumented migrant workers constitute extreme cases, a more common form of disadvantage that migrant workers experience is that of 'de-skilling' in the sense of host country employers failing to recognize the qualifications that the workers gained in their country of origin. There have been a number of insightful studies of this occurring even for state-sanctioned highly skilled migrant knowledge workers. For instance, Purkayastha (2005) focuses upon a group of highly educated women from India who migrated to the US under family reunification clauses for migration, and analyses their attempts to re-establish careers as knowledge workers. She found that their careers were hampered in four main ways: loss of networks, discrimination, responsibility for domestic care work and devalued credentials. Regarding the latter, these women from India were regarded as highly educated in their home countries, but, in the US, many found that 'foreign' degrees became a liability for their careers. The need to retake degrees in US universities was experienced as highly frustrating. One woman noted that 'this degree [from a US university] was just a piece of paper. I had far better, in-depth training in India' (Purkayastha, 2005: 191).

More generally, workers having jobs for which they are overqualified can be experienced as demeaning. Przybyszewska's (2020) study of the experience of Polish workers in Norway brings this out well. One of the people she interviewed, Piotr, worked as a cleaner in Norway after leaving Poland, where he had graduated with a Master's degree and worked as a project manager: 'I've reached such a stage now that my head is filled only with confusion. Because I've lost my self-confidence, I no longer know what I truly desire and what I'm able to achieve.' Sometimes, migrant workers face structures that effectively force them, if they want to migrate, to work in jobs for which they are overqualified. Navallo (2023) shows that the strong restrictions on migrant people entering Japan for nursing roles has pushed many in the care sector into jobs for which they are overqualified. Of 2,600 Philippine-educated nurses who entered Japan between 2009 and 2019, the majority – 2,004 – entered at the lower level of care workers; only 588 entered as nurses.

While many migrant people are overqualified for the jobs that they undertake in the host country, it is still the case that their incomes are likely to be higher than they would have been in their country of birth, despite being likely to work in jobs that matched their qualifications. This is because of the high level of income inequality between countries. It is clear that, overall, cross-border migration still constitutes a pathway to earn higher income for the *individuals* involved. However, sociologists also look beyond outcomes at the level of individual migrants to consider whether the overall process of migration (largely from lower- to higher-income countries) affects the structure of wide income inequality between countries. A key issue to consider here is the degree to which such migration represents a 'brain drain' – a process of stripping key skilled labour, created through education in lower-income countries, from those countries and locating it in higher-income countries. Structurally, this can be seen as a form of international poaching of skilled labour, to the benefit of higher-income countries and the longer-term cost of lower-income countries. Faist's (2016: 323) overview concludes that contemporary migration, even as it helps the income levels of the individuals involved, 'tends to reinforce durable inequalities on a deeper level'. This may be considered the last of many sociological tragedies in the story of contemporary migration within the structure of global inequality.

Sociological imagination – your turn

Consider your own job experience and the job experience of friends and family. Reflect on the sections in this chapter on inequalities relating to gender and inequalities relating to ethnic group membership. Have you or they experienced any of the processes discussed in those sections that contribute to the gender pay gap and/or the ethnicity wage gap? What were those processes? If you think you have *not* experienced any of those processes – either to your advantage (as a male or a white British person) or disadvantage – can you be confident in making this claim?

As noted in Chapter 2, Durkheim (1893: 384) wrote that 'there cannot be rich and poor at birth without there being unjust contracts'. Can this be applied to contemporary inequality, in terms of social class mobility and in terms of global inequality between countries?

9

(Sociology of) Work in Progress

This final chapter considers two key areas in progress. The first section considers artificial intelligence (AI) as one of the most significant emerging developments within the sphere of work. The second section considers the progress made by the sociology of work in the analysis of work.

Technology in progress: artificial intelligence

Some very large claims have been made regarding the likely impact of artificial intelligence (AI) on the nature of work. Jarrahi (2018: 579) states that 'the recent hyperbole surrounding AI and other cognitive technologies has led many to believe that machines will soon outthink humans and replace them in the workplace'. Howcroft and Taylor (2023: 352) note that contemporary imagery regarding AI is 'dominated by images of anthropomorphised robots executing complex tasks and eliminating the need for human labour'. This section assesses these big claims, through considering emerging evidence on the role of AI at work, and, more importantly, through considering wider theoretical approaches within the sociology of work regarding technology at work. We start with the latter.

Sociologists of work point out that the big claims made at the inception of a new wave of technology are often informed by an implicit theoretical approach of *technological determinism*. Technological determinism involves the primary assumption that technology is an 'autonomous development which coerces and determines social and economic organization and relationships' (Grint, 1998: 267). In this approach, not only is technology per se given a determining role, but in addition, what technology does to organizations and work is seen as essentially inscribed within the technology itself. Sociologists of work tend to be very critical of technological determinism as it omits consideration of the social and political creation of the technology and the importance of social relations in influencing the effect of the introduction of forms of technology.

Research within the *social shaping of technology* approach (Mackenzie and Wajcman, 1999; Wajcman, 2006), by contrast, has these considerations as guiding principles. The social shaping of technology approach focuses on the social and political shaping of technology, and on the importance of the social and political in influencing how technology is used in practice at work. Wajcman (2006: 777) states that 'to say that technology is socially shaped is to stress that politics and negotiation are key processes through which technical possibilities are, or are not, put into practice'. Let us consider some examples of what this means in relation to analyses of earlier waves of technology.

In a pioneering study of the printing industry, prior to digitalization, Cockburn (1983) showed how the creation and retention of the heavy (50lb/23kg) printing blocks were a key part of the story of how women were kept out of the craft part of the printing industry, as they were regarded as too weak to be able to manipulate this heavy technology. Cockburn's subsequent (1985) *Machinery and Dominance* is a classic feminist analysis of how the use of new (at the time!) electronic technology in warehousing, clothing manufacture and hospital X-ray were deeply gendered in practice, with assumptions that enabled men, in 'men's jobs', to keep themselves separate from, and above, women, who occupied 'women's jobs'. Cockburn showed that men continued to be the technologists while women were predominantly the low-paid operators of the new technology systems.

Another revealing sociological analysis of a more recent form of technology is Kirkpatrick's (2004) examination of the hidden politics of the development of the personal computer (PC). Kirkpatrick contrasts the 'radical aspirations of the hippy hackers who invented the PC and who saw in it a kind of paradigm for democracy through the equal empowerment of each individual computer user' (p ix) with the development of mass-produced PCs in which individual empowerment is restricted through the strong inhibitions on user experimentation within the given design of the PC. Kirkpatrick argues that the original politics of empowering users with knowledge of the design principles behind the PC has been subverted through the social processes in the creation of the mass commodity of the PC. Further, he argues (p vii):

> Program interfaces [on PCs] are being designed to work with a specific conception of the human as an individual and as a creature with a known set of capacities and endowments. The alternatives – interfaces for more than one person to use at a time; interfaces for people with 'non-standard' sensory configurations or other physical endowments – tend to be left out of the picture.

A key thread in the analysis of the social relations of technology is the idea that technology is rarely neutral: it offers certain potential trajectories in how it is used, and tends to hinder other trajectories. This idea is crystallized in the concept of the *affordances* offered by technology. 'The concept of technology affordance refers to an action potential, that is, to what an individual or organization with a particular purpose can do with a technology or information system' (Majchrzak and Markus, 2013: 572). So, for example, Kirkpatrick's argument can be re-expressed as being about the highly circumscribed affordances in individual user empowerment offered by mass-produced PCs – in contrast to the high degree of affordances for empowerment imagined by the original designers of the PC in the 1960s.

Another important example of technology affordance can be seen in Zuboff's (1988) influential analysis of the role and use of information technology (IT) at work. Although her book *In the Age of the Smart Machine* was written at the end of the 1980s in relation to the first wave of IT, its insights are still relevant in considering the role of AI in the 21st century. Zuboff made the key analytical insight that *information technology* differs from previous forms of technology in that it not only automates (it involves a machine undertaking a task previously undertaken by humans), but it is also *informates*. Informating refers to IT automatically providing data on the (automated) tasks that it undertakes. No previous wave of technology had the capacity to informate. The rise of IT thus opened up vast new arenas of affordances. Zuboff then centred in on the key question of what sort of affordances of IT's informating capacity would become dominant. Specifically, would informating allow the development of whole new areas of information analysis and the generation of new skilled occupation in these areas, or would informating be used by management as part of an IT panopticon system of control (see Chapter 3), where IT allows management's observation of the labour process of workers to increase considerably? Zuboff argues that social and power relations at work will be crucial in the playing out of these different affordances.

Here, the next key questions become what affordances will tend to be supported by the pattern of social relation in a workplace and in an economy, and what affordances will tend to be closed off by those patterns of social relations? For instance, Holman et al's (2009) extensive survey-based study of call centres internationally finds that the use of IT for performance monitoring (IT as panopticon) was systematically less in coordinated market economies (see Chapter 3), where the power of labour is much higher than in liberal market economies.

All this suggests for the analysis of the likely impact of AI on work that we should be wary of predictions based on technological determinism, we should consider carefully the primary affordances of AI and we should consider how the social and political relations in the workplace and in the wider economy are likely to influence which affordances come to dominate. The following sections concentrate on addressing the last two of these points in turn.

Hunt et al's (2023) study found that 'the affordances of AI typically lend themselves to substitute, complement and/or augment human labour (sometimes in combination)'. *Substitution* involves the automation of tasks previously undertaken by humans. As an example of AI as substitution, Hunt et al discuss how an aerospace manufacturing firm turned to AI to automate quality control (the checking for defects) of manufactured items. Rather than people manually checking items, they were scanned by an AI-enabled system. *Complementing* involves AI systems being used by human workers to undertake the existing tasks of their jobs more accurately and/or faster. An example of complementing comes from a study of cancer detection in the images of lymph node cells (Wang et al, 2016). An AI-exclusive approach (substituting) had a 7.5 per cent error rate and human pathologists alone had a 3.5 per cent error rate. An approach combining inputs from both AI and pathologists (complementing) resulted in an error rate of 0.5 per cent. *Augmenting* involves the development of new human labour tasks further to the deployment of AI systems. The example from Hunt et al (2023) here is how the use of AI systems in financial risk modelling led to a substitution of relatively low-skill repetitive tasks in the job and the development of new tasks involving higher-level analytical skills further to the new information generated by the AI system.

Jarrahi (2018) has made an influential argument that the impact of AI in the workplace will involve a mixture of complementing and augmenting. The argument is that these are the primary affordances of AI. Jarrahi (p 571) 'highlights the complementarity of humans and AI and examines how each can bring their own [distinctive] strength in organizational decision-making processes'. He argues that decisions in organizations can be broadly divided into analytical decisions and intuitive decisions. The strength of AI is in its application to cases where there are clear, logically unambiguous, analytical decisions to be made. By contrast, the strength of humans becomes most manifest in cases involving the need for intuitive decision-making. Intuitive decision-making is where 'the individual draws upon past embodied practices, experiences, and judgments to react or decide without conscious attention' (Jarrahi, 2018: 579). Decisions at work can rarely be simply understood as purely analytical decisions, the argument continues. Rather, the common existence of ambiguity in terms of 'uncertainty, complexity, and equivocality' means that intuitive decision-making will continue to remain important. Pettersen (2019: 1058) uses a similar logic in her discussion of the role of AI in knowledge work. Because of the distinct strengths of both AI and humans, Jarrahi makes the case for a 'partnership' between AI and human labour at work.

The discussion so far of the affordances of AI in terms of substituting, complementing and augmenting human labour has focused on the implications for the nature of tasks for human workers. Another important way to think about the affordances of AI is in terms of the implications for the social relations of control and authority at work. Here, Holm and Lorenz (2022: 80) make an important distinction. Their study points to:

> two basic types of AI used in daily work, distinguishing between tasks where the employee receives orders or directions generated automatically by a computer or computerised machinery and tasks where the employee makes use of information compiled automatically by a computer or computerised machinery for further decision-making or for advising clients or customers.

For workers who receive orders or directions from AI systems, the affordance for the use of AI in an (intensified) mode of control appears to be strong.

Overall, the existing analyses of the affordances of AI suggest that there appears to be no clear substantive difference between AI and earlier waves of digital information and communication technology. Indeed, the most insightful studies tend to point to a continuity in the affordance of technology between AI and earlier IT waves.

Having considered the primary affordances of AI, let us turn to analyse how the social and political relations in the workplace and in the wider economy are likely to influence which affordances come to dominate. Valizade et al (2023) argue strongly against a technological-determinist approach to AI at work. They point to the importance of focusing on the interplay between technology (AI), organizational choices and structures. Notably, the findings of their survey-based study point to the impact of workers' collective voice mechanisms in affecting how AI is used in the workplace. This matches the findings of Milanez (2023), who reports an overview of nearly 100 case studies across eight countries. Some cases showed that the direct involvement of workers in AI development and implementation tended to reduce job loss anxiety and to improve workers' willingness to engage with AI technologies.

We can also extrapolate from Jarrahi (2018) regarding social forces leading to the dominance of certain affordances of AI. Jarrahi argues (following his abstract case for productive partnership between AI and human labour in the workplace) that these 'benefits of AI are likely to materialize only in *long-term* partnership with unique human capabilities' (p 583, emphasis added). This becomes problematic to realize when an economy is one dominated by *short-term* financial considerations (see Chapter 3) as 'the business value of AI adoption takes patience and a long-term perspective rather than relying on short-term ROI (return on investment) consideration for assessing immediate financial impacts' (Jarrahi, 2018: 583). In liberal market economies, where the threads of short-term financialized capitalism are woven the deepest, firms are more likely to focus on the use of AI in making short-term cost savings, primarily through job reduction, through automating/substituting.

We end this analysis of AI at work with a consideration of the likely role of AI in knowledge work and service work. A first overview point is that early research suggests there are likely to be significant differences in the implications of AI across these types of work. In high-skill knowledge work, there is a greater likelihood that affordances of complementing and augmenting will materialize. Van den Broek et al's (2021) sensitive ethnographic study of the introduction of AI in the process of hiring job candidates in a human resources department of a large international firm is a case in point. Despite the initial goal of excluding these knowledge workers from the process of technology development, AI-developers and HR-knowledge workers 'arrived at a hybrid practice that relied on a combination of machine learning [a form of AI] and domain [that is, HR] expertise' (p 1573). There was (p 1557): 'a process of mutual learning in which deep engagement with the technology triggered actors to reflect on how they produced knowledge. These reflections prompted the developers to iterate between excluding domain expertise from the machine learning system and including it.' By contrast, the affordance of AI with regard to intensified control may be likely to manifest particularly in call-centre work. Prior to the wave of introducing AI to the workplace, sociologists of work were already discussing the tight nature of control in many call centres – in terms of the combination of close measuring of outputs (for example, sales) and technologically mediated observation of the labour process (see Chapter 3). It is AI's potential to automatically 'read' people's emotions through voice cues that is likely to play a role in intensifying control further (McStay, 2018). McStay explained in an interview (in Lewis, 2019):

What we are talking about is 360-degree surveillance. ...Who benefits from that? I certainly don't think it's the mass of people within an organisation, ie its workers. We have this suite of technologies but then we also have this suite of financial opportunities. And it's whether these financial opportunities are a little bit too lucrative for people to be ethically minded.

The capacity of AI to read emotions may also have a role in the tightening of control through observation in other customer-facing service jobs.

Sociology of work: in progress

While 'in progress' in the previous section referred to the *ongoing nature* of the application of AI, in this section, 'in progress' refers to *progressive development* in the analysis of work that has come through sociology of work scholarship. This section is a concluding rounding-up of the analytical celebration of the sociology of work that has been a driving force through this book. It directly fulfils the promise within the second part of the subtitle of the book: *why we need* the sociology of work.

This section reflects on the considerable strengths of the sociology of work – strengths that have come through in the chapters of the book. The section argues that these strengths of the sociology of work can be usefully highlighted against important gaps and weaknesses in the scholarship in the neighbouring fields of the psychology of work, human resource management, organization studies and economics. Table 9.1 summarizes the main argument of the section. Key individual strengths of the sociology of work are summarized in the first column. The second column presents the contrast to corresponding weaknesses in some of the neighbouring fields of study, or, at least, in main tendencies within those neighbouring fields. This section addresses in turn each of the rows in the table. While I bring key threads of the book together here, I also introduce some additional research that underscores the points to be made. In the discussion of each row of the table, I point to the enduring importance of the sociology of work.

The importance, and distinctive nature, of work

A strong thread throughout this book has been the ways in which much sociology of work scholarship emphasizes the importance and distinctive qualities of work.

Table 9.1: Key strengths of the sociology of work

Key strengths of the sociology of work	Corresponding weaknesses/gaps in neighbouring fields
The importance of, and distinctive nature of, work	*Economics*: denial of anything distinctive in the nature of the employment relationship; *Organizational behaviour* and *organization studies*: focus on organization generally rather than the distinctive nature of *work* organization
The nature of theory: searching for connections between work and society	*HRM* and *organizational behaviour*: theorizing limited to the bounds of the organization
Focus on wider power structures and agency of *collective* workers	*Work psychology*: blindness to analysing wider structures of power; the individual as the unit of analysis

Going back to the set-up of the book in Chapter 1, a key argument of the book is that the social structures of work continue to constitute key structures of society. Chapter 2 shows how this idea has been theorized in a range of revealing ways within the sociology of work. For instance, for Marx, exploitation of labour within the labour process constitutes the (contradictory) heartbeat of the whole society, while, for Weber, seeing corporations as forms of bureaucracy was the key to understanding the nature of modern society. The opening section of Chapter 3 points to important *distinctive* qualities of employment within capitalism: asymmetry of power, the indeterminate nature of the employment relationship and the coexistence of conflict and cooperation. Many people would point to the feminist #MeToo movement as one of the most significant social movements of the early decades of the 21st century, and Chapter 6 makes the case that this movement was embedded in an understanding of the enmeshed structures of patriarchy *and* of employment as the core problem that was being exposed and challenged. Finally, Chapters 7 and 8 lay out how the nature of inequalities in employment is fundamental to the overall nature of inequality both within individual societies and, globally, between societies.

In addition, the theme of the continuing importance of work is strongly present in the examination in Chapter 5 of the ways in which people often create deep meanings around work – even where the structures of work may appear lacking in meaning to outsiders. Doherty's (2009) study of work identity and meaning in routine, low- and medium-skilled jobs across a range of sectors underscores this point. Doherty argues against 'the end of work as identity' thesis which portrays employment as no longer constituting a pillar in people's identities and which suggests that the growth of precarious employment conditions leads to a thinning-out in the meaning of, and attachment to, work. The workers interviewed by Doherty, by contrast, tended to state that work continues to be important to them in a range of ways, even in low- and medium-skill work settings: 'work remains an important source of identity, meaning and social affiliation' (Doherty, 2009: 84). For instance, bus drivers pointed to the 'intrinsic satisfaction in driving for a living and the social interaction with passengers: "Well, I love driving. And I'm a people person too"' (p 91). Retail workers similarly saw meaning and value in their work, in large part in relation to the social interaction with customers: 'People. I love people. Old, young, lovely people' (p 92).

This theme of the importance of work and the distinctive qualities of work is clearly invaluable in helping us to understand work and society. Although it is a core aspect to much sociology of work scholarship, it tends to be overlooked in many neighbouring fields of study. For instance, in neoclassical economics and branches of behavioural economics, the distinctive qualities of employment are implicitly theoretically denied. In neoclassical economics, labour is treated as a good like any other, subject to the laws of supply and demand (Machin, 2006). Sometimes, 'anomalies' like the 'stickiness' of wages may be observed, but are explained away as due to forms of market imperfection. For Oliver Williamson (2010) – whose transaction-cost economics theorizing led to the Nobel Prize for Economics in 2009 – the basic unit of analysis is the transaction. Whether a transaction relates to labour is immaterial in his abstract theorizing. The importance and distinctive qualities of work vanish from our understanding here. The character of Willy Loman in Arthur Miller's play *Death of a Salesman* rages against exactly this way of thinking when he famously exclaims 'a man is not a piece of fruit!' (also referenced in Chapter 3).

Another way for the important and distinctive qualities of work to vanish from analysis is through the placing of the *organization* as the unit of analysis and primary point of interest. Such an approach is often present in the fields of organizational behaviour and organization studies, as, indeed, their names suggest. When organization and organizing become the key focuses, the distinctiveness and importance of the *work* that is organized can easily fade away. Chapters 5 and 6 point to the way in which asymmetry of power becomes quickly absent from analysis within dominant streams of the organizational behaviour field. It is not uncommon for what sociologists of work recognize as worker resistance to be labelled forms of 'dysfunctional' behaviour within organizational behaviour scholarship. A similar logic allows some organizational behaviour scholars to define workers' collective voice as only involving the articulation of ideas that are useful for the improvement of production (Wilkinson et al, 2020).

In the early years of the field of organization studies, there was a clear and consistent central focus on the organization of work, and, as such, there was a rich overlap between that scholarship and sociology of work scholarship. In recent decades, however, the distinctive aspects of the organization of *work* have become increasingly marginalized in that scholarship. The European Group of Organization Studies is the key home of scholarship in the field of organization studies. It is revealing, therefore, that, of the 84 themes for research papers at its 2024 conference, only eight referenced work or employment in the title. The word 'worker/s' was completely absent from the theme titles. The central journal, *Organization Studies*, features rather more articles on the organization of such elements as markets (Geiger and Bourgeron, 2023), strategy (Pettit et al, 2023) and leadership (Tourish and Wilmott, 2023), and rather fewer articles on aspects of the organization of *work* and meaning of *work* for workers. In this context, it becomes almost inevitable that, first, dominant concepts are developed without reference to the importance and distinctiveness of work, and, then, those concepts are applied to the analysis of work and employment. In the process, much is lost. An example is the application of the concept of 'paradox' to analyse worker behaviour and understandings in organizations (Lempiälä et al, 2023). Lempiälä et al's study points to 'the intertwined nature of paradoxical tensions and the relationship between latency and salience in working through paradox'. They also advocate for 'developing a more systematic approach for studying the interactional foundations of organizational paradox' (p 1825). The idea – from the sociology of work – of systematic contradictions in work organization that relate to structural asymmetries of power in the nature of the economy has long since exited the stage. This is why we need the sociology of work.

The nature of theory: searching for connections between work and society

There is a range of ways in which theory is understood and used across the social sciences. Two important overviews of this range have been written by Merton (1967) and by Hirsch and Levin (1999). Fundamentally, they both point to a range in the levels of abstraction at which theory operates. Theory at the highest level of abstraction is described by Merton as driven by the aim of generalizing to abstract concepts such as social systems and society, and is characterized by Hirsch and Levin as undertaken by scholars who are advocates of 'umbrella' concepts and who seek to generalize to create 'a broad perspective'. Chapter 2 of this book notes that postmodern writers use the pejorative label of 'grand narratives' to describe theory at this high level of abstraction. Theory at the lowest level of abstraction is focused on creating discrete hypotheses regarding, or discrete understandings of, narrow empirical settings. Merton (1967) characterizes scholars who operate at this level of theory as 'radical empiricists', while Hirsch and Levin (1999: 200) use the label 'validity police' as a descriptor of the 'more methodologically oriented researchers who call for narrower perspectives that conform to more rigorous standards of validity and reliability'.

While Merton and Hirsch and Levin share this understanding that theorizing operates at a range of levels of abstraction, they differ in terms of the conclusions they draw from this regarding how theorizing should develop. Merton (1967) argues against both macro-level theorizing and against narrow empiricism in making the case for 'middle-range theory'. Middle-range theories consist of limited sets of assumptions from which specific hypotheses are logically derived and confirmed by empirical investigation, with these theories being consolidated into wider networks of theory. Hirsch and Levin (1999), by contrast, praise both the validity police and the umbrella advocates and argue that social scientific knowledge develops productively through a dialectical interplay between scholarship operating at these different levels of abstraction. They argue explicitly *against* thinking about theory progressing cumulatively (p 209): 'We have argued against the orthodox view that organizational behaviour is a field of pure progress; that is, that the field's knowledge [only] grows linearly as new data are added to the existing stock of research findings.' Social science knowledge develops through a constant, but non-regular, push and pull within scholarship at the different levels of abstraction.

Insightful sociology of work tends to be driven by a similar dynamic that Hirsch and Levin outline. Sociologists of work tend to be driven by a constant impulse to seek connections between work and society through theory. Sociologists of work study work settings, but do not see these work settings as isolated islands. Sociologists of work study work settings and seek to understand connections from those settings to other work settings and then to societal patterns and structures. This is why this overview sociology of work book and other overview books devote considerable space to outlining abstract theoretical perspectives that point to key linkages between work and society. Such theorizing is both the point of departure and the aspired-to return point for much sociology of work scholarship. Assumptions are taken from the abstract theorizing, perhaps Marx or Weber or feminism, and are used to underpin studies of work settings, with the findings then taken back to reflect on, and potentially to develop, such abstract theorizing. Theory in the sociology of work tends to be, therefore, a living thing – never complete, always open to adaptation and challenge.

Simmel (1994: 5) puts forward one of the most poetic descriptions of theorizing: 'We are at any moment those who separate the connected or connect the separate.' Applied to the sociology of work, this can refer to the constant attempts to both disaggregate ('separate the connected') abstract linkages between work and society and aggregate ('connect the separate') back up from work to society. These theoretical impulses at the heart of the sociology of work endeavour are present in many of the studies referenced in this book. Chapter 4 outlines the conceptualization in Korczynski (2002) of the organization of contemporary service work as a 'customer-oriented bureaucracy', which is but a disaggregation of Weber's concept of bureaucracy – a concept which, itself, can be positioned as a link to Weber's wider societal concept of the dominance of rational-legal authority. Chapter 3 shows that the concept of precarity is partly based on an aggregation of different forms of non-standard employment – from contingent work to flexible working arrangements. The characterization of post-Fordist society as a society of precarity in Chapter 3 and indeed Standing's (2011) argument that societal-level class politics will increasingly become informed by the precariat both show the impulse of trying to reach up to connect understandings of work to understandings of society.

While these may be the theoretical impulses of much sociology of work, this is not to say that these impulses are always successfully worked through. The sociology of work scholarship is as likely to feature failed attempts to link understandings of work to understandings of society as it is to feature scholarship that makes meaningful connections between work and society. Regardless of whether the dialectical interplay between theory at the work level and theory at the societal level is productive or not, what I want to praise here is the driving theoretical impulse that I have outlined: the search for the theoretical connections between work and society.

By contrast, many neighbouring disciplines rather reside in Merton's middle-range theorizing, where making connections between work and society is a step too far. The fields of human resource management and organizational behaviour, for instance, feature scholarship within the bounds of organizations. They seek to develop a theory in the sense of Merton's concept of the middle range, by seeking to tie together concepts into a network of related ideas. However, this scholarship is not driven by the impulse to make connections from the arenas of employment to wider arenas. Research into high-performance work systems is a case in point. Kaufman's (2020) critical overview of this scholarship points to a number of limitations in this scholarship that seeks to locate clusters of HRM-related factors that contribute to high-performance outcomes. Much of this scholarship seeks to orient itself around middle-range concepts like ability, motivation and opportunity (Kaufman, 2020). However, if one comes to this scholarship from a sociology of work home, there is not just a 'missing environment external to the firm' (Kaufman, 2020: 55), there is also a lack of ambition to make connections between work and society. This is also why we need the sociology of work.

Focus on wider power structures and agency of collective workers

Another driving strength of the sociology of work is its simultaneous focus on wider structures of power and the agency of collective workers. This focus is never far away if you turn to any issue of the key sociology of work journals: *Work, Employment and Society* (for example Hammer and Adham, 2023; Valenzuela-Bustos et al, 2023) and *Work and Occupations* (for example Cornfield, 2023; Vallas and Johnston, 2023). This focus has, of course, been a strong theme in this book. The social theories examined in Chapter 2 put forward different ideas about what constitute the key structures of power – running through both work and society – ranging from Durkheim on the division of labour to feminism on patriarchy. While the social theories surveyed differ regarding what constitutes the key structures of power, they all (apart from postmodernism) share the same foundational question about what the key structures of power are. Chapter 3 continues the examination of debates regarding how to conceptualize contemporary forms of capitalism – understood as a structure of power, as well as an economic system. The final section of Chapter 3 – on control at work – and then Chapter 4 – on the organization of work – take the examination of structures of power down from the macro-societal level to the level of work organization. With these key structures at the level of work and society established, Chapters 5 and 6 focus on the agency and voice of workers within these structures. Although the sociology of work often cedes the floor to the field of organizational behaviour for the analysis of workers creating meaning that is supportive of the structures in which they work, these chapters argue that a good sociology of work should consider the agency and voice of workers, regardless of whether the meanings, practices and voice generated are supportive or resistive of (elements of) the structures in which they labour. A key thread within these two chapters, which together constitute an analytical celebration of the agency and voice of workers, is the importance of not viewing workers as isolated individuals, but understanding them as people who come to *collective* meanings and generate *collective* norms of behaviour, and whose voice can only have real resonance when that voice is a *collective* one. Consider, from Chapter 5, the heart-breaking description of the animal shelter worker killing a dog as part of her job. This was not simply an individual's reaction; it was an individual's reaction within a wider pattern of collective norms and behaviour. Consider too, from Chapter 6, the examination of the #MeToo movement. This was not simply individual women tweeting about their individual experiences; rather, it was a social movement constituted by women acting collectively.

The focus on wider power structures and on the voice and agency of collective workers appears fundamental to understanding the sphere of employment. However, this is not a focus that is shared in some other fields of scholarship that also examine the sphere of employment. Such a focus is most notably absent in the fields of work/ organizational psychology. It is particularly important to be aware of the weaknesses and gaps in the field of work psychology because it is becoming increasingly clear that many debates around work are being dominated by scholarship embedded within psychology. Indeed, the growing colonization of debates by psychology scholars and the negative implications of that are now critiqued through a backlash against the 'psychologization' of the study of the employment relationship (Godard, 2014; Budd, 2020; Kaufman, 2020; Barry and Wilkinson, 2022).

Important limitations in work psychology against the strengths within the sociology of work are illustrated in the argument in Korczynski (2023) pointing to weaknesses in the concept of the psychological contract, and the argument for the alternative, more sociological concept of the social contract of work. The context is that Rousseau's (1995 and 1998) concept of the psychological contract has come to be a mainstream concept within the analysis of work, such that it has even come to be adopted by some sociologists of work. The following definition from Rousseau (1995: 9) has become a pillar for the vast and growing psychological contract field: 'The psychological contract is individual beliefs, shaped by the organization, regarding terms of an exchange agreement between the individual and the organization.' First, in Korczynski (2023), I point to the *individual* as the key unit of analysis in the concept of the psychological contract as a major weakness. This is because there is a considerable body of research which shows that workers' understandings of the nature of give-and-take obligations in the employment relationship tend to be *collective* rather than individual phenomena. Curiously, even Rousseau (1995: 8) herself acknowledges the importance of collectively held understandings, that 'group members interpret contracts together and often come to share a point of view that becomes reality to new members'. In Hodson's (2001: 203) overview of workplace ethnographies, he points to a strong, consistent pattern of co-worker relations being central to '(1) socialization to occupational norms, (2) solidarity and mutual defense, (3) resistance to authority and role distancing'. In other words, the *collective* is central to key elements in the understanding and playing out of the exchange within the employment relationship.

Second, in Korczynski (2023), I argue that the concept of the psychological contract overlooks structures of power in and around the employment relationship. Returning to Rousseau's definition (1995: 9), she postulates that the individual's psychological contract relates to the 'terms of an exchange agreement between the individual and their organization'. Rousseau's placing of the *exchange* agreement as the core substantive content of the psychological contract has the effect of writing out the profound imbalance of power that is present in the *employment* relationship. Cullinane and Dundon (2006) argue that it is little surprise, therefore, that management practitioners are increasingly attracted to the implicitly unitarist concept of the psychological contract. Korczynski (2023) offers a sociological corrective to Rousseau's flawed approach by putting forward *the effort bargain* as the core substantive element to which a group of workers' implicit understanding relates. The term 'effort bargain' is associated with Baldamus' (1961) discussion of the social relations underpinning effort in production. Notably, Baldamus acknowledges the core power imbalance immanent to the employment relationship: 'we shall assume from the start that employer–employee relations present a structure of differentiated power that reflects unequally distributed advantages and disadvantages' (p 7). Further, the concept of the effort bargain suggests that any social order in a workplace is, in effect, a temporary compromise based on the playing out of power of workers and employers respectively.

Overall, Korczynski (2023) puts forward the concept of the social contract of work as an alternative to Rousseau's concept of the psychological contract, defining the social contract of work as 'workers' collective, implicit, and socially embedded, understanding of the effort bargain at work' (p 115). This is a concept rooted in one of the key strengths of the sociology of work: the focus on workers' collective agency as well as the structures of power. This strength shines all the more brightly when highlighted against the limitations and weaknesses of analysis of employment within neighbouring fields (in this instance, work psychology). Thus, I end this book by keeping true to the promise of the book's subtitle and pointing to the final of many important reasons *why we need the sociology of work.*

Sociological imagination – your turn

Artificial intelligence

Talk with your fellow students about how you have used AI in your studies at school, college and university. Do you think your use of AI mainly *substitutes* what you previously did (or what previous students did), *complements* your work or *augments* your work? How might schools, colleges or universities use AI as a surveillance technology to check on students' work?

Sociology of work in progress

Are you persuaded that: a) work is important to people, beyond the wages that they accrue; and b) work has important distinctive elements from other forms of exchange or transaction in contemporary society? Why, or why not?

Reflection

Reflecting on the whole book, has the book helped you to develop your sociological imagination in terms of seeing important connections between work and society that you had not considered before? What are those important connections that you now perceive?

References

Abbott, A. (1988) *The System of Professions*, London: University of Chicago Press.

Abbott, P., Tyler, M. and Wallace, C. (2005) *An Introduction to Sociology: Feminist Perspectives*, London: Routledge.

Acker, J. (1990) 'Hierarchies, jobs, bodies: A theory of gendered organizations', *Gender and Society*, 5: 390–407.

Ackroyd, S. and Thompson, P. (1999) *Organisational Misbehaviour* (1st edition), London: Sage.

Ackroyd, S. and Thompson, P. (2022) *Organisational Misbehaviour* (2nd edition), London: Sage.

Adler, P.S. (1997) 'Work organization: From Taylorism to teamwork', *Perspectives on Work*, 1(1): 61–65.

Adler, P.S. (2015) 'Community and innovation: From Tönnies to Marx', *Organization Studies*, 36(4): 445–471.

Alberti, G., Bessa, I., Hardy, K., Trappmann, V. and Umney, C. (2018) 'In, against and beyond precarity: Work in insecure times', *Work, Employment and Society*, 32(3): 447–457.

Alvesson, M. and Thompson, P. (2005) 'Post-bureaucracy?', in S. Ackroyd, R. Batt, P. Thompson and P. Tolbert (eds) *The Oxford Handbook of Work and Organization*, Oxford: Oxford University Press, pp 485–507.

Anteby, M. and Chan, C.K. (2018) 'A self-fulfilling cycle of coercive surveillance: Workers' invisibility practices and managerial justification', *Organization Science*, 29(2): 247–263.

Apitzsch, B., Wilkesmann, M., Ruiner, C., Bassyiouny, M., Ehlen, R. and Schulz, L. (2022) 'Labour market collectivism: New solidarities of highly skilled freelance workers in medicine, IT and the film industry', *Economic and Industrial Democracy*, doi.org/10.1177/0143831X221120534.

Appelbaum, E. and Batt, R. (2014) *Private Equity at Work: When Wall Street Manages Main Street*, New York: Russell Sage Foundation.

Ashley, L. (2022) *Highly Discriminating: Why the City Isn't Fair and Diversity Doesn't Work*, Bristol: Bristol University Press.

Atkinson, A.B. and Jenkins, S.P. (2020) 'A different perspective on the evolution of UK income inequality', *Review of Income and Wealth*, 66(2): 253–266.

Atzeni, M. (2021) 'Workers' organizations and the fetishism of the trade union form: Toward new pathways for research on the labour movement?', *Globalizations*, 18(8): 1349–1362.

Azzellini, D. (2018) 'Labour as a commons: The example of worker-recuperated companies', *Critical Sociology*, 44(4–5): 763–776.

Baccaro, L., Benassi, C. and Meardi, G. (2019) 'Theoretical and empirical links between trade unions and democracy', *Economic and Industrial Democracy*, 40(1): 3–19.

Bailey, C. and Madden, A. (2017) 'Time reclaimed: Temporality and meaningful work', *Work, Employment and Society*, 31(1): 3–18.

Bain, P. and Taylor, P. (2000) 'Entrapped by the "electronic panopticon"? Worker resistance in the call centre', *New Technology, Work and Employment*, 15(1): 2–18.

Baines, D. (2016) 'Moral projects and compromise resistance: Resisting uncaring in nonprofit care work', *Studies in Political Economy*, 97(2): 124–142.

Baldamus, W. (1961) *Efficiency and Effort*, London: Routledge.

Baldry, C., Bain, P. and Taylor, P. (1998) '"Bright satanic offices": Intensification, control and team Taylorism', in P. Thompson and C. Warhurst (eds) *Workplaces of the Future*, Basingstoke: Palgrave Macmillan, pp 163–183.

Baldry, C., Bain, P., Taylor, P., Hyman, J., Scholarios, D., Marks, A., Watson, A., Gilbert, K., Gall, G. and Bunzel, D. (eds) (2007) *The Meaning of Work in the New Economy*, Basingstoke: Palgrave Macmillan.

Barker, J.R. (1993) 'Tightening the iron cage: Concertive control in self-managing teams', *Administrative Science Quarterly*, 38: 408–437.

Barley, S.R. (1989) 'Careers, identities, and institutions: The legacy of the Chicago School of Sociology', in M.B. Arthur, D.T. Hall and B.S. Lawrence (eds) *Handbook of Career Theory*, New York: Cambridge University Press, pp 41–65.

Barnard, S., Dainty, A., Lewis, S. and Culora, A. (2023) 'Conceptualising work as a "safe space" for negotiating LGBT identities: Navigating careers in the construction sector', *Work, Employment and Society*, 37(6): 1565–1582.

Barry, M. and Wilkinson, A. (2022) 'Employee voice, psychologisation and human resource management', *Human Resource Management Journal*, 32(3): 631–646.

Baruch, Y. (2004) 'Transforming careers: From linear to multidirectional career paths: Organizational and individual perspectives', *Career Development International*, 9(1): 58–73.

Baudrillard, J. (1994) *Simulacra and Simulation*, Ann Arbor, MI: University of Michigan Press.

Bauman, Z. (1989) *Modernity and the Holocaust*, Cambridge: Polity.

Bauman, Z. (2004) *Work, Consumerism and the New Poor*, Cambridge: Polity.

Bayard de Volo, L. (2003) 'Service and surveillance: Infrapolitics at work among casino cocktail waitresses', *Social Politics: International Studies in Gender, State and Society*, 10(3): 346–376.

Beamish, T.D. and Biggart, N.W. (2006) 'Economic worlds of work: Uniting economic sociology with the sociology of work', in M. Korczynski, R. Hodson and P.K. Edwards (eds) *Social Theory at Work*, Oxford: Oxford University Press, pp 233–271.

Beck, U. (2000) *The Brave New World of Work*, London: John Wiley and Sons.

Becker, G. (1991) *A Treatise on the Family*, Cambridge, MA: Harvard University Press.

Bell, E., Mangia, G., Taylor, S. and Toraldo, M.L. (eds) (2018) *The Organization of Craft Work: Identities, Meanings, and Materiality*, London: Routledge.

Belt, V. (2002) Women's Work and Restructuring in the Service Economy: The Case of Telephone Call Centres, PhD thesis, University of Newcastle upon Tyne.

Berggren, C. (1993) *Alternatives to Lean Production: Work Organization in the Swedish Auto Industry*, Ithaca, NY: Cornell University Press.

Bernat, I. and Whyte, D. (2017) 'State-corporate crime and the process of capital accumulation: Mapping a global regime of permission from Galicia to Morecambe Bay', *Critical Criminology*, 25(1): 71–86.

Beynon, H. (1975) *Working for Ford*, London: Penguin.

Bhambra, G. (2007) *Rethinking Modernity: Postcolonialism and the Sociological Imagination*, London: Springer.

Bhambra, G. (2014) *Connected Sociologies*, London: Bloomsbury.

Bhuiyan, J. (2019) 'How the Google walkout transformed tech workers into activists', *LA Times*, latimes.com/business/technology/story/2019-11-06/google-employee-walkout-tech-industry-activism [accessed 1 April 2023].

Bieler, A. and Nowak, J. (2021) 'Labour conflicts in the Global South: Towards a new theory of resistance?', *Globalizations*, 18(8): 1467–1471.

Billig, M. (2013) *Learn to Write Badly: How to Succeed in the Social Sciences*, Cambridge: Cambridge University Press.

Bilton, T., Bonnett, K., Jones, P., Stanworth, M., Sheard, K. and Webster, A. (2002) *Introductory Sociology*, Basingstoke: Macmillan.

Block, F. (2001) 'Introduction' to K. Polanyi, *The Great Transformation*, Boston: Beacon Press, pp xviii–xxxviii.

Blyton, P. and Jenkins, J. (2007) *Key Concepts in Work*, London: Sage.

Blyton, P.R. and Turnbull, P.J. (2004) *The Dynamics of Employee Relations*, Basingstoke: Palgrave Macmillan.

Boland, T. and Griffin, R. (eds) (2015) *The Sociology of Unemployment*, Manchester: Manchester University Press.

Bolton, S.C. (2005) *Emotion Management in the Workplace*, Basingstoke: Palgrave Macmillan.

Bolton, S. and Muzio, D. (2008) 'The paradoxical processes of feminization in the professions: The case of established, aspiring and semi-professions', *Work, Employment and Society*, 22(2): 281–299.

Bond, S. and Sales, J. (2001) 'Household work in the UK: An analysis of the British Household Panel Survey 1994', *Work, Employment and Society*, 15(2): 233–250.

Bone, J. (2006) *The Hard Sell: An Ethnographic Study of the Direct Selling Industry*, Aldershot: Ashgate.

Bourdieu, P. (1984) *Distinction: A Sociological Critique of the Judgement of Taste*, London: Routledge.

Bourdieu, P. (1998) *Acts of Resistance: Against the New Myths of Our Time*, Cambridge: Polity.

Boyer, R. (1996) 'Capital–labour relations in OECD countries: From Fordian golden age to contested national trajectories', in J. Schor (ed) *Capital, the State and Labour*, Aldershot: Edward Elgar, pp 18–69.

Braverman, H. (1974) *Labor and Monopoly Capital*, New York: Monthly Review Press.

Brinkley, I., Fauth, R., Mahdon, M. and Theodoropoulou, S. (2009) *A Knowledge Economy Programme Report*, London: The Work Foundation.

Briskin, L. (2008) 'Cross-constituency organizing in Canadian unions', *British Journal of Industrial Relations*, 46(2): 221–247.

Brown, J.S. and Duguid, P. (1991) 'Organizational learning and communities-of-practice: Toward a unified view of working, learning, and innovation', *Organization Science*, 2(1): 40–57.

Brown, K. and Korczynski, M. (2010) 'When caring and surveillance technology meet: Organizational commitment and discretionary effort in home care work', *Work and Occupations*, 37(3): 404–432.

Budd, J.W. (2020) 'The psychologisation of employment relations, alternative models of the employment relationship, and the OB turn', *Human Resource Management Journal*, 30(1): 73–83.

Bukodi, E. and Goldthorpe, J. (2019) *Social Mobility and Education in Britain: Research, Politics and Policy*, Cambridge: Cambridge University Press.

Bulut, E. (2020) *A Precarious Game: The Illusion of Dream Jobs in the Video Game Industry*, Ithaca, NY: Cornell University.

Burawoy, M. (1979) *Manufacturing Consent: Changes in the Labor Process under Monopoly Capitalism*, Chicago, IL: University of Chicago Press.

Burnett, J. and Whyte, D. (2010) *The Wages of Fear: Risk, Safety and Undocumented Work*, Leeds: Positive Action for Refugees and Asylum Seekers and the University of Liverpool.

Burrell, G. (1988) 'Modernism, post modernism and organizational analysis 2: The contribution of Michel Foucault', *Organization Studies*, 9(2): 221–235.

Burrell, G. (2006) 'Foucauldian and postmodern thought and the analysis of work', in M. Korczynski, R. Hodson and P.K. Edwards (eds) *Social Theory at Work*, Oxford: Oxford University Press, pp 155–181.

Burrell, G. and Morgan, G. (1979) *Sociological Paradigms*, London: Heinneman.

Cañada, E., Izcara, C. and Zapata Campos, M.J. (2023) 'Putting fairness into the gig economy: Delivery cooperatives as alternatives to corporate platforms', *Societies*, 13(3): 68–82.

Cappelli, P., Bassi, L., Katz, H., Knoke, D., Osterman, P. and Useem, M. (1997) *Change at Work*, Oxford: Oxford University Press.

Casey, C. (1995) *Work, Self and Society*, London: Routledge.

Castells, M. (2000) *The Information Age: Economy, Society and Culture, Volume I*, Oxford: Blackwell.

Castles, S. and Miller, M.J. (2019) *The Age of Migration: International Population Movements in the Modern World*, London: Bloomsbury.

Causa, O. and Johansson, Å. (2010) 'Intergenerational social mobility in OECD countries', *OECD Journal: Economic Studies*, 2010(1): 1–44.

Cavendish, R. (1982) *Women on the Line*, London: Routledge.

Charlesworth, S.J. (2000) *A Phenomenology of Working-Class Experience*, Cambridge: Cambridge University Press.

Chen, W. (2023) 'Class performance: An empirical case of Chinese service workers in hair salons', *Regional Science Policy and Practice*, doi: 10.1111/rsp3.12657.

Chertkovskaya, E., Watt, P., Tramer, S. and Spoelstra, S. (2013) 'Giving notice to employability', *Ephemera*, 13(4): 701–716.

China Labour Watch (2010) '"We are extremely tired, with tremendous pressure": A follow-up investigation of Foxconn', chinalaborwatch.org/we-are-extremely-tired-with-tremendous-pressure-a-follow-up-investigation-of-foxconn/ [accessed 9 March 2024].

Chowdhury, R. (2017) 'Rana Plaza fieldwork and academic anxiety: Some reflections', *Journal of Management Studies*, 54(7): 1111–1117.

Ciepley, D. (2023) 'Democracy and the corporation: The long view', *Annual Review of Political Science*, 26: 489–517.

Cini, L., Maccarrone, V. and Tassinari, A. (2022) 'With or without U(nions)? Understanding the diversity of gig workers' organizing practices in Italy and the UK', *European Journal of Industrial Relations*, 28(3): 341–362.

Cioce, G., Korczynski, M. and Però, D. (2022) 'The improvised language of solidarity: Linguistic practices in the participatory labour-organizing processes of multi-ethnic migrant workers', *Human Relations*, 76(12): 1855–1880.

Clark, K. and Nolan, S. (2021) The Changing Distribution of the Male Ethnic Wage Gap in Great Britain, IZA discussion paper no. 14276, Bonn: Institute of Labor Economics (IZA).

Clarke, A. and Smith, C. (2024) 'Reproducing a white elite: The chief officers' "club" in the London Metropolitan Police Service', *Work, Employment and Society*, doi: 10.1177/09500170231199415.

Clarke, S. (1990) 'The crisis of Fordism or the crisis of social democracy', *Telos*, 83: 71–98.

Clegg, S. (1990) *Modern Organizations: Studies in the Postmodern World*, London: Sage.

Cockburn, C. (1983) *Brothers: Male Dominance and Technical Change*, London: Pluto Press.

Cockburn, C. (1985) *Machinery of Dominance: Women, Men and Technical Know-How*, London: Pluto Press.

Cohen, L. and Mallon, M. (2001) 'My brilliant career? Using stories as a methodological tool in careers research', *International Studies of Management and Organization*, 31(3): 48–68.

Cohen, L., Duberley, J. and Smith, P. (2019) 'Losing the faith: Public sector work and the erosion of career calling', *Work, Employment and Society*, 33(2): 326–335.

Cohen, N. and Richards, J. (2015) 'Evaluating self-organised employee coping practices conducted via Facebook', *New Technology, Work and Employment*, 30(3): 222–236.

Cohen, S. and Taylor, L. (2003) *Escape Attempts: The Theory and Practice of Resistance in Everyday Life*, London: Routledge.

Connell, R. (2005) *Masculinities*, Cambridge: Polity.

Cooke, W. (2003) 'The influence of industrial relations systems factors on foreign direct investment', in W. Cooke (ed) *Multinational Companies and Global Human Resource Strategies*, Westport, CT: Quorum, pp 498–508.

Cornfield, D.B. (2023) 'The new labor activism, a new labor sociology', *Work and Occupations*, 50(3): 316–334.

Cornforth, C. (1995) 'Patterns of cooperative management: Beyond the degeneration thesis', *Economic and Industrial Democracy*, 16(4): 487–523.

Costa, S., Boatcă, M. and Franco, G. (2010) 'Postcolonial sociology: State of the art and perspectives', *Sociological Studies*, 28: 335–358.

Cottom, T.M. (2020) 'The hustle economy', *Dissent*, 67(4): 19–25.

Couloigner, S. (2022) Making Sense of Brexit: French Skilled Workers Negotiating their Migration, Intergration and Identification in the UK, PhD thesis, University of Nottingham.

Cova, B. and Dalli, D. (2009) 'Working consumers: The next step in marketing theory?', *Marketing Theory*, 9: 315–339.

Covaleski, M.A., Dirsmith, M.W., Heian, J.B. and Samuel, S. (1998) 'The calculated and the avowed: Techniques of discipline and struggles over identity in Big Six public accounting firms', *Administrative Science Quarterly*, 43(2): 293–327.

Cox, A. (2005) 'What are communities of practice? A comparative review of four seminal works', *Journal of Information Science*, 31(6): 527–540.

Crompton, R. (2008) *Class and Stratification*, Oxford: Polity.

Csikszentmihalhi, M. (2020) *Finding Flow: The Psychology of Engagement with Everyday Life*, London: Hachette.

Cullinane, N. and Dundon, T. (2006) 'The psychological contract: A critical review', *International Journal of Management Reviews*, 8(2): 113–129.

Cushen, J. (2009) 'Branding employees', *Qualitative Research in Accounting and Management*, 6(1/2): 102–114.

De Angelis, M. (2017) *Omnia Sunt Communia: On the Commons and the Transformation to Postcapitalism*, London: Zed Books.

De Certeau, M. (1984) *The Practice of Everyday Life*, London: University of California Press.

Deery, S., Kolar, D. and Walsh, J. (2019) 'Can dirty work be satisfying? A mixed method study of workers doing dirty jobs', *Work, Employment and Society*, 33(4): 631–647.

De Maio, F.G. (2007) 'Income inequality measures', *Journal of Epidemiology and Community Health*, 61(10): 849–852.

Department of Business (2022) *Trade Union Membership, UK 1995–2021*, London: HMSO Statistical Bulletin.

Desmond, M. (2023) *Poverty, by America*, London: Allen Lane.

Devine, F., Britton, J., Mellor, R. and Halfpenny, P. (2000) 'Professional work and professional careers in Manchester's business and financial sector', *Work, Employment and Society*, 14(3): 521–540.

Dickens, L. (2000) 'Still wasting resources? Equality in employment', in S. Bach and K. Sisson (eds) *Personnel Management*, Oxford: Blackwell, pp 137–170.

Dill, J.S. and Morgan, J.C. (2017) 'Employability among low-skill workers: Organizational expectations and practices in the US health care sector', *Human Relations*, 71(7): 1001–1022.

Discenna, T.A. (2016) 'The discourses of free labor: Career management, employability, and the unpaid intern', *Western Journal of Communication*, 80(4): 435–452.

Dobrow, S.R. and Tosti-Kharas, J. (2011) 'Calling: The development of a scale measure', *Personnel Psychology*, 64(4): 1001–1049.

Doellgast, V., Lillie, N. and Pulignano, V. (eds) (2018) *Reconstructing Solidarity: Labour Unions, Precarious Work, and the Politics of Institutional Change in Europe*, Oxford: Oxford University Press.

Doerflinger, N. (2022) 'Social interactions at work: Why interactive work should be an analytical category in its own right', *Employee Relations: The International Journal*, 44(7): 81–95.

Doeringer, P.B. and Piore, M.J. (1970) *Internal Labor Markets and Manpower Analysis*, New York: Routledge.

Doherty, M. (2009) 'When the working day is through: The end of work as identity?', *Work, Employment and Society*, 23(1): 84–101.

Donaghey, J., Cullinane, N., Dundon, T. and Wilkinson, A. (2011) 'Reconceptualising employee silence: Problems and prognosis', *Work, Employment and Society*, 25(1): 51–67.

Donne, J. (1624/1987) *Devotions upon Emergent Occasions*, Oxford: Oxford University Press.

Dorling, D. (2019) *Inequality and the 1%*, London: Verso.

Draper, H. (1978) *Karl Marx's Theory of Revolution: Volume 2*, New York: Monthly Review.

Duménil, G. and Lévy, D. (2018) *Managerial Capitalism: Ownership, Management and the Coming New Mode of Production*, London: Pluto Press.

Dundon, T. and Rollinson, D. (2004) *Employment Relations in Non-Union Firms*, London: Routledge.

Dundon, T., Wilkinson, A., Marchington, M. and Ackers, P. (2004) 'The meanings and purpose of employee voice', *The International Journal of Human Resource Management*, 15(6): 1149–1170.

Dunford, R. and Perrons, D. (2014) 'Power, privilege and precarity: The gendered dynamics of contemporary inequality', in M. Evans, C. Hemming, M. Henry and H. Johnstone (eds) *The Sage Handbook of Feminist Theory*, London: Sage, pp 465–482.

Durkheim, E. (1893/1964) *The Division of Labour in Society*, New York: Free Press.

Edgell, S. and Granter, E. (2020) *The Sociology of Work*, London: Sage.

Edwards, P.K. (1986) *Conflict at Work*, Oxford: Blackwell.

Edwards, P. and Hodder, A. (2022) 'Conflict and control in the contemporary workplace: Structured antagonism revisited', *Industrial Relations Journal*, 53(3): 220–240.

Edwards, P. and Whitston, C. (1993) *Attending to Work: The Management of Attendance and Shopfloor Order*, Oxford: Blackwell.

Edwards, P., Bélanger, J. and Wright, M. (2006) 'The bases of compromise in the workplace: A theoretical framework', *British Journal of Industrial Relations*, 44(1): 125–145.

Edwards, R. (1979) *Contested Terrain: The Transformation of the Workplace in the Twentieth Century*, London: Heinemann.

Egan, R.D. (2006) 'Resistance under the black light: Exploring the use of music in two exotic dance clubs', *Journal of Contemporary Ethnography*, 35(2): 201–219.

EHRC (2014) *Gender-Neutral Job Evaluation Schemes*, Manchester: Equality and Human Rights Commission.

EHRC (2017a) *The Ethnicity Pay Gap*, research report 108, Manchester: Equality and Human Rights Commission.

EHRC (2017b) *The Gender Pay Gap*, research report 109, Manchester: Equality and Human Rights Commission.

El-Sawad, A. and Korczynski, M. (2007) 'Management and music: The exceptional case of the IBM Songbook', *Group and Organization Management*, 32(1): 79–108.

England, P. (1992) *Comparable Worth: Theories and Evidence*, New York: Aldine de Gruyter.

England, P. (2005) 'Emerging theories of care work', *Annual Review of Sociology*, 31(1): 381–399.

England, P. (2010) 'The gender revolution uneven and stalled', *Gender and Society*, 24(2): 49–66.

Ens, N. (2021) Tales of hustling in the digital economy, paper presented at Data and Society workshop, The Hustle Economy.

Erickson, K.A. (2009) *The Hungry Cowboy: Service and Community in a Neighborhood Restaurant*, Jackson, MS: University Press of Mississippi.

Eyles, A., Major, L.E. and Machin, S. (2022) *Social Mobility: Past, Present and Future*, London: The Sutton Trust.

Faist, T. (2016) 'Cross-border migration and social inequalities', *Annual Review of Sociology*, 42(2): 323–346.

Fernie, S. and Metcalf, D. (1998) (Not) Hanging on the Telephone: Payment Systems in the New Sweatshops, working paper no. 390, Centre for Economic Performance, London School of Economics and Political Science.

Fevre, R. (2000) 'Review of Richard Sennett's *Corrosion of Character*', *Work, Employment and Society*, 14(4): 797–800.

Fevre, R. (2003) *The New Sociology of Economic Behaviour*, London: Sage.

Findlay, P., McKinlay, A., Marks, A. and Thompson, P. (2000) 'In search of perfect people teamwork and team players in the Scottish spirits industry', *Human Relations*, 53(12): 1549–1574.

Flaherty, E. (2015) 'Top incomes under finance-driven capitalism, 1990–2010: Power resources and regulatory orders', *Socio-Economic Review*, 13(3): 417–447.

Fleming, P. and Sturdy, A. (2011) '"Being yourself" in the electronic sweatshop: New forms of normative control', *Human Relations*, 64(2): 177–200.

Fligstein, N. (2014) 'The sociology of Picketty's Capital', *Contemporary Sociology*, 43(6): 791–794.

Fligstein, N. and Goldstein, A. (2022) 'The legacy of shareholder value capitalism', *Annual Review of Sociology*, 48: 193–211.

Forde, C., Stuart, M. and Joyce, S. (2017) *The Social Protection of Workers in the Platform Economy*, report PE 614.184, Brussels: European Parliament.

Foreign Policy (2012) 'Mongolia vs. eBay', foreignpolicy.com/2012/02/2urozoneia-vs-ebay [accessed 8 March 2024].

Forrier, A. and Sels, L. (2003) 'Temporary employment and employability: Training opportunities and efforts of temporary and permanent employees in Belgium', *Work, Employment and Society*, 17(4): 641–666.

Foucault, M. (1977) *Discipline and Punish*, London: Penguin.

Fox, A. (1966) Industrial Sociology and Industrial Relations, Royal Commission research paper no. 3, London: HMSO.

Fox, A. (1971) *A Sociology of Work in Industry*, London: Collier-MacMillan.

Fox, A. (1974) *Beyond Contract: Work, Power and Trust Relations*, London: Faber and Faber.

Fox, A. (1985) *History and Heritage*, London: Allen and Unwin.

Frayne, D. (2015) *The Refusal of Work: The Theory and Practice of Resistance to Work*, London: Zed Books.

Frega, R., Herzog, L. and Neuhäuser, C. (2019) 'Workplace democracy: The recent debate', *Philosophy Compass*, 14(4): e12574.

Frenkel, S. (2006) 'Towards a theory of dominant interests, globalization and work', in M. Korczynski, R. Hodson and P.K. Edwards (eds) *Social Theory at Work*, Oxford: Oxford University Press, pp 388–422.

Frenkel, S., Korczynski, M., Donoghue, L. and Shire, K. (1995) 'Re-constituting work: Trends towards knowledge work and info-normative control', *Work, Employment and Society*, 9(4): 773–796.

Frenkel, S., Korczynski, M., Shire, K.A. and Tam, M. (1999) *On the Front Line: Organization of Work in the Information Economy*, Ithaca, NY: Cornell University Press.

Friedland, W.H. (1971) *Migrant: Agricultural Workers in America's Northeast*, New York: Holt, Rinehart and Winston.

Friedman, A.L. (1977) *Industry and Labour: Class Struggle at Work and Monopoly Capitalism*, Basingstoke: Macmillan.

Friedman, S. and Laurison, D. (2019) *The Class Ceiling: Why It Pays to Be Privileged*, Bristol: Bristol University Press.

Friedson, E. (2001) *Professionalism: The Third Logic*, Cambridge: Polity.

Fuller, L. and Smith, V. (1991) 'Consumers' reports: Management by customers in a changing economy', *Work, Employment and Society*, 5(1): 1–16.

Gabriel, Y. and Lang, T. (2015) *The Unmanageable Consumer*, London: Sage.

Gabriel, Y., Korczynski, M. and Rieder, K. (2015) 'Organizations and their consumers: Bridging work and consumption', *Organization*, 22(5): 629–643.

Galtung, J. (1990) 'Theory formation in social research: A plea for pluralism', in E. Oyen (ed) *Comparative Methodology: Theory and Practice in International Social Research*, London: Sage, pp 96–112.

Gamble, J. (2007) 'The rhetoric of the consumer and customer control in China', *Work, Employment and Society*, 21(1): 7–25.

Gegenhuber, T., Ellmer, M. and Schüßler, E. (2020) 'Microphones, not megaphones: Functional crowdworker voice regimes on digital work platforms', *Human Relations*, 74(9): 1473–1503.

Geiger, S. and Bourgeron, T. (2023) 'In the name of transparency: Organizing European pharmaceutical markets through struggles over transparency devices', *Organization Studies*, doi: 01708406231171802.

Gereffi, G. and Korzeniewicz, M. (1994) *Commodity Chains and Global Capitalism*, New York: Bloomsbury.

Giddens, A. (1984) *The Constitution of Society*, Cambridge: Polity.

Giddens, A. and Sutton, P.W. (2021) *Sociology*, Cambridge: Polity.

Giles, A. (2000) 'Globalisation and industrial relations theory', *Journal of Industrial Relations*, 42(2): 173–194.

Ginn, J., Arber, S., Brannen, J., Dale, A., Dex, S., Elias, P. and Rubery, J. (1996) 'Feminist fallacies: A reply to Hakim on women's employment', *British Journal of Sociology*, 47(1): 167–174.

Glavin, P., Bierman, A. and Schieman, S. (2021) 'Über-alienated: Powerless and alone in the gig economy', *Work and Occupations*, 48(4): 399–431.

Glucksmann, M. (1990) *Women Assemble: Women Workers and the New Industries in Inter-War Britain*, London: Taylor and Francis.

Go, J. (2016) *Postcolonial Thought and Social Theory*, Oxford: Oxford University Press.

Godard, J. (2014) 'The psychologisation of employment relations?', *Human Resource Management Journal*, 24(1): 1–18.

Goffman, I. (1990) *The Presentation of Self in Everyday Life*, London: Penguin.

Goldthorpe, J.H., Lockwood, D., Bechhofer, F. and Platt, J. (1969) *The Affluent Worker in the Class Structure*, Cambridge: Cambridge University Press.

Goodrich, C. (1921) *The Frontier of Control: A Study in British Workshop Politics*, London: Harcourt Brace.

GOV.UK (2022) Employment by Occupation, ethnicity-facts-figures.service.gov.uk/work-pay-and-benefits/employment/employment-by-occupation/latest [accessed 8 March 2024].

Graeber, D. (2018) *Bullshit Jobs: A Theory*, London: Penguin Random House.

Green, F. (2001) 'It's been a hard day's night: The concentration and intensification of work in late twentieth-century Britain', *British Journal of Industrial Relations*, 39(1): 53–80.

Green, F. (2013) *Skills and Skilled Work*, Oxford: Oxford University Press.

Green, F., Felstead, A., Gallie, D. and Henseke, G. (2022) 'Working still harder', *ILR Review*, 75(2): 458–487.

Greenberg, E.S. (1986) *Workplace Democracy: The Political Effects of Participation*, Ithaca, NY: Cornell University Press.

Gregory, M.R. (2009) 'Inside the locker room: Male homosociability in the advertising industry', *Gender, Work and Organization*, 16(3): 323–347.

Gregory, P. and Stuart, R. (2013) *The Global Economy and Its Economic Systems*, Mason, OH: Cengage Learning.

Griesbach, K., Reich, A., Elliott-Negri, L. and Milkman, R. (2019) 'Algorithmic control in platform food delivery work', *Socius*, 5, doi: 2378023119870041.

Griffin, E. (2013) *Liberty's Dawn: A People's History of the Industrial Revolution*, New Haven, CT: Yale University Press.

Grimshaw, D. and Rubery, J. (1998) 'Integrating the internal and external labour markets', *Cambridge Journal of Economics*, 22(2): 199–220.

Grint, K. (1998) *The Sociology of Work* (2nd edition), Cambridge: Polity.

Gumbrell-McCormick, R. and Hyman, R. (2019) 'Democracy in trade unions, democracy through trade unions?', *Economic and Industrial Democracy*, 40(1): 91–110.

Gurney, L., Lockington, J., Quinn, L. and MacPhee, M. (2020) 'Why do we need wobble rooms during COVID-19?', *Nursing Leadership*, 33(4): 45–50.

Hakim, C. (2000) *Work-Lifestyle Choices in the 21st Century: Preference Theory*, Oxford: Oxford University Press.

Hall, E.J. (1993) 'Smiling, deferring, and flirting: Doing gender by giving "good service"', *Work and Occupations*, 20(4): 452–471.

Hall, P.A. and Soskice, D. (2001) *Varieties of Capitalism: The Institutional Foundations of Comparative Advantage*, Oxford: Oxford University Press.

Halpin, B.W. (2015) 'Subject to change without notice: Mock schedules and flexible employment in the United States', *Social Problems*, 62(3): 419–438.

Hammer, A. and Adham, A. (2023) 'Mobility power, state and the "sponsored labour regime" in Saudi capitalism', *Work, Employment and Society*, 37(6): 1497–1516.

Hamper, B. (1991) *Rivethead*, New York: Grand Central Publishing.

Hampson, I. and Junor, A. (2005) 'Invisible work, invisible skills: Interactive customer service as articulation work', *New Technology, Work and Employment*, 20(2): 166–181.

Hanser, A. (2008) *Service Encounters: Class, Gender, and the Market for Social Distinction in Urban China*, Stanford, CA: Stanford University Press.

Hardin, G. (1968) 'The tragedy of the commons', *Science*, 162(13): 1243–1248.

Harknett, K., Schneider, D. and Wolfe, R. (2020) 'Losing sleep over work scheduling? The relationship between work schedules and sleep quality for service sector workers', *SSM-Population Health*, 12, 100681.

Hartmann, H.I. (1979) 'The unhappy marriage of Marxism and feminism: Towards a more progressive union', *Capital and Class*, 3(2): 1–33.

Harvey, D. (1989) *The Condition of Postmodernity*, Oxford: Blackwell.

Heckscher, C. and McCarthy, J. (2014) 'Transient solidarities: Commitment and collective action in post-industrial societies', *British Journal of Industrial Relations*, 52(4): 627–657.

Heery, E. (2015) 'Unions and the organising turn: Reflections after 20 years of organising works', *Economic and Labour Relations Review*, 26(4): 545–560.

Heery, E. (2018) 'Fusion or replacement? Labour and the "new" social movements', *Economic and Industrial Democracy*, 39(4): 661–680.

Heery, E., Abbott, B. and Williams, S. (2012) 'The involvement of civil society organizations in British industrial relations: Extent, origins and significance', *British Journal of Industrial Relations*, 50(1): 47–72.

Heery, E., Hann, D. and Nash, D. (2017) 'The Living Wage campaign in the UK', *Employee Relations*, 39(6): 800–814.

Herzenberg, S.A., Alic, J.A. and Wial, H. (1998) *New Rules for a New Economy*, Ithaca, NY: Cornell University Press.

Hipp, L. (2020) 'Feeling secure vs. being secure? Qualitative evidence on the relationship between labour market institutions and employees' perceived job security from Germany and the US', *Contemporary Social Science*, 15(4): 416–429.

Hirsch, P.M. and Levin, D.Z. (1999) 'Umbrella advocates versus validity police: A life-cycle model', *Organization Science*, 10(2): 199–212.

Hirschman, A.O. (1982) 'Rival interpretations of market society: Civilizing, destructive, or feeble?', *Journal of Economic Literature*, 20(4): 1463–1484.

Hirst, A. (2001) *Links between Volunteering and Employability*, research report RR309, Cambridge.

Hislop, D., Bosua, R. and Helms, R. (2013) *Knowledge Management in Organizations: A Critical Introduction*, Oxford: Oxford University Press.

Hoch, P. (1972) *Rip Off the Big Game*, Garden City, NY: Doubleday.

Hochschild, A. (1983) *The Managed Heart: Commercialisation of Human Feeling*, New York: Routledge.

Hodgson, D. and Briand, L. (2013) 'Controlling the uncontrollable: "Agile" teams and illusions of autonomy in creative work', *Work, Employment and Society*, 27(2): 308–325.

Hodson, R. (1995) 'Worker resistance: An underdeveloped concept in the sociology of work', *Economic and Industrial Democracy*, 16(1): 79–110.

Hodson, R. (2001) *Dignity at Work*, Cambridge: Cambridge University Press.

Holm, J.R. and Lorenz, E. (2022) 'The impact of artificial intelligence on skills at work in Denmark', *New Technology, Work and Employment*, 37(1): 79–101.

Holman, D., Frenkel, S., Sørensen, O. and Wood, S. (2009) 'Work design variation and outcomes in call centers: Strategic choice and institutional explanations', *Industrial and Labor Relations Review*, 62(4): 510–532.

Howard, P.N., Duffy, A., Freelon, D., Hussain, M.M., Mari, W. and Maziad, M. (2011) Opening Closed Regimes: What Was the Role of Social Media during the Arab Spring?, working paper, University of Washington Project on IT and Political Islam.

Howcroft, D. and Taylor, P. (2023) 'Automation and the future of work: A social shaping of technology approach', *New Technology, Work and Employment*, 38(2): 351–370.

Huber, E., Petrova, B. and Stephens, J.D. (2022) 'Financialization, labor market institutions and inequality', *Review of International Political Economy*, 29(2): 425–452.

Hunt, W., Terry, E. and Rolf, S. (2023) Substituting, Complementing and Augmenting Human Labour with AI: Evidence from Case Study Research in UK Manufacturing and Finance', paper presented at Work, Employment and Society conference, Glasgow.

Huzell, H. (2009) 'Striving for flexibility, attaining resistance: Culture clashes in the Swedish rail industry', in E. Skorstad and H. Ramsdal (eds) *Flexible Organizations and the New Working Life*, Farnham: Ashgate, pp 163–185.

Hyman, J., Lockyer, C.J., Marks, A. and Scholarios, D.M. (2004) 'Needing a new programme: Why is union membership so low among software workers?', in G. Healy, E. Heery, P. Taylor and W. Brown (eds) *The Future of Worker Representation*, Basingstoke: Palgrave Macmillan, pp 37–61.

Hyman, R. (1997) 'Trade unions and interest representation in the context of globalisation', *Transfer: European Review of Labour and Research*, 3(3): 515–533.

Hyman, R. (2006) 'Marxist thought and the analysis of work', in M. Korczynski, R. Hodson and P.K. Edwards (eds) *Social Theory at Work*, Oxford: Oxford University Press, pp 26–55.

Ilsøe, A. and Jesnes, K. (2020) 'Collective agreements for platforms and workers: Two cases from the Nordic countries', in K. Jesnes and S. Oppegaard (eds) *Platform Work in the Nordic Models*, Copenhagen: Nordic Council of Ministers, pp 53–67.

Jackson, G. and Deeg, R. (2006) How Many Varieties of Capitalism? Comparing the Comparative Institutional Analyses of Capitalist Diversity, discussion paper, 06/2, Max Planck Institute.

Jacoby, S.M. (1998) *Modern Manors*, Princeton, NJ: Princeton University Press.

Jaffe, S. (2018) 'The collective power of #MeToo', *Dissent*, 65(2): 80–87.

Jäger, S., Noy, S. and Schoefer, B. (2022) 'What does codetermination do?', *ILR Review*, 75(4): 857–890.

James, C.L.R. (1938/2001) *The Black Jacobins*, London: Penguin.

Jarrahi, M.H. (2018) 'Artificial intelligence and the future of work: Human-AI symbiosis in organizational decision making', *Business Horizons*, 61(4): 577–586.

Jessop, B. (1992) 'Fordism and post-Fordism: A critical reformulation', in M.J. Storper and A.J. Scott (eds) *Pathways to Regionalism and Industrial Development*, London: Routledge.

Jiang, J. and Korczynski, M. (2023) 'The role of community organisations in the collective mobilisation of migrant workers: The importance of a "community"-oriented perspective', *Work, Employment and Society*, doi: 10.1177/09500170221138008.

Jones, O. (2020) *Chavs: The Demonization of the Working Class*, London: Verso.

Jordan, Z. and Conway, D. (2023) 'Amazon strikes: Workers claim their toilet breaks are timed', BBC News, 23 January, bbc.co.uk/news/business-64384287 [accessed 5 December 2023].

Joyce, S. and Stuart, M. (2021) 'Digitalised management, control and resistance in platform work: A labour process analysis', in J. Haidar and M. Keune (eds) *Work and Labour Relations in Global Platform Capitalism*, London: Edward Elgar, pp 158–184.

Kalberg, S. (1980) 'Max Weber's types of rationality: Cornerstones for the analysis of rationalization processes in history', *American Journal of Sociology*, 85(5): 1145–1179.

Kalleberg, A. (2018) *Precarious Lives*, Cambridge: Polity.

Kan, M.Y. (2007) 'Work orientation and wives' employment careers: An evaluation of Hakim's preference theory', *Work and Occupations*, 34(4): 430–462.

Kara, S. (2017) *Modern Slavery: A Global Perspective*, New York: Columbia University Press.

Karlsson, J.C. (2012) *Organizational Misbehaviour in the Workplace: Narratives of Dignity and Resistance*, London: Springer.

Katz, C. (2004) *Growing Up Global: Economic Restructuring and Children's Everyday Lives*, Minneapolis, MN: University of Minnesota Press.

Kaufman, B.E. (2020) 'The real problem: The deadly combination of psychologisation, scientism, and normative promotionalism takes strategic human resource management down a 30-year dead end', *Human Resource Management Journal*, 30(1): 49–72.

Kay, R. and Hildyard, L. (2020) *Pay Ratios and the FTSE 350*, London: High Pay Centre.

Kearsey, J. (2023) Organising from the Road: Private Hire Drivers, Platforms, and Independent Unionism, PhD thesis, University of Nottingham.

Kelly, J.E. (1982) *Scientific Management, Job Redesign and Work Performance*, London: Academic Press.

Kelly, J.E. (1998) *Rethinking Industrial Relations: Mobilization, Collectivism, and Long Waves*, London: Routledge.

Kessler, I., Bach, S. and Nath, V. (2019) 'The construction of career aspirations amongst healthcare support workers: Beyond the rational and the mundane?', *Industrial Relations Journal*, 50(2): 150–167.

Khaola, P. and Rambe, P. (2021) 'The effects of transformational leadership on organisational citizenship behaviour: The role of organisational justice and affective commitment', *Management Research Review*, 44(3): 381–398.

Khan, M., Mowbray, P.K. and Wilkinson, A. (2023) 'Employee voice on social media: An affordance lens', *International Journal of Management Reviews*, 25(4), doi: 10.1111/ijmr.12326.

Kirkpatrick, G. (2004) *Critical Technology: A Social Theory of Personal Computing*, London: Routledge.

Klein, G., Shtudiner, Z., Kantor, J., Mollov, B. and Lavie, C. (2019) 'Contact theory in the workplace: The case of Jewish–Arab contact in Israel', *Journal of Community and Applied Social Psychology*, 29(2): 146–164.

Klein, N. (2001) *No Logo*, London: Flamingo.

Kochan, T.A., Fine, J.R., Bronfenbrenner, K., Naidu, S., Barnes, J., Diaz-Linhart, Y., Kallas, J., Kim, J., Minster, A., Tong, D., Townsend, P. and Twiss, D. (2023) 'An overview of US workers' current organizing efforts and collective actions', *Work and Occupations*, doi: 07308884231168793.

Kokkonen, A., Esaiasson, P. and Gilljam, M. (2015) 'Diverse workplaces and interethnic friendship formation: A multilevel comparison across 21 OECD countries', *Journal of Ethnic and Migration Studies*, 41(2): 284–305.

Kollmeyer, C. (2018) 'Trade union decline, deindustrialization, and rising income inequality in the United States, 1947 to 2015', *Research in Social Stratification and Mobility*, 57: 1–10.

Kollmeyer, C. and Peters, J. (2019) 'Financialization and the decline of organized labor: A study of 18 advanced capitalist countries, 1970–2012', *Social Forces*, 98(1): 1–30.

Korczynski, M. (2002) *Human Resource Management in Service Work*, Basingstoke: Palgrave Macmillan.

Korczynski, M. (2003) 'Communities of coping: Collective emotional labour in service work', *Organization*, 10(1): 55–79.

Korczynski, M. (2009a) 'The mystery customer: Continuing absences in the sociology of service work', *Sociology*, 43(5): 952–967.

Korczynski, M. (2009b) 'Understanding the contradictory lived experience of service work: The customer-oriented bureaucracy', in M. Korczynski and C. Macdonald (eds) *Service Work: Critical Perspectives*, New York: Routledge, pp 73–90.

Korczynski, M. (2013) 'The customer in the sociology of work: Different ways of going beyond the management–worker dyad', *Work, Employment and Society*, 27(6): NP1–NP7.

Korczynski, M. (2014) *Songs of the Factory: Pop Music, Culture, and Resistance*, Ithaca, NY: Cornell University Press.

Korczynski, M. (2023) 'The social contract of work: Moving beyond the psychological contract', *Human Resource Management Journal*, 33(1): 115–128.

Korczynski, M. and Macdonald, C. (eds) (2009) *Service Work: Critical Perspectives*, New York: Routledge.

Korczynski, M. and Ott, U. (2004) 'When production and consumption meet: Cultural contradictions and the enchanting myth of customer sovereignty', *Journal of Management Studies*, 41(4): 575–599.

Korczynski, M. and Wittel, A. (2020) 'The workplace commons: Towards understandinng within work relations', *Sociology*, 54(4): 711–726.

Korczynski, M., Hodson, R. and Edwards, P. (2006) 'Introduction: Competing, collaborating and reinforcing theories', in M. Korczynski, R. Hodson and P.K. Edwards (eds) *Social Theory at Work*, Oxford: Oxford University Press, pp 1–25.

Korczynski, M., Shire, K., Frenkel, S. and Tam, M. (2000) 'Service work in consumer capitalism: Customers, control and contradictions', *Work, Employment and Society*, 14(4): 669–687.

Kordos, M. and Vojtovic, S. (2016) 'Transnational corporations in the global world economic environment', *Procedia-Social and Behavioral Sciences*, 230: 150–158.

Kornberger, M., Pflueger, D. and Mouritsen, J. (2017) 'Evaluative infrastructures: Accounting for platform organization', *Accounting, Organizations and Society*, 60(1): 79–95.

Korpi, W. (1983) *The Democratic Class Struggle*, London: Routledge.

Kost, D., Fieseler, C. and Wong, S.I. (2018) 'Finding meaning in a hopeless place? The construction of meaningfulness in digital microwork', *Computers in Human Behavior*, 82(1): 101–110.

Kost, D., Fieseler, C. and Wong, S.I. (2020) 'Boundaryless careers in the gig economy: An oxymoron?', *Human Resource Management Journal*, 30(1): 100–113.

Kougiannou, N.K. and Mendonça, P. (2021) 'Breaking the managerial silencing of worker voice in platform capitalism: The rise of a food courier network', *British Journal of Management*, 32(3): 744–759.

Koumenta, M. and Williams, M. (2019) 'An anatomy of zero-hour contracts in the UK', *Industrial Relations Journal*, 50(1): 20–40.

Kroezen, J., Ravasi, D., Sasaki, I., Żebrowska, M. and Suddaby, R. (2021) 'Configurations of craft: Alternative models for organizing work', *Academy of Management Annals*, 15(2): 502–536.

Kunda, G. (1992) *Engineering Culture: Control and Commitment in a High-Tech Corporation*, Philadelphia, PA: Temple University Press.

Laaser, K. and Karlsson, J.C. (2022) 'Towards a sociology of meaningful work', *Work, Employment and Society*, 36(5): 798–815.

Lamont, M. (2000) *The Dignity of Working Men: Morality and the Boundaries of Race, Class, and Immigration*, Cambridge, MA: Harvard University Press.

Langman, L. and Smith, D. (eds) (2018) *Twenty-First Century Inequality and Capitalism: Piketty, Marx and Beyond*, London: Brill.

Lash, S. and Urry, J. (1987) *The End of Organized Capitalism*, Madison, WI: University of Wisconsin Press.

Lave, J. and Wenger, E. (1991) *Situated Learning: Legitimate Peripheral Participation*, Cambridge: Cambridge University Press.

Layder, D. (1994) *Understanding Social Theory*, London: Sage.

Lazazzara, A., Tims, M. and De Gennaro, D. (2020) 'The process of reinventing a job: A meta-synthesis of qualitative job crafting research', *Journal of Vocational Behavior*, 116: 103267.

Leadbetter, C. (1999) *Living on Thin Air*, London: Viking.

Legge, K. (2005) *Human Resource Management: Rhetoric and Realities*, Basingstoke: Palgrave Macmillan.

Leidner, R. (1993) *Fast Food, Fast Talk: Service Work and the Routinization of Everyday Life*, Berkeley, CA: University of California Press.

Lemert, C. (2012) *Social Things: An Introduction to the Sociological Life*, New York: Rowman and Littlefield.

Lempiälä, T., Tiitinen, S. and Vanharanta, O. (2023) 'Paradox as an interactional resource: An ethnomethodological analysis into the interconnectedness of organizational paradoxes', *Organization Studies*, 44(11): 1825–1852.

Lepanjuuri, K., Wishart, R. and Cornick, P. (2018) *The Characteristics of Those in the Gig Economy: Final Report*, London: Department of Business, Energy and Industrial Strategy.

Lewis, T. (2012) 'Tacit knowledge and the labour process', in P. Gibb (ed) *Learning, Work and Practice: New Understandings*, Dordrecht: Springer, pp 33–50.

Lewis, T. (2019) 'AI can read your emotions. Should it?', *The Guardian* (online), 17 August, theguardian.com/technology/2019/aug/17/emotion-ai-artificial-intelligence-mood-realeyes-amazon-facebook-emotient [accessed 2 January 2024].

Li, Y., Bechhofer, F. and Stewart, R. (2002) 'A divided working class? Planning and career perceptions in the service and working class', *Work, Employment and Society*, 16(3): 617–636.

Littler, C.R. (1978) 'Understanding Taylorism', *British Journal of Sociology*, 29(2): 185–202.

Littler, C.R. (1990) 'The labour process debate: A theoretical review, 1974–1988', in D. Knights and H. Wilmott (eds) *Labour Process Theory*, Basingstoke: Macmillan, pp 46–94.

Liu, H.Y. (2023a) '"When nobody listens, go online": The "807" labor movement against workplace sexism in China's tech industry', *Gender, Work and Organization*, 30(1): 312–328.

Liu, H.Y. (2023b) 'The role of the state in influencing work conditions in China's internet industry: Policy, evidence, and implications for industrial relations', *Journal of Industrial Relations*, 65(1): 3–21.

Locke, R.M. (2013) *The Promise and Limits of Private Power: Promoting Labor Standards in a Global Economy*, Cambridge: Cambridge University Press.

Long, M. (2012) 'Merchantry, usury, villainy: Capitalism and the threat to community integrity in *The Merchant of Venice*', *Anthropoetics*, 17(2), anthropoetics.ucla.edu/ap1702/1702long [accessed 6 March 2024].

Low Pay Commission (1999) *National Minimum Wage: The Story So Far*, London: Low Pay Commission.

Low Pay Commission (2016) *National Minimum Wage: Low Pay Commission Report 2016*, London: Low Pay Commission.

Lundemo, T. (2011) 'Charting the gesture', *Eurozine*, eurozine.com/articles/2011-06-21-lundemo-en.html [accessed 2 January 2024].

Lysova, E.I. and Khapova, S.N. (2019) 'Enacting creative calling when established career structures are not in place: The case of the Dutch video game industry', *Journal of Vocational Behavior*, 114: 31–43.

Macdonald, C. and Merrill, D. (2009) 'Intersectionality in the emotional proletariat', in M. Korczynski and C.L. Macdonald (eds) *Service Work: Critical Perspectives*, New York: Routledge, pp 113–134.

Macdonald, C.L. and Sirianni, C. (1996) 'The service society and the changing experience of work', in C.L. Macdonald and C. Sirianni (eds) *Working in the Service Society*, Philadelphia, PA: Temple University Press, pp 1–26.

MacDonald, K. (2006) 'Professional work', in M. Korczynski, R. Hodson and P.K. Edwards (eds) *Social Theory at Work*, Oxford: Oxford University Press, pp 356–387.

Machin, S. (2006) 'The economic approach to the analysis of the labour market', in M. Korczynski, R. Hodson and P.K. Edwards (eds) *Social Theory at Work*, Oxford: Oxford University Press, pp 182–207.

Mackenzie, D. and Wajcman, J. (1999) *The Social Shaping of Technology*, Milton Keynes: Open University Press.

Majchrzak, A. and Markus, M.L. (2013) 'Technology affordances and constraints in management information systems (MIS)', in E. Kessler (ed) *Encyclopedia of Management Theory*, New York: Sage, pp 572–577.

Major, L.E. and Machin, S. (2018) *Social Mobility: And Its Enemies*, London: Penguin.

Major, L.E. and Machin, S. (2020) *What Do We Know and What Should We Do About Social Mobility?*, London: Sage.

Manning, A. and Swaffield, J. (2008) 'The gender gap in early-career wage growth', *The Economic Journal*, 118(530): 983–1024.

Marsden, R. (1999) *The Nature of Capital*, London: Routledge.

Mathews, J.A. (1994) *Catching the Wave: Workplace Reform in Australia*, Ithaca, NY: Cornell University Press.

Marx, K. (1844/1992) 'Economic and philosophical manuscripts', in *Early Writings*, London: Penguin, pp 279–401.

Marx, K. (1845/1978) 'Theses on Feuerbach', in *Marx and Engels Collected Works*, Volume 5, London: Lawrence and Wishart, pp 3–5.

Marx, K. (1859/1954) *The Eighteenth Brumaire of Louis Bonaparte*, London: Progress.

Marx, K. (1867/1934) *Capital, Volume One*, London: Lawrence and Wishart.

Marx, K. (1885/1956) *Capital, Volume Two*, London: Lawrence and Wishart.

Marx, K. (1894/1959) *Capital, Volume Three*, London: Lawrence and Wishart.

Marx, K. (1970) *A Contribution to the Critique of Political Economy*, New York: International Publishers.

Marx, K. and Engels, F. (1848/1969) *Manifesto of the Communist Party*, London: Lawrence and Wishart.

Mazmanian, M., Orlikowski, W.J. and Yates, J. (2013) 'The autonomy paradox: The implications of mobile email devices for knowledge professionals', *Organization Science*, 24(5): 1337–1357.

McGovern, P., Hill, S., Mills, C. and White, M. (2007) *Market, Class, and Employment*, Oxford: Oxford University Press.

McMurray, R. and Ward, J. (2014) '"Why would you want to do that?": Defining emotional dirty work', *Human Relations*, 67(9): 1123–1143.

McStay, A. (2018) *Emotional AI: The Rise of Empathic Media*, London: Sage.

Mefteh, K.Y., Mulugeta, G.M. and Teshome, W.L. (2022) 'The lived experience of waitresses in hospitality sector: A phenomenological study on work related abuse and its coping mechanisms among selected waitresses in hospitality sector in Bahirdar City, northwestern Ethiopia', *Qualitative Report*, 27(6): 1607–1622.

Merton R.K. (1967) *On Theoretical Sociology*, New York: Free Press.

Milanez, A. (2023) The Impact of AI on the Workplace: Evidence from OECD Case Studies of AI Implementation, Social, Employment and Migration working paper, no. 289, OECD.

Milanovic, B. (2015) 'Global inequality of opportunity: How much of our income is determined by where we live?', *Review of Economics and Statistics*, 97(2): 452–460.

Miller, A. (1949) *Death of a Salesman*, New York: Morehouse and Gibbs.

Miller, D. and Lee, J. (2001) 'The people make the process: Commitment to employees, decision making and performance', *Journal of Management*, 27(2): 163–189.

Mills, C.W. (1956) *White Collar*, Oxford: Oxford University Press.

Mills, C.W. (1959) *The Sociological Imagination*, New York: Routledge.

Miraglia, M. and Johns, G. (2021) 'The social and relational dynamics of absenteeism from work: A multilevel review and integration', *Academy of Management Annals*, 15(1): 37–67.

Mishel, L. and Davis, A. (2015) 'Top CEOs make 300 times more than typical workers', *Economic Policy Institute*, 21(1): 1–14.

Moen, P. and Roehling, P. (2005) *The Career Mystique*, Boulder, CO: Rowman and Littlefield.

Mirza, H.S. and Warwick, R. (2022) *Race and Ethnicity*, London: Institute for Fiscal Studies.

Mumby, D.K., Thomas, R., Martí, I. and Seidl, D. (2017) 'Resistance redux', *Organization Studies*, 38(9): 1157–1183.

Musacchio, A., Lazzarini, S.G. and Aguilera, R.V. (2015) 'New varieties of state capitalism: Strategic and governance implications', *Academy of Management Perspectives*, 29(1): 115–131.

Navallo, K.S. (2023) 'From nurses to care workers: Deskilling among Filipino nurses in Japan', in R. Adhikari and E. Plotnikova (eds) *Nurse Migration in Asia*, London: Routledge, pp 95–114.

Nickson, D.P., Warhurst, C., Witz, A. and Cullen, A.M. (2001) 'The importance of being aesthetic: Work, employment and service organization', in A. Sturdy, I. Grugulis and H. Willmott (eds) *Customer Service: Empowerment and Entrapment*, Basingstoke: Macmillan, pp 170–190.

Nixon, D. (2009) '"I can't put a smiley face on": Working-class masculinity, emotional labour and service work in the new economy', *Gender, Work and Organization*, 16(3): 300–322.

Noon, M. and Blyton, P. (2013) *The Realties of Work*, Basingstoke: Palgrave Macmillan.

Oakley, A. (1974) *Housewife*, London: Allen Lane.

OECD (The Organisation for Economic Co-operation and Development) (2019) 'Indicators of employment protection', https://www.oecd.org/employment/emp/oecdindicatorsofemploymentprotection.htm [accessed 2 October 2023].

OECD (2022) 'Gender wage gap', OECD Data, data.oecd.org/earnwage/gender-wage-gap.htm [accessed 13 March 2024].

Oesch, D. and Piccitto, G. (2019) 'The polarization myth: Occupational upgrading in Germany, Spain, Sweden, and the UK, 1992–2015', *Work and Occupations*, 46(4): 441–469.

Offe, C. (1985) *Disorganized Capitalism*, Cambridge, MA: MIT Press.

Olsen, W. and Walby, S. (2004) Modelling Gender Pay Gaps, working paper series no. 18, Equal Opportunities Commission.

Olsen, W., Gash, V., Vandecasteele, L., Walthery, P. and Heuvelman, H. (2010a) *The Gender Pay Gap in the UK: 1995–2007: Part 1*, research report, Government Equalities Office.

Olsen, W., Heuvelman, H., Gash, V. and Vandecasteele, L. (2010b) *The Gender Pay Gap in the UK: 1995–2007: Part 2*, research report, Government Equalities Office.

Olsen, W., Gash, V., Sook, K. and Zhang, M. (2018) *The Gender Pay Gap in the UK: Evidence from the UKHLS*, report no. DFE-RR804, Department for Education.

ONS (2020) *Ethnicity Pay Gaps: 2019*, London: Office for National Statistics.

ONS (2022) *Gender Pay Gap in the UK: 2022*, London: Office for National Statistics.

ONS (2023) *A09: Labour Market Status by Ethnic Group*, London: Office for National Statistics.

Organ, D.W. (1988) *Organizational Citizenship Behavior: The Good Soldier Syndrome*, New York: Lexington.

Ormaechea, J.M. (1993) *The Mondragon Co-operative Experience*, Mondragón: Mondragon Co-operative Corporation.

Ouchi, W.G. (1979) 'A conceptual framework for the design of organizational control mechanisms', *Management Science*, 25(9): 833–848.

Ozkazanc-Pan, B. (2019) 'On agency and empowerment in a #MeToo world', *Gender, Work and Organization*, 26(8): 1212–1220.

Patel, V., Burns, J.K., Dhingra, M., Tarver, L., Kohrt, B.A. and Lund, C. (2018) 'Income inequality and depression: A systematic review and meta-analysis of the association and a scoping review of mechanisms', *World Psychiatry*, 17(1): 76–89.

Pattison, P. and McIntyre, N. (2021) 'Revealed: 6,500 migrant workers have died in Qatar since World Cup awarded', *The Guardian* (online), 23 February, theguardian.com/global-development/2021/feb/23/revealed-migrant-worker-deaths-qatar-fifa-world-cup-2022 [accessed 13 March 2024].

Peacock, M., Bissell, P. and Owen, J. (2014) 'Shaming encounters: Reflections on contemporary understandings of social inequality and health', *Sociology*, 48(2): 387–402.

Perales, F. (2013) 'Occupational sex-segregation, specialized human capital and wages: Evidence from Britain', *Work, Employment and Society*, 27(4): 600–620.

Però, D. (2020) 'Indie unions, organizing and labour renewal: Learning from precarious migrant workers', *Work, Employment and Society*, 34(5): 900–918.

Pettersen, L. (2019) 'Why artificial intelligence will not outsmart complex knowledge work', *Work, Employment and Society*, 33(6): 1058–1067.

Pettit, K.L., Balogun, J. and Bennett, M. (2023) 'Transforming visions into actions: Strategic change as a future-making process', *Organization Studies*, 44(11): 1775–1799.

Pfau-Effinger, B. (1993) 'Modernisation, culture and part-time employment: The example of Finland and West Germany', *Work, Employment and Society*, 7(3): 383–410.

Phillips, A. and Taylor, B. (1986) 'Sex and skill', in Feminist Review (ed) *Waged Work: A Reader*, London: Virago, pp 54–66.

Pickett, K.E. and Wilkinson, R.G. (2015) 'Income inequality and health: A causal review', *Social Science and Medicine*, 128(3): 316–326.

Pike, K. (2020) 'Voice in supply chains: Does the better work program lead to improvements in labor standards compliance?', *ILR Review*, 73(4): 913–938.

Piketty, T. (2013) *Capital in the Twenty-First Century*, Cambridge, MA: Harvard University Press.

Pilling, R. (2020) Where's Your #Wobbleroom? The Impact of Creating Safe Spaces for Staff during COVID and Beyond, paper at Institute of Health Management No Going Back conference.

Piore, M.J. and Sabel, C.F. (1984) *The Second Industrial Divide: Possibilities for Prosperity*, New York: Basic Books.

Piore, M. and Safford, S. (2006) 'Changing regimes of workplace governance, shifting axes of social mobilization and the challenge to industrial relations theory', *Industrial Relations*, 45(3): 299–325.

Plummer, K. (2016) *Sociology: The Basics*, London: Routledge.

Pocock, B. (2008) 'Equality at work', in P. Blyton, N. Bacon, J. Fiorito and E. Heery (eds) *The Sage Handbook of Industrial Relations*, London: Sage, pp 572–587.

Polanyi, K. (1944/2001) *The Great Transformation: The Political and Economic Origins of Our Time*, Boston, MA: Beacon Press.

Pollert, A. (1981) *Girls, Wives, Factory Lives*, Basingstoke: Macmillan.

Powell, M. (2023) The Beginning Never Ends: The Erratic Temporality of Platform Couriers' Collective Action, paper presented at British Sociological Association conference, University of Manchester.

Pradella, L. (2016) 'Postcolonial theory and the making of the world working class', *Critical Sociology*, 43(4–5): 573–586.

Prasad, A. and Prasad, P. (2001) '(Un)willing to resist? The discursive production of local workplace opposition', *Studies in Cultures, Organizations and Societies*, 7(1): 105–125.

Prasad, P. and Prasad, A. (2000) 'Stretching the iron cage: The constitution and implications of routine workplace resistance', *Organization Science*, 11(4): 387–403.

Price, R. and Bain, G.S. (1983) 'Union growth: Dimensions, determinants and destiny', in G. Bain (ed) *Industrial Relations in Britain*, Oxford: Blackwell, pp 3–33.

Przybyszewska, A. (2020) 'Habitus mismatch and suffering experienced by Polish migrants working below their qualification level in Norway', *Central and Eastern European Migration Review*, 9(2): 71–88.

Purcell, C. and Brook, P. (2022) 'At least I'm my own boss! Explaining consent, coercion and resistance in platform work', *Work, Employment and Society*, 36(3): 391–406.

Purkayastha, B. (2005) 'Skilled migration and cumulative disadvantage: The case of highly qualified Asian Indian immigrant women in the US', *Geoforum*, 36(2): 181–196.

Putnam, R.D. (2000) *Bowling Alone: The Collapse and Revival of American Community*, New York: Simon and Schuster.

Quillian, L. and Midtbøen, A.H. (2021) 'Comparative perspectives on racial discrimination in hiring: The rise of field experiment', *Annual Review of Sociology*, 47: 391–415.

Quinn, R.W. (2005) 'Flow in knowledge work: High performance experience in the design of national security technology', *Administrative Science Quarterly*, 50(4): 610–641.

Rabinow, P. (1996) *Making PCR: A Story of Biotechnology*, Chicago, IL: University of Chicago Press.

Rahman, H. (2018) Invisible Cages: Algorithmic Evaluations in Online Labor Markets, PhD dissertation, Stanford University.

Raikes, P., Friis Jensen, M. and Ponte, S. (2000) 'Global commodity chain analysis and the French filière approach: Comparison and critique', *Economy and Society*, 29(3): 390–417.

Rainnie, A. (1991) 'Just-in-time, sub-contracting and the small firm', *Work, Employment and Society*, 5(3): 353–375.

Ravenelle, A.J. (2019) *Hustle and Gig: Struggling and Surviving in the Sharing Economy*, Berkeley, CA: University of California Press.

Reed, M. and Burrell, G. (2019) 'Theory and organization studies: The need for contestation', *Organization Studies*, 40(1): 39–54.

Rees, C. (2023) Employee Voice, Corporate Governance Reform, and the Prospects for Workplace Democracy, paper at the British Sociological Association conference, April.

Reinecke, J. and Donaghey, J. (2015) 'After Rana Plaza: Building coalitional power for labour rights between unions and (consumption-based) social movement organisations', *Organization*, 22(5): 720–740.

Reinecke, J. and Donaghey, J. (2023) *Stitching Governance for Labour Rights*, Cambridge: Cambridge University Press.

Richards, J. and Marks, A. (2007) 'Biting the hand that feeds: Social identity and resistance in restaurant teams', *International Journal of Business Science and Applied Management*, 2(2): 42–57.

Rieder, K. and Voß, G.G. (2013) 'The working customer – a fundamental change in service work', in W. Dunkel and F. Kleemann (eds) *Customers at Work: New Perspectives on Interactive Service Work*, Houndmills: Palgrave Macmillan, pp 177–196.

Riordan, C.A. and Kowalski, A.M. (2021) 'From Bread and Roses to #MeToo: Multiplicity, distance, and the changing dynamics of conflict in IR theory', *ILR Review*, 74(3): 580–606.

Ritzer, G. (1998) *The McDonaldization Thesis: Explorations and Extensions*, London: Pine Forge Press.

Ritzer, G. (2011) *The McDonaldization of Society*, Thousand Oaks, CA: Pine Forge Press.

Ritzer, G., Dean, P. and Jurgenson, N. (2012) 'The coming of age of the prosumer: Introduction', *American Behavioral Scientist*, 56(3): 379–398.

Rivera, L.A. (2015) *Pedigree: How Elite Students Get Elite Jobs*, Princeton, NJ: Princeton University Press.

Rogers, E.M. and Larsen, J.K. (1984) *Silicon Valley Fever: Growth of High-Technology Culture*, New York: Basic Books.

Rolfe, H., Dhudwar, A., George, A. and Metcalf, H. (2009) *Perceptions of Discrimination in Employment*, London: Government Equalities Office.

Rose, N. (1990) *Governing the Soul: The Shaping of the Private Self*, London: Routledge.

Rousseau, D.M. (1995) *Psychological Contracts in Organizations*, Thousand Oaks, CA: Sage.

Rousseau, D.M. (1998) 'The "problem" of the psychological contract considered', *Journal of Organizational Behavior*, 19(4): 665–671.

Roy, D. (1954) 'Efficiency and the "fix"', *American Journal of Sociology*, 60(3): 255–266.

Roy, D. (1959) '"Banana time": Job satisfaction and informal interaction', *Human Organization*, 18(4): 158–168.

Safi, M. (2020) *Migration and Inequality*, London: Polity.

Sallaz, J.J. (2013) *Labor, Economy, and Society*, New York: John Wiley and Sons.

Sallaz, J.J. (2015) 'Permanent pedagogy: How post-Fordist firms generate effort but not consent', *Work and Occupations*, 42(1): 3–34.

Sandoval, M. (2013) 'Foxconned labour as the dark side of the information age: Working conditions at Apple's contract manufacturers in China', *TripleC: Communication, Capitalism and Critique*, 11(2): 318–347.

Santino, J. (1991) *Miles of Smiles, Years of Struggle: Stories of Black Pullman Porters*, Urbana-Champaign, IL: University of Illinois Press.

Saxenian, A. (1996) 'Beyond boundaries: Open labor markets and learning in Silicon Valley', in M. Arthur and D. Rousseau (eds) *The Boundaryless Career*, Oxford: Oxford University Press, pp 23–39.

Sayer, A. (2005) *The Moral Significance of Class*, Cambridge: Cambridge University Press.

Schachar, A. (2009) *The Birthright Lottery: Citizenship and Global Inequality*, Cambridge, MA: Harvard University Press.

Schierup, C.U., Hansen, P. and Castles, S. (2006) *Migration, Citizenship, and the European Welfare State: A European Dilemma*, Oxford: Oxford University Press.

Schnake, M. (1991) 'Organizational citizenship: A review, proposed model, and research agenda', *Human Relations*, 44(7): 735–759.

Schneider, A., Subramanian, D., Suquet, J.B. and Ughetto, P. (2022) 'Situating service work in action: A review and a pragmatist agenda for analysing interactive service work', *International Journal of Management Reviews*, 24(1): 25–50.

Scholarios, D. and Taylor, P. (2011) 'Beneath the glass ceiling: Explaining gendered role segmentation in call centres', *Human Relations*, 64(10): 1291–1319.

Scott, J.C. (1990) *Domination and the Arts of Resistance: Hidden Transcripts*, New Haven: Yale University Press.

Scott, J. and Marshall, G. (eds) (2005) *Oxford Dictionary of Sociology*, Oxford: Oxford University Press.

Sennett, R. (1999) *The Corrosion of Character: The Personal Consequences of Work in the New Captialism*, New York: Norton.

Sennett, R. (2008) *The Craftsman*, New Haven, CT: Yale University Press.

Sennett, R. and Cobb, J. (1973) *The Hidden Injuries of Class*, New York: Random House.

Shade, L.R. and Jacobson, J. (2015) 'Hungry for the job: Gender, unpaid internships, and the creative industries', *The Sociological Review*, 63(2): 188–205.

Shaw, P. (2008) *Patti Smith: Horses*, London: Continuum.

Sherman, R. (2007) *Class Acts: Service and Inequality in Luxury Hotels*, Berkeley, CA: University of California Press.

Shildrick, T., MacDonald, R., Webster, C. and Garthwaite, K. (2012) *Poverty and Insecurity: Life in Low-Pay, No-Pay Britain*, London: Policy Press.

Silver, B.J. (2003) *Forces of Labor: Workers' Movements and Globalization since 1870*, Cambridge: Cambridge University Press.

Silver, D. (2023) 'Meaningful work and the purpose of the firm', *Journal of Business Ethics*, 185: 825–834.

Simmel, G. (1994) 'Bridge and door', *Theory, Culture and Society*, 11(1): 5–10.

Simms, M. (2005) Organising Service Sector Workers, PhD thesis, Cardiff Business School, Cardiff University.

Simms, M., Holgate, J. and Heery, E. (2017) *Union Voices: Tactics and Tensions in UK Organizing*, Ithaca, NY: Cornell University Press.

Smart, B. (ed) (1999) *Resisting McDonaldization*, London: Sage.

Smith, A. (1776/2016) *The Wealth of Nations*, London: Aegitas.

Smith, C. (2006) 'The double indeterminacy of labour power: Labour effort and labour mobility', *Work, Employment and Society*, 20(2): 389–402.

Soffia, M., Wood, A.J. and Burchell, B. (2022) 'Alienation is not "bullshit": An empirical critique of Graeber's theory of BS jobs', *Work, Employment and Society*, 36(5): 816–840.

Sölvell, Ö. and Zander, I. (1995) 'Organization of the dynamic multinational enterprise: The home-based and the heterarchical MNE', *International Studies of Management and Organization*, 25(1/2): 17–38.

Sønderskov, K.M. and Thomsen, J. (2015) 'Contextualizing intergroup contact: Do political party cues enhance contact effects?', *Social Psychology Quarterly*, 78(1): 49–76.

Spenner, K.I. (1990) 'Skill: Meanings, methods, and measures', *Work and Occupations*, 17(4): 399–421.

Spradley, J.P. and Mann, B.E. (1975) *The Cocktail Waitress: Woman's Work in a Man's World*, New York: Waveland Press.

Stacey, C.L. (2011) *The Caring Self: The Work Experiences of Home Care Aides*, Ithaca, NY: Cornell University Press.

Standing, G. (2011) *The Precariat: The New Dangerous Class*, London: Bloomsbury.

St-Denis, X. and Hollister, M. (2023) 'Are all the stable jobs gone? The transformation of the worker–firm relationship and trends in job tenure duration and separations in Canada 1976–2015', *Work, Employment and Society*, doi: 09500170221146916.

Stewart, H. (2023) 'Why, even now, do we think that women's work is worth less?', *The Guardian* (online), 11 August, theguardian.com/world/2023/aug/11/why-even-now-do-we-think-a-womans-work-is-worth-less [accessed 12 December 2023].

Stiglitz, J.E. (2003) *The Roaring Nineties: A New History of the World's Most Prosperous Decade*, New York: WW Norton and Company.

Strangleman, T. (2015) 'Rethinking industrial citizenship: The role and meaning of work in an age of austerity', *The British Journal of Sociology*, 66(4): 673–690.

Streeck, W. (2009) *Re-Forming Capitalism: Institutional Change in the German Political Economy*, Oxford: Oxford University Press.

Streeck, W. (2018) 'E Pluribus Unum? Varieties and commonalities of capitalism', in M. Granovetter (ed) *The Sociology of Economic Life*, New York: Routledge, pp 419–455.

Stroebaek, P.S. (2013) 'Let's have a cup of coffee! Coffee and coping communities at work', *Symbolic Interaction*, 36(4): 381–397.

Suwandi, I., Jonna, R.J. and Foster, J.B. (2019) 'Global commodity chains and the new imperialism', *Monthly Review*, 70(10): 1–24.

Sweet, S. and Meiskins, P. (2008) *Changing Contours of Work: Jobs and Opportunities in the New Economy*, London: Pine Forge Press.

Tallberg, L. and Jordan, P.J. (2022) 'Killing them "softly"(!): Exploring work experiences in care-based animal dirty work', *Work, Employment and Society*, 36(5): 858–874.

Tam, M.Y.M., Korczynski, M. and Frenkel, S.J. (2005) 'Organizational and occupational commitment: Knowledge workers in large corporations', in S. Little and T. Ray (eds) *Managing Knowledge: An Essential Reader*, London: Sage, pp 171–198.

Tapia, M., Lee, T.L. and Filipovitch, M. (2017) 'Supra-union and intersectional organizing: An examination of two prominent cases in the low-wage US restaurant industry', *Journal of Industrial Relations*, 59(4): 487–509.

Tassinari, A. and Maccarrone, V. (2020) 'Riders on the storm: Workplace solidarity among gig economy couriers in Italy and the UK', *Work, Employment and Society*, 34(1): 35–54.

Taylor, F. (1948) *Scientific Management*, New York: Harper and Row.

Taylor, P. and Bain, P. (1999) '"An assembly line in the head': Work and employee relations in the call centre', *Industrial Relations Journal*, 30(2): 101–117.

Taylor, S. and Tyler, M. (2000) 'Emotional labour and sexual difference in the airline industry', *Work, Employment and Society*, 14(1): 77–95.

Thieme, T.A. (2018) 'The hustle economy: Informality, uncertainty and the geographies of getting by', *Progress in Human Geography*, 42(4): 529–548.

Thomas, H. and Walsh, D. (1998) 'Modernity/postmodernity', in C. Jenks (ed) *Core Sociological Dichotomies*, London: Sage, pp 363–390.

Thompson, E.P. (1991) *Customs in Common: Studies in Traditional Popular Culture*, London: New Press/ORIM.

Thompson, P. (2003) 'Disconnected capitalism, or why employers can't keep their side of the bargain', *Work, Employment and Society*, 17(2): 359–378.

Thompson, P. (2016) 'Dissent at work and the resistance debate: Departures, directions and dead ends', *Studies in Political Economy*, 97, 106–123.

Thompson, P. and Ackroyd, S. (1995) 'All quiet on the workplace front? A critique of recent trends in British industrial sociology', *Sociology*, 29(4): 615–633.

Thompson, P. and McHugh, D. (1990) *Work Organisations*, Basingstoke: Macmillan.

Thompson, P. and Smith, C. (2009) 'Labour power and labour process: Contesting the marginality of the sociology of work', *Sociology*, 43(5): 913–930.

Tonnies, F. (1887/2002) *Community and Society*, London: Courier.

Topa, G., Aranda-Carmena, M. and De-Maria, B. (2022) 'Psychological contract breach and outcomes: A systematic review of reviews', *International Journal of Environmental Research and Public Health*, 19(23): 15527.

Tope, D., Chamberlain, L.J., Crowley, M. and Hodson, R. (2005) 'The benefits of being there: Evidence from the literature on work', *Journal of Contemporary Ethnography*, 34(4): 470–493.

Tourish, D. and Willmott, H. (2023) 'Despotic leadership and ideological manipulation at Theranos: Towards a theory of hegemonic totalism in the workplace', *Organization Studies*, 44(11): 1801–1824.

Townley, B. (1994) *Reframing Human Resource Management: Power, Ethics and the Subject at Work*, Basingstoke: Macmillan.

Treem, J.W. and Leonardi, P.M. (2012) 'Social media use in organizations: Exploring the affordances of visibility, editability, persistence, and association', in C.T. Salmon (ed) *Communication Yearbook*, New York: Routledge, pp 143–189.

Trentham, S. and Larwood, L. (1998) 'Gender discrimination and the workplace: An examination of rational bias theory', *Sex Roles*, 38(1–2): 1–28.

Tridico, P. (2018) 'The determinants of income inequality in OECD countries', *Cambridge Journal of Economics*, 42(4): 1009–1042.

Umney, C. (2018) *Class Matters: Inequality and Exploitation in 21st Century Britain*, London: Pluto Press.

Umney, C., Stuart, M., Bessa, I., Joyce, S., Neumann, D. and Trappmann, V. (2024) 'Platform labour unrest in a global perspective: How, where and why do platform workers protest?', *Work, Employment and Society*, doi-org.nottingham.idm.oclc.org/10.1177/09500170231209676.

Unger, R. (2019) *The Knowledge Economy*, London: Verso.

Upchurch, M. (2020) 'Time, tea breaks and the frontier of control in UK workplaces', *Historical Studies in Industrial Relations*, 41(1): 37–64.

Valenzuela-Bustos, A., Gálvez-Mozo, A. and Alcalde-Gonzalez, V. (2023) 'Invisible room attendants: Outsourcing as a dispositive of (in)visibility and the resistance of Las Kellys in Spain', *Work, Employment and Society*, 37(6): 1646–1663.

Valizade, D., Schulz, F. and Stuart, M. (2023) Working for or Working with AI? An Empirical Investigation into the Relationship between AI Technologies, Job Autonomy and (Management) Control in UK Establishments, paper presented at Work, Employment and Society conference, Glasgow.

Vallas, S.P. and Johnston, H. (2023) 'Labor unbound? Assessing the current surge in labor activism', *Work and Occupations*, 50(3): 376–384.

Vallas, S. and Schor, J.B. (2020) 'What do platforms do? Understanding the gig economy', *Annual Review of Sociology*, 46: 273–294.

Van den Broek, E., Sergeeva, A. and Huysman, M. (2021) 'When the machine meets the expert: An ethnography of developing AI for hiring', *MIS Quarterly*, 45(3): 1557–1580.

Van Doorn, N. and Vijay, D. (2021) 'Gig work as migrant work: The platformization of migration infrastructure', *Environment and Planning A: Economy and Space*, doi: 10.1177/0308518X211065049.

Van Doorn, N., Ferrari, F. and Graham, M. (2023) 'Migration and migrant labour in the gig economy: An intervention', *Work, Employment and Society*, 37(4): 1099–1111.

Vargas, T.L. (2021) 'Consumer redlining and the reproduction of inequality at dollar general', *Qualitative Sociology*, 44(2): 205–229.

Vidal, M. (2013) 'Postfordism as a dysfunctional accumulation regime: A comparative analysis of the USA, the UK and Germany', *Work, Employment and Society*, 27(3): 451–471.

Waitling, D. and Snook, J. (2003) 'Work councils and trade unions: Complementary or competitive? The case of SAGCo', *Industrial Relations Journal*, 34(3): 260–270.

Wajcman, J. (2006) 'New connections: Social studies of science and technology and studies of work', *Work, Employment and Society*, 20(4): 773–786.

Walby, S. (2011) *The Future of Feminism*, Cambridge: Polity.

Wallerstein, I. (1979) *The Capitalist World-Economy*, Cambridge: Cambridge University Press.

Wang, D., Khosla, A., Gargeya, R., Irshad, H. and Beck, A.H. (2016) 'Deep learning for identifying metastatic breast cancer', arxiv.org/pdf/1606.05718 [accessed 13 March 2024].

Warhurst, C. and Nickson, D. (2020) *Aesthetic Labour*, London: Sage.

Watts, J.H. (2009) 'Leaders of men: Women "managing" in construction', *Work, Employment and Society*, 23(3): 512–530.

Webb, T. and Cheney, G. (2014) 'Worker-owned-and-governed co-operatives and the wider co-operative movement: Challenges and opportunities within and beyond the global economic crisis', in M. Parker, G. Cheney, V. Fournier and C. Land (eds) *The Routledge Companion to Alternative Organization*, London: Routledge, pp 64–88.

Weber, M. (1904/1976) *The Protestant Ethic and the Spirit of Capitalism*, New York: Charles Scribner.

Weber, M. (1921/1978) *Economy and Society*, London: University of California Press.

Weick, K.E. (1995) *Sensemaking in Organizations*, London: Sage.

Weil, D. (2014) *The Fissured Workplace: Why Work Became So Bad for So Many and What Can Be Done to Improve It*, Cambridge, MA: Harvard University Press.

West, P. (2012) *From Modern Production to Imagined Primitive: The Social World of Coffee from Papua New Guinea*, Durham, NC: Duke University Press.

Wheen, F. (1999) *Karl Marx*, London: Fourth Estate.

Wicks, D. (1998) *Nurses and Doctors at Work*, Buckingham: Open University Press.

Wiksell, K. and Henriksson, A. (2023) 'Friends against capitalism: Constructive resistance and friendship compliance in worker cooperatives', *Current Sociology*, 71(7): 1272–1294.

Wilkinson, A., Barry, M. and Morrison, E. (2020) 'Toward an integration of research on employee voice', *Human Resource Management Review*, 30(1) (no page numbering).

Wilkinson, A., Knoll, M., Mowbray, P.K. and Dundon, T. (2021) 'New trajectories in worker voice: Integrating and applying contemporary challenges in the organization of work', *British Journal of Management*, 32(3): 693–707.

Wilkinson, R. and Pickett, K. (2010) *The Spirit Level*, London: Penguin.

Wilkinson, R. and Pickett, K. (2013) 'Reply to reviews', *Work, Employment and Society*, 27(1): 175–177.

Williams, C.L., Muller, C. and Kilanski, K. (2012) 'Gendered organizations in the new economy', *Gender and Society*, 26(4): 549–573.

Williamson, O.E. (2010) 'Transaction cost economics: The natural progression', *American Economic Review*, 100(3): 673–690.

Willis, P. (1977) *Learning to Labour: How Working Class Kids Get Working Class Jobs*, London: Gower.

Wills, J. (2008) 'Making class possible: Organizing contract cleaners in London', *International Journal of Urban and Regional Research*, 32(2): 305–323.

Wills, J. and Linneker, B. (2014), 'In-work poverty and the Living Wage in the United Kingdom: A geographical perspective', *Transactions of the British Institute of Geographers*, 39(2): 82–194.

Witz, A. (1992) *Professions and Patriarchy*, London: Routledge.

Wong, Y.L.A. and Charles, M. (2020) 'Gender and occupational segregation', in N. Naples (ed) *Companion to Women's and Gender Studies*, New York: Wiley, pp 303–325.

Wood, A.J. (2020) *Despotism on Demand: How Power Operates in the Flexible Workplace*, Ithaca, NY: Cornell University Press.

Wood, A.J. and Lehdonvirta, V. (2021) 'Antagonism beyond employment: How the "subordinated agency" of labour platforms generates conflict in the remote gig economy', *Socio-Economic Review*, 19(4): 1369–1396.

Wood, M., Hales, J., Purdon, S., Sejersen, T. and Hayllar, O. (2009) *A Test for Racial Discrimination in Recruitment Practice in British Cities*, research report 607, Department for Work and Pensions.

Woodcock, J. (2020) 'The algorithmic panopticon at Deliveroo: Measurement, precarity, and the illusion of control', *Ephemera*, 20(3): 67–95.

Woodcock, J. (2021) *The Fight against Platform Capitalism: An Inquiry into the Global Struggles of the Gig Economy*, London: University of Westminster Press.

Wozniak, S.R. (2022) "Sexual Harassment Is My Job": The Impact of Display Work on Bikini Barista Interactions, thesis, University of Montana.

Wright, E.O. (2015) *Understanding Class*, New York: Verso.

Yan, Z. and Luo, B. (2023) "'It's your Liangxin that tells you what to do': Interpreting workplace-induced emotions in a Chinese nursing home', *Journal of Aging Studies*, 64, 101111.

Yu, X. (2008) 'Impacts of corporate code of conduct on labor standards: A case study of Reebok's athletic footwear supplier factory in China', *Journal of Business Ethics*, 81(3): 513–529.

Zibechi, R. (2006) 'Another world is possible: The ceramics of Zanon', in T. Ballvé and V. Prashad (eds) *Dispatches from Latin America: On the Frontlines against Neoliberalism*, New York, South End Press, pp 350–358.

Zimbardo, P. (2011) *The Lucifer Effect: How Good People Turn Evil*, New York: Random House.

Zuboff, S. (1988) *In the Age of the Smart Machine: The Future of Work and Power*, New York: Basic Books.

Zuboff, S. (2019) *The Age of Surveillance Capitalism: The Fight for a Human Future at the New Frontier of Power*, New York: Profile Books.

Author Index

A

Abbott, A. 67, 84
Abbott, P., Tyler, M. and Wallace, C. 24
Acker, J. 25, 163, 165
Ackroyd, S. and Thompson, P. 90, 109
Adler, P.S. 77, 85, 98, 111
Alberti, G., Bessa, I., Hardy, K., Trappmann,
    V. and Umney, C. 46
Alvesson, M. and Thompson, P. 45
Anteby, M. and Chan, C.K. 109
Apitzsch, B., Wilkesmann, M., Ruiner, C.,
    Bassyiouny, M., Ehlen, R. and Schulz, L. 48
Appelbaum, E. and Batt, R. 49
Ashley, L. 156
Atkinson, A.B. and Jenkins, S.P. 143
Atzeni, M. 119, 120
Azzellini, D. 133, 134

B

Baccaro, L., Benassi, C. and Meardi, G. 131
Bailey, C. and Madden, A. 95
Bain, P. and Taylor, P. 61
Baines, D. 95, 103, 105, 112
Baldamus, W. 186
Baldry, C., Bain, P. and Taylor, P. 77
Baldry, C., Bain, P., Taylor, P., Hyman, J.,
    Scholarios, D., Marks, A. and Watson, A. 96,
    98, 100, 101
Barker, J.R. 60, 71
Barley, S.R. 96
Barnard, S., Dainty, A., Lewis, S.
    and Culora, A. 101
Barry, M. and Wilkinson, A. 117, 185
Baruch, Y. 72
Baudrillard, J. 26, 27
Bauman, Z. 1, 18, 27
Bayard de Volo, L. 110
Beamish, T.D. and Biggart, N.W. 57
Beck, U. 45, 46, 54
Becker, G. 163
Bell, E., Mangia, G., Taylor, S. and Toraldo,
    M.L. 75
Belt, V. 161, 162
Berggren, C. 67
Bernat, I. and Whyte, D. 171
Beynon, H. 60, 102
Bhambra, G. 32, 169

Bhuiyan, J. 123
Bieler, A. and Nowak, J. 120
Billig, M. 11
Bilton, T., Bonnett, K., Jones, P., Stanworth,
    M., Sheard, K. and Webster, A. 24
Block, F. 21
Blyton, P. and Jenkins, J. 3, 128, 130
Blyton, P.R. and Turnbull, P.J. 41, 51, 54, 63
Boland, T. and Griffin, R. 91
Bolton, S.C. 105
Bolton, S. and Muzio, D. 163
Bond, S. and Sales, J. 25
Bone, J. 59
Bourdieu, P. *see* subject index
Boyer, R. 44
Braverman, H. 76, 79, 80, 81, 83
Briskin, L. 128
Brown, J.S. and Duguid, P. 84
Brown, K. and Korczynski, M. 112, 113
Budd, J.W. 185
Bukodi, E. and Goldthorpe, J. 154
Bulut, E. 48
Burawoy, M. 57, 58, 90
Burnett, J. and Whyte, D. 172
Burrell, G. 11, 13, 26, 27, 30
Burrell, G. and Morgan, G. 30

C

Cappelli, P., Bassi, L., Katz, H., Knoke, D.,
    Osterman, P. and Useem, M. 58
Casey, C. 62, 63
Castells, M. 54
Castles, S. and Miller, M.J. 170, 171
Causa, O. and Johansson, A. 155
Cavendish, R. 70
Charlesworth, S.J. 148
Chen, W. 149
Chertkovskaya, E., Watt, P., Tramer, S. and
    Spoelstra, S. 73, 74
China Labour Watch 79
Chowdhury, R. 55
Ciepley, D. 131
Cini, L., Maccarrone, V. and Tassinari, A. 124, 125
Cioce, G., Korczynski, M. and Pero, D. 129
Clark, K. and Nolan, S. 168
Clarke, A. and Smith, C. 168
Clarke, S. 44

Clegg, S. 26
Cockburn, C. 102, 176
Cohen, L. and Mallon, M. 97
Cohen, L., Duberley, J. and Smith, P. 98
Cohen, N. and Richards, J. 108
Cohen, S. and Taylor, L. 10
Connell, R. 25
Cooke, W. 55
Cornfield, D.B. 120, 128, 184
Cornforth, C. 134
Costa, S., Boatcă, M. and Franco, G. 32
Cottom, T.M. 74, 75
Couloigner, S. 101
Cova, B. and Dalli, D. 4
Covaleski, M.A., Dirsmith, M.W., Heian, J.B. and Samuel, S. 37, 38
Cox, A. 84
Crompton, R. 150, 151
Csikszentmihalhi, M. 93
Cullinane, N. and Dundon, T. 186
Cushen, J. 99

D

De Angelis, M. 70
De Certeau, M. 31
Deery, S., Kolar, D. and Walsh, J. 96
De Maio, F.G. 138
Department of Business 128
Desmond, M. 75
Devine, F., Britton, J., Mellor, R. and Halfpenny, P. 72, 73
Dickens, L. 162
Dill, J.S. and Morgan, J.C. 73, 74
Discenna, T.A. 74
Dobrow, S.R. and Tosti-Kharas, J. 97
Doellgast, V., Lillie, N. and Pulignano, V. 129
Doerflinger, N. 107
Doeringer, P.B. and Piore, M.J. 71
Doherty, M. 181
Donaghey, J., Cullinane, N., Dundon, T. and Wilkinson, A. 116, 118
Donne, J. 2
Dorling, D. 138, 143
Draper, H. 14
Dumenil, G. and Levy, D. 151
Dundon, T. and Rollinson, D. 119
Dundon, T., Wilkinson, A., Marchington, M. and Ackers, P. 116, 117
Dunford, R. and Perrons, D. 161
Durkheim, E. *see* subject index

E

Edwards, P. 41
Edwards, P. and Hodder, A. 109
Edwards, P. and Whitston, C. 109
Edwards, P., Belanger, J. and Wright, M. 90
Edwards, R. 57, 72, 77
Egan, R.D. 113
El-Sawad, A. and Korczynski, M. 62
England, P. 162
EHRC 162, 163, 164, 166

Ens, N. 75
Erickson, K.A. 98, 105
Eyles, A., Major, L.E. and Machin, S. 153, 154, 155, 156, 159

F

Faist, T. 169, 170, 173
Fernie, S. and Metcalf, D. 61
Fevre, R. 24, 36, 61
Findlay, P., McKinlay, A., Marks, A. and Thompson, P. 71
Flaherty, E. 145
Fleming, P. and Sturdy, A. 64
Fligstein, N. 145
Fligstein, N. and Goldstein, A. 49, 144, 145, 146
Forde, C., Stuart, M. and Joyce, S. 6
Foreign Policy 53
Foucault, M. *see* subject index
Fox, A. 1, 21, 61
Forrier, A. and Sels, L. 73
Frayne, D. 92
Frega, R., Herzog, L. and Neuhauser, C. 132
Frenkel, S. 53, 54
Frenkel, S., Korczynski, M., Donoghue, L. and Shire, K. 64, 105
Frenkel, S., Korczynski, M., Shire, K.A. and Tam, M. 61, 84
Friedland, W.H. 104
Friedman, A.L. 57, 59
Friedman, S. and Laurison, D. 154, 156, 157
Friedson, E. 83
Fuller, L. and Smith, V. 60, 82

G

Gabriel, Y. and Lang, T. 4, 88
Gabriel, Y., Korczynski, M. and Rieder, K. 4
Galtung, J. 13, 34
Gamble, J. 60
Gegenhuber, T., Ellmer, M. and Schusler, E. 119
Geiger, S. and Bourgeron, T. 182
Gereffi, G. and Korzeniewicz, M. 56
Giddens, A. 31
Giddens, A. and Sutton, P.W. 2, 5, 25
Giles, A. 54
Ginn, J., Arber, S., Brannen, J., Dale, A., Dex, S., Elias, P. and Rubery, J. 93
Glavin, P., Bierman, A. and Schieman, S. 101
Go, J. 32
Godard, J. 185
Goffman, I. 31
Goldthorpe, J.H., Lockwood, D., Bechhofer, F. and Platt, J. 92
Goodrich, C. 109
GOV.UK 73, 161
Graeber, D. 92
Green, F. 67, 68
Green, F., Felstead, A., Gallie, D. and Henseke, G. 68, 69
Greenberg, E.S. 102, 106
Gregory, M.R. 164
Gregory, P. and Stuart, R. 39

Griffin, E. 76
Grimshaw, D. and Rubery, J. 58
Grint, K. 30, 175
Gumbrell-McCormick, R. and Hyman,
R. 131, 132
Gurney, L., Lockington, J., Quinn, L.
and MacPhee, M. 123

H

Hakim, C. 93
Hall, E.J. 34
Hall, P.A. and Soskice, D. 50, 51, 52
Halpin, B.W. 48, 82
Hammer, A. and Adham, A. 184
Hamper, B. 110
Hampson, I. and Junor, A. 82
Hanser, A. 149
Hardin, G. 70
Harknett, K., Schneider, D. and Wolfe, R. 48
Hartmann, H.I. 30
Harvey, D. 54
Heckscher, C. and McCarthy, J. 122
Heery, E. 126, 127, 129
Heery, E., Abbott, B. and Williams, S. 125,
126, 127
Heery, E., Hann, D. and Nash, D. 125, 126
Herzenberg, S.A., Alic, J.A. and Wial, H. 83, 84
Hipp, L. 51
Hirsch, P.M. and Levin, D.Z. 182, 183
Hirschman, A.O. 30, 31
Hirst, A. 4
Hislop, D., Bosua, R. and Helms, R. 5, 44, 46, 84
Hoch, P. 78
Hochschild, A. 7, 8, 80, 81, 95, 110
Hodgson, D. and Briand, L. 118
Hodson, R. 69, 90, 92, 100, 106, 107, 109, 111,
117, 186
Holm, J.R. and Lorenz, E. 178
Holman, D., Frenkel, S., Sorensen, O.
and Wood, S. 177
Howard, P.N., Duffy, A., Freelon, D., Hussain,
M.M., Mari, W. and Maziad, M. 120
Howcroft, D. and Taylor, P. 175
Huber, E., Petrova, B. and Stephens, J.D. 145
Hunt, W., Terry, E. and Rolf, S. 177
Huzell, H. 100
Hyman, J., Lockyer, C.J., Marks, A. and
Scholarios, D.M. 131
Hyman, R. 14, 16, 30, 128, 129, 131, 132

I

Ilsoe, A. and Jesnes, K. 35

J

Jackson, G. and Deeg, R. 73
Jacoby, S.M. 62, 72
Jaffe, S. 120, 121
Jager, S., Noy, S. and Schoefer, B. 132
James, C.L.R. 32
Jarrahi, M.H. 175, 178, 179
Jessop, B. 44

Jiang, J. and Korczynski, M. 127, 128
Jones, O. 148, 149
Jordan, Z. and Conway, D. 68
Joyce, S. and Stuart, M. 108, 111, 146

K

Kalberg, S. 17
Kalleberg, A. 45, 47, 48
Kan, M.Y. 93
Kara, S. 172
Karlsson, J.C. 110, 112
Katz, C. 106
Kaufman, B.E. 105, 184, 185
Kay, R. and Hildyard, L. 144
Kearsey, J. 102, 104, 113
Kelly, J.E. 67, 126, 127
Kessler, I., Bach, S. and Nath, V. 98
Khaola, P. and Rambe, P. 106
Khan, M., Mowbray, P.K. and Wilkinson,
A. 115, 122
Kirkpatrick, G. 176
Klein, G., Shtudiner, Z., Kantor, J., Mollov, B.
and Lavie, C. 101
Klein, N. 55, 56, 57, 135, 136
Kochan, T.A., Fine, J.R., Bronfenbrenner, K.,
Naidu, S., Barnes, J., Diaz-Linhart, Y.,
Kallas, J., Kim, J., Minster, A., Tong, D.,
Townsend, P. and Twiss, D. 122, 128
Kokkonen, A., Esaiasson, P. and Gilljam, M. 101
Kollmeyer, C. 146
Kollmeyer, C. and Peters, J. 49
Korczynski, M. 5, 34, 46, 59, 60, 63, 67, 68, 70,
79, 80, 81, 82, 99, 101, 102, 103, 107, 108,
110, 119, 158, 162, 163, 184, 185, 186
Korczynski, M. and Macdonald, C. 5
Korczynski, M. and Ott, U. 81, 107
Korczynski, M. and Wittel, A. 4, 70, 71
Korczynski, M., Hodson, R. and Edwards, P. 30
Korczynski, M., Shire, K., Frenkel, S.
and Tam, M. 63
Kordos, M. and Vojtovic, S. 53
Kornberger, M., Pflueger, D. and Mouritsen, J. 88
Korpi, W. 52
Kost, D, Fieseler, C. and Wong, S.I. 74, 98
Kougiannou, N.K. and Mendonca, P. 119
Koumenta, M. and Williams, M. 48
Kroezen, J., Ravasi, D., Sasaki, I., Żebrowska, M.
and Suddaby, R. 75, 76, 83, 93
Kunda, G. 37, 62

L

Laaser, K. and Karlsson, J.C. 91, 94
Lamont, M. 149
Langman, L. and Smith, D. 145
Lash, S. and Urry, J. 26
Lave, J. and Wenger, E. 84
Layder, D. 30
Lazazzara, A., Tims, M. and De Gennaro, D. 131
Leadbetter, C. 45
Legge, K. 26, 62, 99
Leidner, R. 68, 107

Subject Index

Printed and bound by CPI Group (UK) Ltd, Croydon, CR0 4YY

23/04/2025

14661026-0004